Developmental Experiences

Treatment of Developmental Disorders in Children

DAVID SCOTT LEVIN

Jason Aronson, Inc.

New York and London

Copyright © 1985 by David Scott Levin

10 9 8 7 6 5 4 3 2 1

Library of Congress Cataloging in Publication Data

Levin, David Scott.
  Developmental experiences.

  Bibliography: p. 313
  Includes index.
  1. Child psychopathology. 2. Child psychotherapy.
3. Parent and child. I. Title. [DNLM: 1. Child
Behavior Disorders—therapy. 2. Child Development
Disorders—therapy. 3. Parent-Child Relations.
WS 350.6 L665d]
RJ499.L389 1985   618.92'89   84-24318
ISBN 0-87668-760-5

  Manufactured in the United States of America.

For Veda and Adam

Foreword

Those who have worked with autistic children know that the type and degree of their disability is the overriding factor in the fascination these children have held for clinicians and researchers. That they present with a lack of ability (or interest) to relate to other human beings is not only baffling but also frightening. Their behavior subjects to question the basic assumption that all children want and need parenting. The quandary is all the more complex because "helpers" and their "treatments" have traditionally depended upon social and, in particular, verbal interactions with their "patients."

In 1943 Dr. Leo Kanner published his report on the group of children whose condition he called "early infantile autism." Kanner characterized this disorder as one in which there is a defect ". . . in the child's ability to relate in the ordinary way to people and situations from the beginning of life." Similar children had, no doubt, existed before Kanner observed the commonalities among them and arrived at the diagnosis. They had probably even been described in the literature prior to this century (as "feral" children). Kanner's clinical descriptions in his original paper and in the ones that followed made the condition into a subject of scientific inquiry. The stage was set for the dramatic debate over etiology, diagnosis, and treatment that has continued ever since.

In the years since Kanner identified these children as a diagnostic subgroup, early infantile autism has been declared by some to result from irrevocable damage caused by poor parenting. Others, with equal pessimism, have concluded that autism is a biological disorder and not particularly amenable to the talking cure and its variations.

Recently the emphasis in autism research has been fundamentally directed at the neurobiology of the disorder. The distinctions drawn previously between early infantile autism, childhood psychoses, and other severe developmental disorders have blurred. Indeed, the issues of nosology and specific diagnostic criteria are lively areas of investigation. Despite the many advances in the technical aspects of biological research, moreover, the etiology of autism remains unclear. Treatment research has, similarly, yielded little despite the claims of various individuals (including one Nobel laureate) that they have found the cure. One must also be careful not to be trapped by the belief that even a successful treatment means that one has somehow intervened with and corrected "the" etiological agent.

Levin's contribution to the treatment of pervasive developmentally disordered children represents a breakthrough. He has defined new concepts for treating the immature, deficient, or disturbed person—ideas which fit with new knowledge about the early development of human beings. His thinking is solidly anchored in the work of Greenspan and of Sander, who have emphasized the key role of adaptational and interactional phases of early development, respectively, in the psychological structuralization of the human being. His concepts are informed, as well, by those of Mahler, Pine, Kohut, and Alexander. He shows how treatment at the precursory stages of individuation and mental representation reflects an understanding of life span development as a continuous and coherent epigenetic sequence. He extends to the preindividuated and preconceptual-level child the adult treatment concepts formulated originally from clinical experience with the psychologically structured person—one who has achieved a first state of psychological representation and differentiation (30 to 36 months)—then proceeds to delineate systematically what this treatment involves.

Levin's key concept, the *Corrective Developmental Experience,* stems from the work of Alexander, but differs from it importantly. Unlike Alexander's Corrective Emotional Experience, the Corrective Developmental Experience is not based on the manipulation or gratification of the transference. Instead, Levin argues, it is a treatment aimed at falling in with and complementing the developmental mandate of the maturing and differentiating organism. The Corrective Developmental Experience is an inevitable product of the treatment process because the therapist is not locked into the same caregiving patterns as the parent and can therefore apprehend, complement, and expand upon the developmental needs of the pre-individuated organism. With this clear differentiation from Alexander's concepts, Levin has moved to the leading edge of current psychoanalytic thinking regarding the treatment of self-pathologies (see Kohut, Tolpin, Goldberg, and Wolf).

But Levin goes further than this and herein is his major contribution: he identifies the actual therapeutic processes of the Corrective Developmental Experience. His are not adultomorphic interpretations of infantile experience but, rather, phenomenologically anchored observations of the individual's experiential capabilities. Levin puts into words what others have led up to but fallen short of articulating—that "the therapeutic domain of the preconceptual, pre-individuated organism is interactional" and that "the interactional forms the intrapsychic."

He then posits *how* the interactive structures the intrapsychic. According to Levin, recognition, the foundation for memory traces, leads to anticipatory responses, which in turn lead to action patterns. The capacity for recognition, anticipation, and action, early bio-psychological structures which begin to unfold from birth, forms the basis for mental representation and the establishing of object relationships. These capacities—recognition, anticipation, and action—are the infrastructure of both empathy and transference.

Empathy with the infant is possible because the earliest developmental experiences, though not available to the adult in coherent symbolic representations and memories, are inherent in all patterning of recognition, anticipation, and action. They persist, therefore, in the psychological life of the person as basic organizing factors for all subsequent experiences. Levin takes issue with Kohut's claim that the therapist as adult can no longer retrieve the pre-symbolic experiences of infancy and that empathy with the infant state is hence unattainable.

Transference, too, Levin argues, is a concept applicable to the treatment of infants. The capacity for transference is within the developmental capabilities of the infant and is evident from birth. Distortions in recognition, anticipation, and actions occur in early infancy, as illustrated by Fraiberg's work (1982) on the mechanisms of defense in infancy. It is this which mandates the therapeutic workability of the transference even in the very young.

In Levin's framework, verbal communication by the therapist at this early stage is not primarily for the purpose of symbolic communication, but for the regulation of all kinds of experience— the physical, affective, cognitive, social, and the symbolic. At this stage, in other words, the melody and its phrasing—the sentient aspects of the communication—are more important than the words themselves. The words acquire significance in the treatment (as well as in development) only as recognition and memory become organized and gain structure.

In his case presentation of a pervasive developmentally disordered child, Kathy M., and her mother, Ms. L., Levin illustrates how the therapeutic process takes place in the mutually regulated patterns of action and interaction between therapist and child, as well as in the intensive treatment of the mother. Moving from clinical theory to clinical work, Levin describes how the therapist establishes therapeutic contact with the immature, disturbed, or developmentally deviant person and learns to identify what in the child draws or coerces a maladaptive response from the interactive partner. The therapist must do no less for the adult caregiving person. This strategy resolves transference distortions simultaneously for both child and mother.

The concept of a Corrective Developmental Experience addresses an issue basic not only to treating developmental disturbances but also to understanding them. Levin's model is "interactional" and, therefore, confronts the most disturbing aspects of these disorders. The model also allows a more developmentally appropriate view of the psychosocial contributions to the pathology. To say that bad parenting causes developmental psychopathology is no longer acceptable. Rather, it is the distorted and compromised capacity of the child to interact with the environment that leads to the expression of symptoms. Through interactional interventions remediation of symptoms may be possible. It was for Kathy.

It honors us that Levin developed these ideas during his training at the Child Psychiatry Clinic of the Department of Psychiatry at the University of Chicago and, in particular, in the course of ongoing teaching, research, and clinical practice with the Parent-Infant Development Services for 0–3.

Bennett L. Leventhal, M.D.
Director, Child Psychiatry
The University of Chicago

Chaya H. Roth, Ph.D.
Director, 0-3 Programs
Child Psychiatry Clinic
The University of Chicago.

Acknowledgments

I wish to gratefully acknowledge the many colleagues, teachers and patients whose influence runs throughout but whose contributions for the most part go unnoted.

Impetus for the present work began with the encouragement of Dr. Bernard Gold, Dean, The Chicago School of Professional Psychology, who maintained the need for such a reevaluation of developmental psychopathology and clinical intervention. Without his support much of what is written here would not likely have made it to print. I am similarly indebted to Doctors Zanvel Klein, Myra Leifer, and Bennett Leventhal of the Child Psychiatry Clinic and Parent-Infant Development Service at the University of Chicago for their invaluable contributions throughout. In the formulation of this work, I owe much to Dr. Chaya Roth, whose thoughts on development, babies, empathy, and treatment provided a foundation for many of the concepts which I have tried to develop here. Doctors Bernard Aronov and Michael Basch were helpful in illuminating the psychotherapeutic process through their teaching and example. Finally, I must thank my patients, whose struggle to find new solutions to old problems has been a continuous source for speculation and a proving ground for new ideas about treatment.

Contents

Introduction

Which of us, having worked psychotherapeutically with very young or very disturbed children, has not wondered from time to time whether we have gotten through—whether our intended communication has made an impact, or whether in a broader sense we have helped the child to move ahead with the work of growing up. At an extreme, speculations of this sort can lead to a sense of futility and withdrawal from the child: "Why am I talking like this to a baby when she can't possibly understand what I'm saying?" More frequently, however, particularly as the child grows, begins to speak, and develops the capacity for complex conceptualization, we may succeed in getting through, only to be misunderstood or, worse yet, ignored. While communication and understanding are of course the concern of any invested caregiver, parent or therapist, issues of meaning, message, delivery, and impact assume a special significance in the work of the psychotherapist for whom verbal and nonverbal exchanges of special kinds of information are believed to have curative properties and are at the heart of the therapeutic process.

In working psychotherapeutically with the most severely disturbed children who have come to my professional attention, children from 3 months to 4 years of age who have failed in varying degrees to develop capacities for psychophysiological self-regulation, emotional attachment, mental representation, or receptive and expressive verbal facility, I have often pondered the questions of understanding and therapeutic effect. Does a little girl of 3, for example, whose entire lexicon consists of five or six words, and who still seems to believe that her needs and wishes are magically apprehended by others (who may not even exist for her as such), understand me when I interpret that she is throwing a block because she's angry or is stroking a doll's hair as her own mother sometimes strokes hers because she loves her?

If one looks long and hard enough, it is I suppose possible to find a rationale for almost any procedure and an affirmation for almost any apparent result. The psychotherapeutic literature is certainly no exception. For many years psychoanalytic and object relations investigators have maintained that even the earliest natal and prenatal experiences are registered and represented in consciousness and, moreover, that once registered, such experiences are retrievable, reconstructible, and subject to reintegration within a more developmentally mature and adaptive psychic organization. Freud himself (1900) maintained that while all thinking is the result of a detour from the direct path towards instinctual gratification and therefore a somewhat later developmental acquisition, the generation of ideation in the primary process is a capacity of basic human endowment with distinct phylogenetic underpinnings. The elaboration of this hypothetical ideational capacity by early object relations theorists into highly complex and differentiated representational schema is well known and persists as an underlying assumption in the work of most current investigators (see Kernberg 1976, 1980). Only more recently, however, with the proliferation of studies based on the direct observation of infants, toddlers, and preschool children, have these early theoretical assumptions, based primarily on the reconstructed memories of adult psychoanalytic patients, been tempered by the direct observational assessment of what biologically, psychologically, and socially immature human beings are actually capable of in terms of cognitive affective organization, integration, and differentiation (Lichtenberg 1983). Modern infants as we know them today are beings endowed with and adapted for so much more yet at the same time so much less than most investigators had once believed.

It would appear, however, that complex mental representation during the first days, weeks, even months of life is not one of these primary endowments. Furthermore, until such time as this capability has been achieved, it makes little sense to assume that the active agent in almost any kind of therapeutic or extratherapeutic communication with the child is the semantic, ideational, or symbolic representational component. If our dialogue appears to produce an effect, particularly one in the direction of enhanced functioning, we must look to some other aspect of the interaction in order to account for the apparent change. Such was the case with the pervasively disordered child whom I described briefly above. Very rarely was I convinced that the meaning of my communication had in and of itself been the agent of change in our treatment interactions, yet, gradually, the child seemed to grow. In other words, there must have been something else, something about the dialogue as a complex amalgam of affective, sensory, and representational components, each having specific repercussions at any or all levels of the child's bio-psycho-social functioning, that had facilitated her taking what the therapist had offered and making it her own. From one regulated to one relating, from one disinterested to one attached, from one locked into the immediacy of the moment to one capable of carrying aspects of the physical and interpersonal environment within herself: each of these developmental transitions began to unfold in a remarkable stagewise sequence.

In some respects Kathy's development unfolded much as one might have expected of a normal infant over the course of the first two years of life. But Kathy was not an infant: she was already three years old and a radically different psychophysiological being from the normal infant-toddler. While the end product of the therapeutic intervention was the negotiation and renegotiation of key developmental phases, the quality of "interactive fit" or "coherence" (Sanders 1983) was radically different from what Kathy had experienced in the past with her own mother. In other words, the treatment situation had created an experience that was essentially new, yet which seemed to free certain emotional and cognitive processes that would normally have emerged much earlier in the child's developmental history. I will have more to say about this later on as I examine the case of Kathy M. in greater detail.

Let me state at the outset what should already be apparent: I do not believe it is possible to account for psychotherapeutic effects (adaptive interactive processes [Roth et al. in press]) in very young (preoedipal) children such as Kathy or even older children or adults having severe structural psychopathology, on the basis of a purely interpretive model of treatment intervention. Nor do I believe that we can accurately assess the treatment situation in these kinds of cases if we insist on defining an isolated, unidirectional relationship between what the therapist as an outside intervening agent says or does and the way in which the child as a presumedly wholly autonomous, self-regulating, self-righting, self-directing individual (which the child clearly is not) responds. In order to make sense out of the treatment process, one must take into consideration certain non-interpretive or "background" (Pine 1979) characteristics of the treatment situation and the functions which these characteristics serve in the context of the emerging biopsychological structures of the child's nascent personality organization. While the actual clinical conveyance of these "background characteristics" may take the form of conceptual level verbal-linguistic motifs—for this is how adult-functioning psychotherapists tend to organize and represent the conscious level concomitants of processes occurring at almost every level of functioning—it would be a mistake to assume that what the child understands or assimilates derives directly from those same aspects of the interaction. Once again, this is not to say that the conceptual-level therapist has no way of getting through to the preconceptual-level child, for process we believe recapitulates content at multiple levels of psychological and physiological organization. We say only that we have not yet ascertained a comprehensive mapping of the primitive experiential states which correspond to and register these nuances of human interaction. Constructing such a cartography of early developmental experiences, or at least establishing an effective methodology for doing so, will constitute the principal aim of this work.

In light of the extreme uncertainty inherent in a clinical approach of this kind, which attempts to account systematically for the impact of complex interactions between persons functioning at radically different levels of psychological and physiological organization, it is not surprising to find that many clinicians currently working with developmentally disordered youngsters tend to steer away from treatment models which rely so heavily upon difficult-to-confirm experiential complexes such as human understanding and responsiveness. We are not as confident in our empathy perhaps as in our other forms of information processing. Clinical research in this area in recent years seems to have moved in the direction of physiological and behavioral explanations reflecting what I believe to be a sense of futility surrounding psychodynamic approaches. Not surprisingly, methodology in these disciplines has made steady progress which is reflected in a continual refinement of clinical technique. Until quite recently, psychodynamic investigators have simply not kept pace. As Ornstein (1976) noted in this regard, overextension of psychoanalytic principles based on clinical work with neurotic or relatively well-integrated children to youngsters whose psychological difficulties are related primarily to structural deficits or developmental arrest rather than internalized conflict has led to predictably disappointing results. There have, of course, been any number of important departures from basic technique. Psychoanalytic investigators such as Mahler and Fraiberg have for many years addressed themselves and their theories to the problems associated with the severe developmental disturbances, but these classic tracts were written 10, 15, even 20 years ago and very little has followed in their wake. There remain as well the psychoanalytically oriented inpatient treatment programs such as Bettelheim's Orthogenic School. What you will find today, however, should you walk through the halls of the school on the Midway, is a far cry from what Bettelheim wrote about in *The Empty Fortress* (1967) and *Home for the Heart* (1974). Today's residents are a troubled lot, to be sure, yet they have for the most part developed some competency along linguistic, cognitive, and affective lines and are relatively capable of establishing at least a modicum of social rapport. These are not, by and large, the remotely inaccessible autistic and symbiotic children of a generation ago.

This is not to say that there is no interest in the evaluation, description, and treatment of the pervasive developmental disorders, but that the thrust of research and development seems to have moved off into other directions. Take for example a recent (and fairly representative) issue of the *Journal of Autism and Developmental Disorders*. This particular publication is relatively nonpartisan and can give us a good sense of the current state of study of these syndromes. Looking through the table of contents, we find papers pertaining to the communicative behavior of adults with an autistic 4-year-old; childhood psychosis and computed tomographic brain scan findings; stimulus-evaluation processes in autistic subjects; and developmental effects in the cerebral lateralization of autistic, retarded, and normal children. There is nothing here, however, which pertains to the child as a self-experiencing human being in whose awareness each of these biological, physiological, biochemical, and behavioral processes may produce a variety of subjective sequellae.

What is it like for the psychotic child? What is it like to be a psychotic child? Finally, just how much can we learn from being with the psychotic child and to what extent can processes occurring at biopsychological-behavioral levels of organization be influenced within the context of this interactional process? These and other phenomenological questions, the kinds of questions which psychodynamically oriented clinicians have been asking themselves for close to a century now, seem to have been forgotten about in the

study of the violently troubled youngsters whose peculiar disturbances of affect, relatedness, and cognition render them so ill-
equipped to meet the challenge of growing up.

There are, perhaps, other, more mundane reasons for the decline of psychoanalytic psychotherapy with developmentally disordered youngsters. For many different reasons, even the most well
thought out models of psychotherapeutic intervention had a limited
success rate and those children who were helped seldom attained or
maintained normal developmental progress. Almost every paper
written during the 1940s, 1950s, and 1960s pertaining to the treatment of the early onset psychoses concluded with talk of "guarded
prognosis." Those treatments that were most successful typically
consumed countless years and countless thousands of dollars. Moreover, these treatments were often methodologically and theoretically unsystematic; no one could be quite sure why a particular
child had or had not improved. The emphasis in recent years has
clearly been on cost-effectiveness and short-term gains, and this is
the stuff of which psychopharmacology and behavioral interventions are made. Again, in these areas there has been steady and
gratifying progress. Still, I am concerned that while we may be
doing a good job of modifying behaviors and altering neurochemical metabolisms, we are rapidly losing sight of the child as an
experiencing, organizing, and adapting human being struggling,
like the rest of us, to bring some semblance of order and coherence
to a remarkably unpredictable world.

It is my contention that practicing clinicians have relented
prematurely in pursuing a psychodynamic treatment model for the
pervasive developmental disorders of early childhood and that with
recent advents in developmental psychology and psychoanalytic
psychology we are once again in a position to reassess our strategies
and make certain key technical and conceptual modifications in
our treatment interventions to reflect these advances in our understanding of the first years of life. With these considerations in
mind, I wish to offer the corrective developmental experience as a
model for the evaluation and treatment of the psychopathology of
infancy and early childhood and related manifestations in the psychopathology of adulthood and later life.

However, before looking into a new solution to what we shall
soon see is a very old problem, I believe that it is important that we
understand the nature of the problem itself. To this end, I will
begin with a review of the various vantage points from which this
group of disorders has been conceptualized and the methods of
evaluation and treatment that have followed each model. It should

be understood from the outset, however, that despite the organizational convenience of treating these theoretical disciplines as relatively independent lines of thought, the object of study remains a child embedded in a complex system in which psychological, physiological, and psychodynamic processes converge. In reality no one of these levels of understanding is independent or isolated. Processes occurring at one level resonate and filter through processes at any or all other levels of system functioning. The clinical phenomena with which we will concern ourselves are not exclusively biological, psychological, or psychodynamic—they are all of these. As I hope will become increasingly clear, the pervasive developmental disorders will, in all likelihood, continue to defy understanding as unitary etiological processes. The most that can be said with certainty at this point is that each of this group of disorders seems to represent a generic or nonspecific reaction to any of a range of physiological and psychological traumas and most likely represents a complex interaction of events at physiological, genetic, behavioral, and psychodynamic levels of organization. Thus, we are talking not about absolute causes but about relative contributions. From the standpoint of clinical intervention, the complexity of these complementary processes is, I believe, cause for hopefulness rather than despair, for if, in fact, the pervasive developmental disorders represent a complex "anlage" of constitutional and experiential factors, as Mahler described them (1952), or a final common pathway for diverse etiological factors, as I will later describe them, then we have the potential for and possibility of successful intervention at multiple points of entry into what can only be understood as a disturbed and disrupted biological, psychological, social interactional system.

Psychological investigators have observed the infant-toddler, the preindividuated, preconceptual-level child, from the vantage point of adult reconstructions and representations of the earliest phases in the life cycle. They have observed the same child from naturalistic and empirical points of view, meticulously documenting action, interaction, and every mode of psychopathological and behavioral process through direct observation. The task remaining, then, is for the analytically informed investigator, the investigator of subjective experience and internal states, to assume a position as closely allied with the actual experience of the child as his empathy will permit.

I will begin by considering the state of the art in the clinical assessment and treatment of the pervasive developmental disorders of infancy and early childhood as a function of the first two of these three observational positions: the direct observation and assessment of behavioral and psychopathological processes and adult reconstructions of early developmental experiences. I will then develop the foundations for a model of assessment and intervention based on the third position, that of the empathically attuned participant observer. A comprehensive case presentation will illustrate the application of the revised clinical model—the corrective developmental experience—to the case of a pervasively disordered 3½-year-old girl and her mother. In conclusion, I will describe the relationship of a reformulated corrective developmental paradigm to Franz Alexander's original conceptualization of the corrective developmental experience.

PART ONE

Historical and Critical Review of the Literature

Chapter One

Historical Aspects

It seems that psychosis is the sad prerogative of the human species. It is not confined to adults alone.
—Margaret Mahler

Severe psychopathological disturbances of infancy and early childhood, disturbances of psychotic proportion, are a relatively rare but tragic variation in human development. Presumably this has always been the case, though, prior to the mid-1800s, medical chronicles and literary characterizations alike allude only occasionally to the violently troubled child who from birth seemed oddly ill-equipped to adapt to life's exigencies. It is unlikely, however, that Esquinol's "little homicidal maniacs" (Kanner 1971) could have been overlooked. As Macmillan (1960) suggested, the peculiar silence surrounding the place of the psychotic child in history reflects, in all likelihood, a combination of both scientific and extra-scientific influences.

At least part of the problem may have stemmed from the ambiguous classification of all "defective" children according to educational level. Children manifesting severe intellectual impairments were treated as a relatively homogeneous group. Psychotic children became objects of study in their own right only with the refinement of classificatory schemes based on etiology and pathological type. A more incorrigible obstacle to the study of childhood psychosis, however, may have had less to do with the state of the art in diagnosis than with a certain reluctance on the part of both scientific and lay communities to accept the notion of insanity among the very young. This reluctance faded more slowly.

Clinical recognition of psychotic disturbances in children has gained wide acceptance only since the late 1930s. Twenty years later, Ekstein et al. (1958) pondered the tendency of many clinicians, who were still uncomfortable with the idea of pathological mental states in the young, to deny the existence of the childhood psychoses. Thus it comes as no surprise that when, in 1867, Maudsley, a noted British psychiatrist, published a 34-page tract on "The Insanity of Early Life," he was criticized by his colleagues for so brazenly impugning to children this most "unnatural" condition of adult life. In prefacing the 1880 edition of *Physiology and Pathology of the Mind*, Maudsley wrote: "How unnatural! is an exclamation of pained surprise which some of the more striking instances of insanity in young children are likely to provoke. However, to call a thing unnatural is not to take it out of the domain of natural law."

Compelling, perhaps, but apparently not convincing. More than half a century later, in 1938, Franz Kallmann's pioneering work, *Genetics of Schizophrenia*, describing recurring patterns of familial incidence and twin concordance for schizophrenic disorders, was all but ignored because of what Bender (1971) later interpreted as a "wish to disbelieve." Taken together, the first 45 volumes of the *American Journal of Insanity* (1844–1889) show not a single paper pertaining to children, let alone children with psychotic disturbances (Kanner 1971).

First Clinical Studies of Childhood Psychosis

Maudsley's 1867 textbook chapter, mentioned above, constitutes a seminal work in the study of early onset psychosis and a first attempt at correlating symptomatology with developmental status. His 7-point classificatory system, though couched in the antiquated psychiatric idiom of his day, is certainly not far removed from contemporary systems.

A short time following the second edition of Maudsley's text, Spitzka devoted space in his *Treatment of Insanity* (1883) to a discussion of infantile psychosis, a condition which he attributed to heredity, fright, sudden changes in temperature, and masturbation. Following Morel, who in 1860 proposed that "dementia [was in certain cases nothing but] the final outcome of a fetal evolution, the seed of which has been carried from birth," DeSanctis described children whose mental deficiency ("phrenasthenia") was accompanied by certain psychoticlike or "versonic" features reminiscent of those described by Kraeplin in his studies of adult forms of dementia praecox (Szurek and Berlin 1973). The designation "dementia praecocissima" was reserved for those children among the mentally deficient "with a type of mentality truly insane." The possibility of an intellectual deficit with causation other than mental deficiency gave DeSanctis reason for optimism that children so afflicted might ultimately be cured: "I used to believe that all forms and variations of dementia praecox were incurable. Now I believe that some children regarded as mentally deficient who present a clearly insane mentality not only have improved but can be cured" (Szurek and Berlin 1973, p. 40). DeSanctis went on to suggest that the prospect for recovery was, in fact, the feature which distinguished dementia praecocissima from "the insanity of mental deficiency."

Two years after DeSanctis's description of dementia praecocissima, Heller (1908) reported six cases of infantile psychosis with onset in the third to fourth years following an otherwise normal development. The course of the illness began with an increasing malaise, diminution of interest, and loss of speech and sphincter control, and ended with a complete cognitive, social, and emotional regression. Heller labeled the syndrome "dementia infantalis" and at first believed it to be a functional disorder. In 1931, however, in performing an autopsy on an afflicted child, he noted an acute degeneration of ganglion cells in the lower cortex, suggesting a distinct organic etiology.

Across the Atlantic in the United States, Lightner Witmer established the first psychological clinic for maladjusted children at the University of Pennsylvania in 1896. Using response to psychotherapy as a means of differentiating childhood psychosis from mental deficiency, Witmer, like DeSanctis, proposed a distinction between two types of feeblemindedness, the first resulting from congenital defects (as in what is now called Down's syndrome) and the second resulting from what he described as "arrested development." Where the latter pertained, Witmer believed cure was possible provided that treatment began early enough (Szurek and Berlin 1973, p. 48)

Perhaps the major impetus to clinical research in the area of childhood psychosis came not from the ranks of child psychiatry, but from awakened interest around the turn of the century in psychotic disorders among adult psychiatric patients. Although the term "dementia praecox" had been used by Morel as early as 1860 and by Pick in 1891 (Arieti 1974) to describe the early or precocious onset of psychotic symptomatology, Kraepelin broadened the significance of the term to include what he believed to be an inevitable and progressive deterioration of cognitive and affective functioning to the point of complete mental impairment. Kraepelin recognized four variations of the disease—hebephrenia, catatonia, paraphrenia, and simple—though in each case the prognostic outlook was progressive dementia.

Bleuler

Eugen Bleuler, whose 1911 monograph on dementia praecox is perhaps best known for its renaming of the syndrome schizophrenia (implying a splitting of the various psychic functions), took issue with Kraepelin's notion of a single disease entity defined by an inevitable outcome. Instead, he proposed a group of schizophrenias based on the appareance of fundamental symptoms present to some degree in every case of schizophrenia (e.g., disorder of association, "autism") and a group of "accessory" symptoms (e.g., delusions, hallucinations, posturing) that may or may not be present depending on the specific manifestation of the disorder (Arieti 1974). Dementia, a total deterioration of the personality, was by no means an inevitability. For Bleuler, the elements common to schizophrenic disorders were the characteristic disturbances of association and a splitting of basic personality functions.

Curiously, Bleuler had virtually nothing to say about schizophrenic or other psychotic disorders of childhood, yet his term "autism" continues to be identified with what is perhaps the most distinct syndrome within the current classification of Pervasive Developmental Disorders (*DSM III:* Early Infantile Autism). Rutter (1978) has commented on the ambiguous usage of the term and the confusion that has arisen from its misapplication. In the context of Bleuler's original work autism referred to both a turning away from reality and a characteristic quality of thinking that accompanied this withdrawal: "It is unlogical and permits the greatest degree of contradiction with the outer world and in itself" (Arieti, 1974, p. 15).

In contrast, Kanner's later use of the term implied a failure to develop relations in the external world rather than a withdrawal from relations already extant. Furthermore, the rich "deriestic" inner life to which Bleuler's schizophrenic patients seemed to withdraw had little in common with the bleak preoccupations and impoverished imaginations of Kanner's original group of autistic children (Kanner 1943). The impact of Bleuler's "group of schizophrenias," however, was not reflected immediately in the still lagging classification of the psychotic disorders of childhood.

Potter

H. W. Potter's criteria for the diagnosis of "childhood schizophrenia" (1933), among the first of their kind following Maudsley, were clearly influenced by Bleuler's classificatory schema, but they further clarified ways in which the child's relative immaturity and verbal and cognitive limitations altered the clinical course of the disease.

Potter described six primary features (Goldfarb 1980): generalized retraction of interest from the environment; unrealistic thinking, feeling, and acting; thought disturbance; impaired emotional rapport; diminution, rigidity, and distortion of affect; and behavioral abnormalities manifesting increased motility, decreased motility, complete immobility, perseveration, or stereotyped behavior. Lending empirical evidence to the new classificatory schema, Bradley and Bowen (1941) were able to discriminate 14 psychotic youngsters from a group of 38 children in residential care on the basis of Potter's criteria.

Bender

The trend in classifying early onset psychotic disorders following Potter was in a sense a throwback to earlier pre-Bleulerian thinking. Childhood schizophrenia was regarded largely as a unitary disorder and children so affected as belonging to a single homogenous population. In contrast to Bleuler, whose primary and accessory symptomatology recognized considerable variation in the form, course, and prognosis of the adult schizophrenic disorders, Bender (1947, 1953, 1971) proposed a single diagnostic entity, "childhood schizophrenia," to cover the diverse manifestations of all childhood psychoses.

Bender believed that the primary disorder was a pervasive one with pathological manifestations at every level of central nervous system functioning. Those diagnostic variations that were noted—pseudodefective, pseudoneurotic, pseudopsychopathic—represented a common disease process with distinct manifestations determined by age of onset and developmental status. But these variations did not constitute fundamentally different forms of the basic schizophrenic disorder. Even later onset adult schizophrenias could be shown to fall along a continuum with childhood disorders if developmental factors were taken into consideration.

Bolstered by Kallmann's findings of "remarkable recurring patterns" of family incidence and twin concordance for schizophrenic illness, Bender (1971) adopted the position that the diverse symptomatology of childhood schizophrenia, by virtue of its exceedingly precocious onset, necessarily had to involve either an inherited predisposition, an early physical or organic crisis, or a failure in the consolidation of adequate defense mechanisms at a "somatopsychic" level of organization: "The time from birth to the appearance of deviancy in the autistic child [Bender used "autistic" and "schizophrenic" synonymously] is too short to allow environmental factors to cause such an inexorable lifetime disorder" (Bender 1971, p. 116).

Kanner

With the publication of Kanner's seminal work, "Autistic Disturbances of Affective Contact" (1943), the study of childhood psychosis reached a new level of description and classification. Much as DeSanctis had been struck by the presentation of a "type of mentality truly insane" in certain of his feebleminded patients, so did Kanner note among children diagnosed as schizophrenic a group of youngsters whose penchant for "extreme aloneness" seemed to have existed from birth.

Some 30 years following Bleuler's "group of adult schizophrenias" came the realization that as a unitary process, "childhood schizophrenia" was inadequate for classifying what, upon closer inspection, appeared to be diverse phenomena. While the 11 children in Kanner's 1943 case study evidenced certain "basic schizophrenic phenomena"—extreme autism, obsessiveness, stereotypy, and echolalia—other characteristics, most notably the children's nearly complete inability to "relate themselves in the ordinary way to people and situations from the beginning of life" suggested a distinct syndrome. In this context, autism acquired a strikingly different connotation from that which it held in Bleuler's use of the term:

> This is not, as in schizophrenic children or adults, a departure from an initially present relationship. . . . There is from the start an extreme autistic aloneness that wherever possible disregards, ignores, [and] shuts out anything that comes to the child from the outside (Kanner 1943, p. 127).

Other features characteristic of Kanner's 11 children included: failure to assume an anticipatory posture upon approach of a parental figure, failure to mold to the parenting figure's body when held, delayed acquisition of speech or mutism, failure to develop communicative language use, delayed echolalia, confusion of personal pronouns (pronominal fixation), refusal of food, anxiously obsessive desire for the maintenance of sameness coupled with a dread of change and incompleteness, and repetitious behaviors suggesting "masturbatory orgastic gratification." At the same time, however, Kanner's children were distinguished for their good cognitive potential, excellent rote memory and fine motor control, and "strikingly intelligent physiognomies."

While the majority of Kanner's pathognomonic signs remain in current use, more recent studies (Rutter 1975, Rutter and Lockyer 1967) have cast doubt upon Kanner's original contention of "good intelligence" and negative neurological findings. Given that all children are better at some things than others, however, the overall variability in autistic intellectual functioning is greater than normal. Similarly, while many current studies support Kanner's contention of an innate predisposition to autistic disturbances, there are, with few exceptions (such as Massie 1978, King 1975), no clear findings to support the notion that parents of autistic children are any more obsessive or less warmhearted than the parents of normal or dysphasic children (Cox et al. 1975, DeMyer et al. 1972, Goldfarb et al. 1976).

Studies of Childhood Psychosis After 1943

Of the many psychoanalytically oriented workers in the field of childhood and infantile psychosis, most came late and left early. Little in this area was written before the early 1940s or after the late 1960s. Hartman (1953) pondered the fact that so little use had been made of the hints Freud provided (1914, 1924) on the metapsychology of schizophrenia and the establishment of a systematic theory of the psychoses. Freud himself, however, had not always been so optimistic about the relationship between psychoanalysis and what he described as the "narcissistic neuroses," despite the fact that his original interest in primary and normal narcissism arose in an effort to explain the problem of dementia praecox in terms of the prevailing libido theory. Patients whom he described as "paraphrenics" exhibited two troublesome characteristics—megalomania and an extreme withdrawal of interest from the human and physical world—which set them apart from the neurotically afflicted. The latter of these changes in particular caused Freud to lament that such persons "are inaccessible to the influence of psychoanalysis and cannot be cured by our endeavors" (1914, p. 56).

Perhaps this is the hint that contemporary clinicians have taken in their reluctance to investigate the psychology of early onset psychotic disorders. Even beyond the realm of psychosis, however, it is possible to detect, at least in the early days of psycho-analysis, a gap between clinical psychoanalysts and the direct observation of children in general. As Hartman pointed out, it was the study of regressive phenomena among adult psychotics, rather than the direct inspection of developmental processes in normal children, that dominated the study of child development for some time. The work of testing regression-based hypotheses against first-hand developmental data has been a relatively recent endeavor.

Mahler

Margaret Mahler, whose interest in early psychotic disturbances evolved from the study of "tic syndrome" in children (Harley and Weil 1979, Mahler 1979a, was among the first psychoanalytically oriented clinicians to integrate theoretical notions of psychological development with the direct observation of normal and severely disturbed children. Taken in a historical context, the immediate effect of Mahler's work was a dramatic refinement in the discrimination and differentiation of phenomenal subtypes among psychotic disorders. Her refinement, the third of its kind, was preceded by DeSanctis's recognition of a "dementia praecox mentality" among certain mentally deficient children and Kanner's discrimination of autistic from schizophrenic psychopathologies.

Mahler (1979b, 1979c) described two distinct groups of early onset psychoses. In the first, autistic psychosis, the mother as a representative of the outside world "never seems to have been perceived emotionally by the infant." Rather, the maternal figure remains a part object, "seemingly devoid of specific cathexis and not distinguished from inanimate objects." In the second subtype, symbiotic psychosis, the early mother–infant symbiotic relationship is marked but does not progress to the stage of object-libidinal cathexis: "The mental representation of the mother remains or is regressively fused with . . . that is to say, not separated from the self" (1979b, p. 138). Neither symbiotic nor autistic pathology need be mutually exclusive, however, and depending on shifting developmental demands, may oscillate in the same child. The self-sufficient contentedness of the primarily autistic infant is viewed by Mahler as a defensive orientation aimed at gating, or shutting out, sources of stimulation which threaten to overwhelm the infant's primitive and perhaps congenitally vulnerable ego organization. Human contact, particularly contact with the mothering figure whose empathic reading of the infant's needs allows her to serve as an external executive ego (Mahler 1980), imposes upon the child's "halucinatory delusional need" to control a constricted inanimate environment. Only by maintaining a severely limited intensity of experience is the child able to approximate a state of relative homeostatic equilibrium.

Symbiotic psychotic phenomena, which typically reach crisis proportion between the ages of two and one-half and five, aim at a restoration of the "symbiotic-parasitic delusion" of oneness with the mother. Children so disposed are characterized by an abnormally low, perhaps congenitally limited tolerance for frustration or delay. Reality sense for the symbiotic youngster depends largely upon his ability to maintain a primitive delusional fusion with the primary caregiver or caregivers. A craving to unite with and incorporate the mothering partner and to maintain the "double frame of reference" of the symbiotic unit alternates with the struggle against reengulfment and the obliteration of whatever fragmentary vestiges of self have taken hold.

Mahler expanded the language of psychoanalytic metapsychology to include the phenomenology of primitive mental states in the separation–individuation process. It is doubtful, however, that Mahler ever intended to explain fully the genesis of early onset psychopathology in the same way in which she explained its course, that is, in purely psychological terms. Too often, the parents of severely disturbed children seemed neither so obsessive and emotionally distant nor unusually lacking in acceptance, love, and empathy as would account for such a catastrophic and intractable abnormality in the development of an otherwise healthy infant.

Mahler (1979b, p. 135) speculated that a primary psychophysiological vulnerability, a "constitutional anlage," must predispose the characteristic lack or loss of ability to utilize the need-satisfying object. The deficient tension-regulating capabilities and volatile temperaments of these infants could not be complemented by even the most sensitive, well-attuned parenting. In either case, whether because of a constitutional deficit or severe and early postnatal trauma, the tragic unfolding of infantile psychosis as conceived by Mahler took place not within the intrapsychic world of the infant— for as yet there could be no well differentiated intrapsychic structuralization—but within the "symbiotic dual unity" of the mother-child interaction.

Bergman and Escalona

Mahler was not alone among psychoanalytic investigators searching for a constellation of innate vulnerabilities predisposing to severe disturbances in early development. Bergman and

Escalona (1949) were struck by the "unusual sensitivities" of certain very young children in several, if not all, sensory modalities. Slight variations in color, light intensity, sound, tactile stimulation, taste, smell, or temperature seemed to have an extraordinary pleasurable or painful impact on these children. Though it was possible that this acuity might predispose the giftedness, the authors suggested that further investigation might indicate a more likely relationship to childhood psychosis.

The infant protected insufficiently from stimuli because of either a thin protective barrier or the failure of maternal protection was believed to compensate through "the premature formation of an ego." When this precocious but vulnerable adaptation broke down as a consequence of trauma, however, the infant would be left with only restitutive psychotic mechanisms with which to adapt. Recognized early, vulnerable children predisposed to sensory inundation might be provided with supplemental protection against intense stimuli allowing a more gradual consolidation of the barrier function.

Role of the Maternal Figure in the Etiology of Childhood Psychosis

Not all of the early psychoanalytic investigators shared a belief in the importance of congenital factors in the genesis of childhood psychosis. Mothers who were "extremely immature . . . with narcissistic cathexis incapable of mature emotional relationships" (Rank 1949) or "hostile overprotective [and] rejecting" (Spitz 1951) also began to appear in the literature. The "schizophrenogenic mother" (Fromm-Reichman 1948) emerged as the archetypal villain of child psychiatry—a malignant composite of indecipherable "double bind" communication (Bateson et al. 1965), narcissistic preoccupations, and unknowable genetic loadings, pitted against a hapless infant struggling to adapt in a world of senseless contradictions. Certainly there were indications of these phenomena in some cases, but few therapists had actually encountered the dreaded multipathological Medusa in clinical practice.

Bettelheim

Bettelheim (1967) shared with Bender (1959) and Goldstein (1959) the belief that autistic psychoses represented a defensive reaction against unbearable anxiety. He disagreed, however, with their interpretation of the reaction as a response to an inborn

impairment of the central nervous system, seeing it instead as a response of the child to life conditions perceived as being "utterly destructive."

The pathogenesis of autism, according to Bettelheim, was a relationship experienced by the child as persecutory, and defended against through withdrawal. In order for the full autistic syndrome to unfold, the maternal figure must have adopted a style of responding to the child's rejections (intentional or unintentional) with counterrejections of her own. The child's eventual withdrawal would be coerced by a sense of hopelessness, of being unable to alter a reality perceived as wholly destructive. Thus, as a defensive reaction, autism prevented painful stimuli from intruding upon awareness and curtailed the "temptation to act" where action could only meet with failure—a hellish scenario for which Bettelheim believed the parents were culpable yet blameless: "The parents of autistic children simply lived their own lives, reacting to its conditions out of their own psychological makeup. True they did so with little regard for the nature of the child, but this they did not know" (1967, p. 71).

Classificatory Systems for Childhood Psychoses

Classificatory systems for early onset psychotic disorders proliferated following the pioneering efforts of such workers as Kanner, Bender, and Mahler. Each advance in theory seemed to bring with it a new designation, and designations were continually broadened in scope to include an ever-widening range of clinical phenomena.

As late as 1970, Kanner, in a personal communication to Rimland (1973), estimated that no more than one child in ten diagnosed as autistic actually fit the syndrome as originally conceived. Where attempts have been made to achieve greater specificity through the distillation of "essential symptoms" (Eisenberg and Kanner 1956), results have often led to the use of oversimplified diagnostic criteria based on the appearance of only one or two symptoms. Not infrequently, similar symptoms are characteristic of a variety of disorders. Menal and Simon (1965) pointed out, for example, that social withdrawal may be common to early infantile autism, childhood schizophrenia, central language disorders, acute situational stress reactions, and encephalitis.

Some have gone so far as to question the usefulness of any single category or categories as compared to a unified continuum based on a gradient of disturbance from neurotic to psychotic (Szurek and Berlin 1973). Others (Rutter 1972) continue to stand by the objectification of criteria as a worthwhile and workable goal for descriptive psychiatry. Currently in favor are the multiaxial systems, of which *DSM III* (American Psychiatric Association 1980) is perhaps best known.

The first viable approach to standardization in the diagnosis of childhood psychosis came from the British Working Party under the authorship of Creak (1961). Nine criteria were included in the new system: gross and sustained impairment of emotional relationships (including both symbiotic and autistic phenomena); apparent unawareness of personal identity to a degree inappropriate to the child's age; pathological preoccupation with particular objects or characteristics of objects without regard to their accepted functions; sustained resistance to change; abnormal perceptual experiences in the absence of discernible organic abnormality; acute, excessive, and seemingly illogical anxiety; speech that has been lost, never acquired, or is developmentally delayed; distortion of motility; and a background of serious retardation in which islets of normal, near normal, or exceptional functioning may appear.

Creak's diagnostic criteria were effective in diagnosing early childhood psychosis, but they did so broadly and without adequate discrimination between differing etiological factors. There seemed to be a tendency beginning with Creak to disregard age of onset as a primary diagnostic criterion, with the result that disorders beginning in early infancy were grouped together with psychotic disorders of later childhood and adolescence (Rutter 1978). In response to this deficiency, the Group for the Advancement of Psychiatry (GAP 1966) issued a classificatory system based on that of the British Working Party but emphasizing differences in clinical presentation at different ages and developmental stages of onset. Psychoses of infancy and early childhood were characterized by onset prior to 5 years of age, and three subtypes were recognized: early infantile autism, interactional psychotic disorder (psychoses related to or emerging around attachment and separation issues), and other psychoses of infancy and early childhood. Psychoses of later childhood were defined by onset between 6 and 12 years of age, and two subtypes were recognized: schizophreniform psychotic disorders with manifestations comparable to those found among adult schizophrenics, and other psychoses with atypical presentations.

Chapter Two

Current Classifications

In 1943, Kanner first described the diagnostic syndrome of early infantile autism, having observed a condition that differed "so markedly and uniquely from anything reported so far that each case merits a detailed consideration of its fascinating peculiarities." Believing his sample of 11 autistic children to have been of essentially normal intelligence, Kanner excluded from this category those children who showed signs of pervasive cognitive retardation or neurological impairment. Insult to the central nervous system, however, is difficult to rule out. Gross lesions may only appear symptomatically over time, while subclinical manifestations of organicity may never reveal their presence to direct or mechanical observation. Rutter and Lockyer (1967) reported that in a sample of preschool autistic children showing negative neurological findings, 18 percent developed seizure disorders by adolescence.

Difficulties encountered in the discrimination of cases of true Kannerian autism from cases of so-called "secondary autism" (secondary to neurological dysfunction or mental retardation) led to the use of multicategorical systems such as *DSM II* (American Psychiatric Association 1968) and the multiaxial system in current use, *DSM III* (American Psychiatric Association 1980). Both systems allow for a greater discrimination of etiological factors and associated or atypical features.

In *DSM III*, the terms "childhood schizophrenia" and "childhood psychosis" do not appear. In place of these generic terms the new system recognizes three classificatory subtypes—Infantile Autism, Childhood Onset Pervasive Developmental Disorder, and Atypical Pervasive Developmental Disorder of Childhood. Residual states are also classified for cases in which the current clinical picture no longer meets all criteria for the full syndrome despite the persistence of certain signs or symptoms of the original illness. Schizophrenic disorders of childhood showing a clinical course similar to that found among adult schizophrenics (such as presence of hallucinations and delusions) are classified under the adult headings and subtypes for schizophrenic disorders. The move toward clear differentiation of schizophrenic and developmental disorders may, in part, have been a response to followup studies (DeMyer et al. 1973, Rutter and Lockyer 1967) indicating that lower-functioning autistic children do not resemble adult schizophrenics at maturity but more often appear mentally retarded. Moreover higher-functioning autistic adults, though often disabled by certain social and intellectual impairments, are not diagnosed generally as schizophrenic (Watt 1978, Roff et al. 1976). A recent review of clinical studies (DeMyer et al. 1981) which examined the relationship between diagnostic categories of childhood psychotic disorders suggested a continuum along the dimension of cognitive disability. Autistic children fall at the lowest level of functioning, early onset schizophrenic children intermediate, and borderline children at the highest level. Delusional ideation and hallucinations, primary symptoms in the schizophrenias, are seldom found among autistic children or adults.

Among the 3 major subtypes of Pervasive Developmental Disorder, early infantile autism, with recognition before 30 months, is paradigmatic. The second subtype (and the one of greatest interest to the current study), Childhood Onset Pervasive Developmental Disorder, overlaps with infantile autism symptomatically at many points but represents, overall, a less severe adaptive impairment and only emerges in full syndrome after 30 months of age. Atypical Pervasive Developmental Disorder is a third diagnostic category used in those cases when psychological distortions crossing multiple developmental lines defy classification as either infantile autism or childhood onset pervasive developmental disorder.

With the exception of early infantile autism, which has been studied comprehensively over the past 40 years, the use of childhood onset pervasive developmental disorder and atypical pervasive developmental disorder classifications for either clinical or research purposes is problematic. The proposed diagnostic criteria and even the terms themselves are only a few years old and of unknown validity and reliability. As of this writing, I have been able to locate only two systematic examinations of the pervasive developmental disorders and associated phenomena (Goldfarb 1980, DeMyer et al. 1981). In neither case were statistical evaluations presented. Thus, the paradox: in order to define a diagnostic subtype within a system designed to eliminate ambiguities and overlap, it is necessary to review an earlier literature in which, quite often, the syndrome being described (typically identified indiscriminately as autism or childhood schizophrenia) is nonspecific and may refer to any number of clinical manifestations subsumed under the generic heading of childhood psychosis.

Childhood Onset Pervasive Developmental Disorder

Childhood Onset Pervasive Developmental Disorder, the second class of Pervasive Developmental Disorders, is characterized by an extreme and pervasive disturbance in human relations together with a variety of bizarre behaviors, all of which emerge in full syndrome between 30 months and 12 years of age. Although the full syndrome may include many of the primary and associated features of infantile autism—gross and sustained impairments in attachment behavior, delays in language and cognitive development, and bizarre repetitive behaviors—the essential characteristics of the condition are defined below more broadly.

Diagnostic criteria and clinical features of childhood onset pervasive developmental disorders consists of

A. Gross and sustained impairment in social relations, for example, lack of appropriate affective responsivity, inappropriate clinging, asociality, and lack of empathy.
B. At least three of the following are present:

   1. Sudden, excessive anxiety manifesting in free-floating anxiety, catastrophic reactions to everyday occurrences, inconsolability, and unexplained panic attacks.
   2. Constricted or inappropriate affect, including lack of appropriate fear reactions, unexpected rage reactions, and extreme mood lability.
   3. Resistance to change in the environment or insistence on sameness.

    4. Oddities of motor movement such as peculiar posturing, peculiar hand or finger movements, and walking on tiptoe.
    5. Abnormalities of speech.
    6. Hyper- or hyposensitivity to sensory stimuli.
    7. Self-mutilation.

C. Onset of the full syndrome occures between 30 months and 12 years of age.
D. Additional criteria are absence of delusions, hallucinations, incoherence, and marked loosening of association.
    (Adapted from American Psychiatric Association 1980)

In the final analysis, the extreme early onset of the autistic child's impairment in human relations and speech development allows for the objective differentiation of autistic and childhood onset pervasive developmental disorders. Even this distinction, however, is frequently ambiguous in clinical practice. It would be a mistake to assume that the designation "childhood onset" implies in every instance a sudden and unprecedented appearance of psychotic symptoms during the post-infancy years in the total absence of premorbid signs. Chess (1977) has suggested that insidious or subclinical behavioral or developmental impairments may appear prior to 30 months in a form that does not prove disruptive or abnormal enough to trigger immediate family or professional concern. In other words the fact that a child is not brought in for clinical evaluation until after 30 months is probably not a reliable indicator of either age of onset or clinical course. Thus, a working definition of childhood onset pervasive developmental disorder would most likely include psychotic manifestations early in actual onset but late in recognition and treatment.

Even if we consider this syndrome as merely a special instance of infantile autism, however, the importance of age of onset relative to the ultimate course of the illness cannot be overemphasized. Children of 12 months, 24 months, and 30 months are remarkably different human beings, physiologically and psychologically, and can be expected to show equally dissimilar responses to serious disruptions in development, regardless of the reasons for their occurrence. Older, late onset "autistic" children as recognized by the current classificatory system are very possibly not autistic at all but instead children whose massive developmental disturbances have taken a form and course commensurate with their own maturational stage and its associated tasks, milestones and achievements. Hence, the separate classification of childhood onset pervasive developmental disorder is employed.

Demography and Epidemiology

In view of the recent reclassification of diagnostic criteria in *DSM III*, exact demographic statistics for each of the 3 subtypes of Pervasive Developmental Disorder are unavailable as yet. Recent epidemiological studies, however, seem to agree that the incidence of severe developmental disturbances is relatively low, occurring in 4 to 5 per 10,000 children under the age of 15 (Wing et al. 1976, Lotter 1976). Some workers, however, believe this to be a minimum estimate due to frequent misdiagnosis (Ornitz and Ritvo 1978). Sex ratios in populations described as autistic show that male autistic children outnumber females by a 5 to 1 margin (Ando and Tsuda 1975).

Consistent with Kanner's original findings, parents of psychotic children tend to represent a population of higher than average socioeconomic status (Cox et al. 1975, O'Moore 1972), although, in a more recent study, Schopler (1980) reported that among a sample of 264 autistic children in North Carolina, 74 percent came from families at lower socioeconomic levels. It remains to be demonstrated that discrepant findings are more than artifacts of sampling techniques, intake procedures, and differences in diagnostic classification utilized by service providers representing different sectors of the population. Confusion in diagnostic terms, availability of funding or treatment facilities, and differences in service utilization across different socioeconomic groups may also influence the apparent distribution of cases.

Prognosis

Despite advances in treatment and educational intervention, about two-thirds of psychotic (autistic) children remain completely dependent through adulthood (Goldfarb 1980, Rutter and Lockyer 1967). (Other classifications of pervasive developmental disorders are too recent to have yielded meaningful statistics in this area.) Only one child in six ultimately achieves what could be considered a good social adjustment and self-sustaining employment. An extremely small minority, 1 or 2 percent, resolve all psychotic manifestations and establish a vital, independent adult adjustment.

The relatively favorable outcome of a small percentage of autistic children correlates most highly with measured intelligence (DeMyer 1973, Rutter and Lockyer 1967). Children who have IQs below 50 invariably remain seriously impaired throughout life, while approximately 50 percent of those with IQs over 70 show some signs of improvement (such as employability and continued schooling). In almost all cases, adult autistics (including those who are higher functioning) continue to demonstrate serious impairments across multiple lines of functioning. Frequently, such persons show a striking lack of social intelligence and are unable to understand and respond to the feelings of others.

The effect of early intervention on the adult outcome of early psychotic disorders has been difficult to assess. While some workers (Bettelheim 1967) claim significant therapeutic inroads into the natural history of the disease process, others (Rimland 1964) have gone as far as to suggest that untreated children actually achieve a higher spontaneous recovery rate than children receiving intensive psychotherapy. For the majority of children, treated or untreated, however, recovery to any significant degree is not at issue. By adolescence or early adulthood, many persons with an original diagnosis of autism lose their diagnostic distinction and are institutionalized as "mentally retarded."

Chapter Three

A Psychophysiological Perspective

In 1895 Freud, in his "Project for a Scientific Psychology," proposed the possibility of linking the theoretical and observational data of psychoanalysis to discrete physiological correlates in the central nervous system (Freud 1895). Others have also called for the reconciliation of neurophysiological with psychoanalytical findings though, as one recent example illustrates (Holt 1981), the end result is often more inspirational or diversionary than explanatory. Nevertheless, the call for a unified systems theory, a metapsychology of forces, structures, and dynamics linked to a neurophysiology of metabolites and brain structures, seems a worthy one and movement in this direction is inevitable. If, as Holt proposes, we begin with the assumption of a unitary psychobiological system, then the identification of structural-functional analogues that are neither exclusively psychoanalytic nor exclusively neurophysiological will evolve quite naturally and provide ultimately a common idiom for both disciplines.

A science of human behavior such as this, however, is still only a vision. Current literature rarely offers solid demonstrations of psychophysiological processes underlying personality theory or psychopathology. Thus, it is heartening to find in the study of childhood psychosis a relatively recent body of work in the area of psychophysiology that merges with certain psychodynamic speculations regarding etiology and causation. To begin, I will examine some of the more promising work from the side of physiology.

Summarizing a review of psychophysiological mechanisms in early onset psychosis, James and Barry (1980) have supported a hypothesis of perceptual and physiological abnormalities in sensory integration and selective attention. As a group, psychotic children demonstrate difficulties in attending to, selecting, and assimilating incoming sensory stimulation. In some instances (Lovaas 1971), abnormal responses to sensory input have been characterized by a "stimulus overselectivity" in which responding is limited to a single stimulus dimension in a multisensory array, a form of perceptual centration. Ornitz and Ritvo (1968) in a classic study of neurophysiological mechanisms underlying perceptual abnormalities among autistic and schizophrenic children proposed an inadequate homeostatic regulation of sensory input resulting in a condition of "perceptual inconstancy." Psychotic phenomena, from this point of view, are believed to involve a quality of consciousness resembling that of REM sleep in which periods of state tonic inhibition are periodically interrupted by intervals of phasic excitation. Fluctuations between these states of excitation and inhibition are likened by the authors to the rapidly alternating states of behavioral excitement (hand flapping, darting, lunging) and inhibition observed among certain autistic children.

Ornitz and Ritvo (1968) have attributed autistic manifestations of perceptual inconstancy to a failure of the vestibular system in mediating paired reactions involving sensory input and motor output. Other workers, primarily in the area of adult schizophrenia, have postulated chronically elevated levels of ascending reticular activating system activity resulting in a blocking of sensory pathways. This idea is based on the observation that social withdrawal among chronic schizophrenics is associated with elevations in physiological arousal (Hutt and Hutt 1968). Along similar lines, Broen and Nakamari (1972) and Bush (1977) have proposed a deficit in the "central selection mechanism" that normally facilitates the screening of irrelevant stimuli and irrelevant responses, leading to stimulus overload.

Waters et al. (1977) have developed the concept of "habituation of phasic autonomous response measures": selective gating mechanisms or filters which differentially facilitate or inhibit stimuli impinging from the environment. By filtering out repeated but unimportant stimuli, these mechanisms free attentional capacities for novel or more significant events. Deficiencies in habituation (offered by the authors as a likely mechanism in the psychophysiology of schizophrenia) would result in an inability either to attend to stimuli selectively or to attend to a sufficiently wide range of sensory input.

The majority of theories pertaining to abnormal perceptual processes, faulty arousal mechanisms, and stimulus overselectivity were originally formulated to account for certain pathological manifestations encountered among adult schizophrenic patients. Ornitz (1971), however, has suggested that similar abnormalities imposed upon the maturationally primitive central nervous system of the infant or young child could account for a range of related phenomena though in a form and presentation commensurate with the child's developmental stage. From this point of view, states of perceptual dysfunction thought to be associated with early onset psychoses may anticipate the more elaborate sensory disturbances of adult schizophrenic disorders.

Electroencephalographic Studies

Evidence for RAS dysfunction of phasic responses in early onset psychosis comes primarily from electroencephalographic (EEG) studies. Contrary to Kanner's 1943 findings of essentially normal EEG patterns among his eleven autistic children, more recent studies have demonstrated spontaneous EEG irregularities indicative of central nervous system dysfunction in anywhere from 13 percent (Ritvo et al. 1970) to 85 percent (Creak and Pampiglione 1969) of children diagnosed with psychotic disorders. Reported abnormalities include dysrhythmias and instability (Hinton 1963, Kennard 1959), paroxysmal slow wave activity of 4 to 6 Hz. (Colbert et al. 1959), and spike wave paroxysms (DeMyer 1973). Hutt et al. (1965), have demonstrated a constellation of waking EEG abnormalities characterized by generalized low voltage irregular activity without established rhythm. The authors noted that reduced stereotyped behavior and more synchronous high voltage EEG patterns were obtained when the children in the study were placed in a simpler, less stimulating environment. These findings were interpreted to mean that for at least some psychotic children, the nonspecific activity of the RAS is chronically elevated. Stereotypies or other behaviors aimed at a reduction of stimulation may act as a safeguard against excessive sensory input, thereby protecting the organism from the potentially harmful effects of intense excitation.

Overall, the literature of EEG profiles of psychotic children, while consistent in demonstrating central nervous system abnormalities, has by no means reached consensus as to the exact source, site, or direction (over or underarousal) of the hypothetical dysfunction. The current debate runs in favor of studies pointing to a hyperarousal of central nervous system functioning (Hutt et al. 1965, Kolvin et al. 1971), but others (Creak and Pampiglione 1969, Hermelin and O'Connor 1979) still maintain findings of central nervous system hypoarousal among heterogeneous populations of psychotic children. From one study to the next, there is little uniformity with respect to type, distribution, or severity of abnormalities. In some instances children presenting similar symptoms yield irregular but dissimilar EEG patterns, while in other instances children presenting strikingly dissimilar symptoms yield comparable response records. In studies comparing EEGs of autistic children with those of nonpsychotic children of subnormal intelligence, for example, similar records are often obtained (DeMyer 1973), suggesting a higher correlation with cognitive dysfunction than with psychotic process. Taken together, these highly variable findings were interpreted by Rimland (1964) as evidence for a final common pathway phenomenon wherein any number of different pathological processes eventually converge into an apparently similar symptomatic outcome.

Cardiovascular and Vasomotor Activity

Cardiovascular activity, which has been shown to be elevated in adult schizophrenics (Fenz and Velner 1970), has also been studied as a possible correlate to disturbances in arousal mechanisms among psychotic children. MacCulloch and Williams (1971) have reported a significant increase in heart rate variability for a group of autistic children as compared with normals and retardates. Based on this finding, the authors have postulated a dysfunction in central control of heart rate modulation related to a partial failure of negative feedback between accelerating and decelerating tracts of the brainstem cardio-regulating centers. Irregular activity of the RAS filter mechanisms associated with variable heart rate levels would also explain fluctuating abnormalities in arousal, sensory threshold, and vestibular dysfunction characteristic of some psychotic children. Hutt et al. (1975) have reported clinically significant cardiac arrhythmias in a population of psychotic youngsters as compared with normals. Furthermore, the extent of arrhythmia appeared to be dependent upon the nature of the accompanying behaviors, becoming most pronounced during attentional tasks. The authors interpreted signs of heightened arrhythmia (indicative of a labile and sympathetically dominated autonomic nervous system), together with the EEG irregularities cited above, as further evidence for increased cortical arousal among autistic children.

Vasomotor response—blood pressure and peripheral vascular resistance—also shows promise as a sensitive indicator of emotional and attention states. Changes in peripheral blood flow may, for example, indicate whether a person is actively taking in or rejecting sensory input. Cohen and Johnson (1977), in a comparison of ten autistic children between 5 and 20 years of age with ten matched normals and ten normal adults, have reported that the psychotic children displayed higher mean blood flow and lower vascular resistance during both sensory intake and sensory rejection tasks. In normals this type of vasomotor response was characteristic during sensory rejection tasks, while decreased peripheral blood flow and increased peripheral vasomotor resistance accompanied sensory intake tasks. Although it was not entirely clear whether relatively high blood flow in the psychotic group represented a primary deficit in the regulation of cortical arousal or a temporary psychophysiological adjustment to a strange experimental environment, the authors interpreted these data to mean that autistic children may be perpetually engaged in sensory rejection, with resultant abnormalities in information coding and processing.

Overall, psychotic children tend to have more physical signs than normals and are nearly equivalent to nonpsychotic retardates in the presentation of clinically significant neurological abnormalities (Hingten and Bryson 1972). In fact, autistic phenomena have been associated with a variety of physical disorders including congenital rubella and phenylketonuria. This close association of autistic features with otherwise dissimilar conditions led Ornitz and Ritvo to conceptualize autism as a syndrome rather than a single disease entity—a common symptomatic pathway, as it were, for certain infectious, genetic, and traumatically induced disorders.

The range of physical abnormalities associated with autism in particular is extensive. Minor physical anomalies range from abnormal fingerprint patterns (Alter and Shulenberg 1966) and diminutive stature (Campbell 1980) to low-set ears, "electric hair," and high arched palate (Steg and Rapaport 1975). DeMyer (1979) has identified possible biological factors in 88 percent of those cases of childhood psychotic disorders with onset prior to three years. Of these, 48 percent involve troubled pregnancy and 37 percent complications in labor. In a study of autistic children in Western Australia, Lobascher et al. (1970) reported a high incidence of postmaturity, approaching 65 percent. Among those prenatal and perinatal complications associated with later psychotic disturbances (including fetal anoxia and forceps delivery), prenatal bleeding was reported most frequently, with an incidence of 13 percent (Campbell et al. 1978).

Although few studies pertaining to psychiatrically disturbed children appear in the literature of computerized axial tomography, the use of CAT scan technology holds great promise for future investigation of disorders like autism with a presumed psychophysiological etiology. In one recent study utilizing CAT technology, Hier et al. (1978) have reported an enlargement of the right parieto-occipital region in 7 out of 9 (.77) autistic children as compared to 11 out of 41 (.27) nonautistic retardates. The authors speculated that a reversed pattern of asymmetry is indicative of a left hemisphere dysfunction among autistics.

In conclusion, all that can be said with any real certainty regarding the psychophysiology of early onset psychoses is that children suffering from any of these disorders display characteristic response forms that are different from normals and in many instances comparable to those observed in nonpsychotic retardates. Psychotic children vary widely from one another in terms of specific dysfunctions, but the idiosyncrasies of each individual child tend to remain constant over time. Typically, motoric development appears to be spared, this being an important criterion for differentiating low-functioning psychotic children from nonpsychotic retardates, many of whom do not walk until age three or four. More complex motor skills, such as ball play and imitation, are often abnormal, but psychotic children tend to be handicapped at almost any activities in which multiple aspects of a situation must be dealt with simultaneously. Thus, it is likely that motoric peculiarities, much like other dysfunctional characteristics, have more to do with abnormal attention mechanisms than with specific disturbances in motor coordination.

The exact source or site of the psychotic child's hypothetical central nervous system abnormalities is as yet unclear, though a number of studies implicate RAS, vestibular, and brainstem mechanisms. Dysfunction in the central nervous system seems to occur in the direction of hyperreactivity or overarousal, with associated abnormalities in stimulus gating, stimulus habituation, and random perceptual inconstancy.

Interrelated Physiological and Psychodynamic Processes

Taken in its own right, current psychophysiological research presents a number of intriguing if inconclusive corollaries to the understanding of the pervasive developmental disorders. The cross-validation found the psychoanalytic literature comes largely from a body of relatively early work based on the direct clinical observation of severely disturbed infants. Thinking back, for example, to Bergman and Escalona's (1949) study of very young children with "unusual sensitivities," I am reminded of more recent findings of central nervous system hyperreactivity among autistic and schizophrenic children. The striking vulnerability of certain children to even the slightest variations in sensory stimulation is corroborated from a psychophysiological standpoint by EEG findings of near chronic cortical hyperarousal. Even the unusually sensitive neonate, however, is not without adaptive mechanisms, and here again it is possible to draw a number of parallels between the earliest vestiges of personality organization and certain underlying psychophysiological processes.

Following Freud, Bergman and Escalona described a "protective barrier against stimuli" that functioned in the neonate as a sensory precursor to the ego prior to its emergence from an undifferentiated ego-id matrix. Hartman (1958) also recognized the role of a protective sensory barrier in the newborn, but relegated this function to a constitutionally given ego apparatus relatively autonomous from the id, an innate regulating mechanism. Having developed a capacity for the binding, neutralization, and transformation of instinctual energy, the ego, according to Hartman, then acquires a capacity for automatic reactions or automatizations which further enhances the stimulus-regulating function of the mental apparatus.

Recognizing the inherent vulnerability of any form of primitive, innate stimulus barrier, Mahler and McDevitt (1980) have emphasized the importance of early mother–child interactions. During the normal autistic phase, the child's limited capacities for self-regulation of internal and external stimuli must be augmented by the mother's mature capacity for attuned empathic responding. The infant, for his or her part, develops an increasingly differentiated repertoire of affective and motor discharge patterns with which to summon or signal the mother's need-gratifying ministrations, thereby circumventing a buildup of tension that might otherwise engender a state of "organismic distress." In other words, the primary caregiver serves as an "external auxiliary ego," augmenting the child's limited capacity for binding instinctual energies and delaying discharge. Here the infant's innate but precarious stimulus barrier is enhanced by the remarkable complementarity of the mother–child interaction. The success of the interacting dyad in maintaining internal regulation and outer-directed interest in face of disintegrative stress experiences will largely determine the extent to which the infant will move ahead to richer, better-differentiated relations in the external world.

Regardless of the theoretical point of view from which we start, we can recognize that the neonatal organization of a primitive stimulus barrier—an innate constellation of functional-structural characteristics designed to modulate the intensity of sensory impressions, either autonomously or in conjunction with the mother's responsiveness—represents, on a psychophysiological level, the way in which the central nervous system and autonomic nervous system regulate arousal, attention, and reactivity. Within certain broad parameters, we can even localize these functions. Current findings would seem to suggest that the site of stimulus regulation in both normal and pathological states lies somewhere within the brainstem reticular activating system. The same children who impress clinicians as unusually vulnerable to variations in stimuli also show, on EEG evaluation, a peculiar inability to gate incoming stimuli or to habituate selectively to repeated sources of sensory input. Once having made this connection, it is difficult not to begin considering ego capacities such as impulse delay, synthesis, and sensory regulation in terms of their neurophysiological correlates. Though it is still premature to begin mapping the neuroanatomy of intrapsychic processes, it is nevertheless an important step along the way to have isolated what appear to be distinct regions or structures whose functional organization bears a striking resemblance to what we regularly refer to as ego. The implications of this metapsychological-neurophysiological interface for the study of early ego and pre-ego deficits are equally intriguing.

According to Bergman and Escalona, the clinical course of children protected insufficiently against stimuli because of either a constitutionally thin protective barrier or a massive failure in maternal empathy will, under certain circumstances, lead to a "premature formation of the ego"—a precocious developmental adaptation subject to breakdown under stress. What form would such a premature ego take, both behaviorally and physiologically? It is interesting to recall Hutt's findings (1964, 1965) of reduced stereotyped behavior among psychotic children placed in a relatively simple, stress-free environment. Hutt concluded that stereotypies may act as "safety devices" to reduce the massive influx of sensory input, thereby protecting the primitive organism from the potentially devastating effects of excessive excitation.

One little girl in our program, Katy, frequently became overstimulated during the course of her own solitary play. A series of odd convulsing hand gestures (reminiscent of the theatrical motions of a stage hypnotist) interspersed at regular intervals seemed to help her reestablish distance from her play and momentarily discharge the tensions which had accrued. As though placing a spell, her raised hands twisted peculiarly before her face and her entire body became rigid. Seconds later, quite as if nothing had happened, she was able to resume her play or move off to another activity. What might have been accomplished normally simply by slowing down for a moment, pulling back or turning away—some form of brief, mild respite from activity—required of Katy an extensive mobilization of behavioral and physiological adaptations. Other children suffering from similar disturbances in the gating or regulating of stimulation were noted to use a variety of sterotypical or ritualistic facial and postural movement complexes in much the same way.

Perhaps in the oddly repetitive but seemingly senseless behavior of psychotic children we can see something of the precocious manifestations of a primitive ego talked about by Bergman and Escalona (that is, an organization of complex motor patterns aimed at maintaining equilibrium and adaptedness in face of massive internal and external stimuli). A child unable to modulate sensory reactivity internally, because, let us say, of a hypothetical RAS abnormality, must, in order to compensate, develop a complex behavioral organization designed to distract, distort, or otherwise obstruct attention and in this way limit excitation and arousal. In this sense, certain of the behaviors of psychotic children become sensible as secondary defensive reactions associated with inborn impairments of the central nervous system, a position taken early on by both Goldstein (1959) and Bender (1959). As Bergman and Escalona or Hutt et al. might have predicted, the interruption of a psychotic child's behavior is often observed to elicit a violent and disintegrative response. Perhaps the "sense of annihilation" cited by some writers to describe the experience of loss of self during periods of profound psychotic disorganization represents the phenomenological concomitant of sensory thresholds inundated and overwhelmed by internal or external stimulation, that is, arousal mechanisms gone awry. In any event, these are both unusual and tragic sensitivities.

Chapter Four

The Biochemistry and Genetics of Early Onset Psychoses

Over the past decade a multitude of neurochemical studies have investigated the role of neurotransmitter substances in the pathogenesis of psychiatric disorders. Findings are inconclusive: few specific biological markers have been identified to date. At least a part of the problem is methodological. Studies continue to be plagued with diagnostic ambiguities, poor standardization, and uncontrolled factors such as age, sex, intellectual status, and activity level, any or all of which may have an indeterminate effect on brain chemistry.

The most promising of the recent biochemical studies of early onset psychosis have focused on serotonin metabolism, utilizing such techniques as the measurement of blood serum platelet levels or the assay of cerebral spinal fluid and urine for serotonin and indolamine metabolites. The study of the role of serotonin in the biochemistry of psychotic disorders is a long one, spanning 30 years. The first "serotonin hypothesis" of schizophrenia was presented in the literature by Woolley and Shaw (1954), who hypothesized that mental changes associated with the disorder might be attributed to a cerebral deficiency of serotonin caused, presumably, by a metabolic abnormality. Evidence for the serotonin hypothesis came from clinical studies of the psychotomimetic effects of LSD, a drug which Woolley speculated had an inhibitory effect on serotonin levels. Other studies, however, yielded contradictory findings. For example, iproniazid, an inhibitor of monoamine oxidase (MAO) that is known to increase cerebral serotonin levels also produced a toxic psychosis. In 1961, Schain and Freedman reported elevated platelet serotonin levels in a subpopulation of autistic children. Campbell et al. (1974) more recently found a similar elevation in platelet serotonin among brain damaged children, which has led to some speculation that hyperserotonia may be a more frequent factor in ideopathic mental retardation than in autism or other psychotic disorders.

At present, it is generally agreed that a subgroup of up to 40 percent of autistic persons show elevated blood serotonin levels as compared with normal persons of the same age and sex (Geller et al. 1982). The exact linkage between serotonin metabolism and psychopathology is unclear, though several models have been proposed in the literature. Ciaranello (1982) has suggested that elevated serotonin levels interfere with the normal coordinated functioning of other neuronal systems. In certain areas of the brain, serotoninergic and noradrenenergic neurons mediate reciprocal events, with normal functioning reflecting a balance between opposing stimuli. This type of model has been constructed to account for dopaminergic-cholinergic interactions in Parkinson's Disease and tardive dyskinesia and for serotoninergic-noradrenenergic imbalances in certain types of endogenous depression. A second hypothesis proposes that serotonin, like other neurotransmitter substances, may modulate neuronal morphogenesis. It is known from animal studies that certain neurotransmitters or neurotrophic substances (of which serotonin may be one) can alter or arrest the development of brain neurons.

Despite some hopeful preliminary results in the pharmacological treatment of autistic children with fenfluramine, an anorexigenic drug which produces long-lasting decreases in brain serotonin levels (see p. 50), it is difficult to implicate hyperserotonia as a specific pathogenic factor in early onset psychotic illnesses. Individual variability within diagnostic categories is common, and elevated serotonin levels have been observed in nonautistic individuals as well. The most compelling evidence supports a relationship between blood serotonin levels and intellectual status rather than psychiatric diagnosis (Hanley et al. 1978). There is, of course, the additional risk of assuming a unidirectional cause-and-effect relationship. Whether elevated serotonin levels result in specific dysfunctions, are associated tangentially with specific dysfunctions, or occur adjunctively in response to other characteristic changes in the central nervous system linked more directly to a specific dysfunction is a distinction as yet unclear.

Research into other biochemical correlates to early onset psychosis has been inconclusive and generally less successful than serotonin studies in demonstrating a causal linkage. There is some evidence to suggest lower catecholamine levels in autistic children as compared with normals (Young et al. 1978). Studies of dopamine B-hydroxylase (DBH), a synthesizing catecholamine enzyme involved in the conversion of dopamine to norepinephrine, have demonstrated both elevated (Belmaker et al. 1978) and decreased levels (Lake et al. 1977) in autistic as compared with normal children. Lake et al. observed significantly higher norepinephrine levels in the same group of psychotic children. Studies of platelet MAO activity have failed to demonstrate significant differences between autistic and normal children.

As many as 87 percent of children with early onset psychoses have been shown to manifest various forms of endocrinopathy. In a study examining adrenal, pituitary, and thyroid status in a group of 16 children with psychotic disorders, Brambella et al. (1966) found cortico-hyposecretion in 62 percent of children examined, gonadohyposecretion in 75 percent, and thyrotropic hyposecretion in 50 percent. Overall, children with more debilitating psychotic disorders showed higher rates of endocrinopathy.

Other indices of endocrine functioning, free fatty acid (FFA) metabolism and endocrine stress response, have also been studied in young psychotic children. Mahler et al. (1975) have reported that a group of autistic children as compared with matched normals maintained elevated cortisol levels in response to stress for longer periods of time and recovered normal glucose levels more slowly. The authors interpreted these findings as indicating a functional abnormality in endocrine stress-coping mechanisms among autistic children. DeMyer et al. (1971), studying FFA metabolism in autistic, schizophrenic, and emotionally disturbed children, found that plasma FFA levels were more variable in psychotic children than in other groups, 66 percent of the autistics had normal lowering of FFA in response to exogenous insulin, and no differences were obtained in the FFA response to endogenous insulin as tested by glucose stimulation. The authors hypothesized a poorly functioning regulatory feedback mechanism as one possible abnormality underlying these findings.

Mahler's and DeMyer's studies are particularly interesting when considered together with psychophysiological research into dysfunctional attention-arousal mechanisms among psychotic children. Whether we target a specific structure such as the reticular activating system or a particular endocrine reaction such as the endocrine stress response, the effects of disruption to baseline functioning are similar. Across both measures, psychotic children show greater difficulty than normals in reestablishing equilibrium and maintaining viable homeostatic limits. They are slower than normal children in recovering from stress and, because of heightened baseline cortical arousal levels, are more susceptible to stressful situations in the first place. Again we are reminded that when we speak in the context of defective ego functioning in psychotic children, what we refer to represents a specifiable constellation of psychophysiological correlates. But psychology does not end with psychophysiology. Far from obviating the need for a psychology or even metapsychology of psychotic process, the findings of psychophysiological studies can only broaden our understanding of normal and pathological adaptation while enhancing the specificity of our interventions. The physiology of autistic and symbiotic psychotic phenomena may be represented in terms of behavioral adaptation to defects in cortical arousal mechanisms, platelet serotonin levels, or insulin stress response. The phenomenology of psychosis, however, can be represented only by analogy and metaphor. A psychophysiology of complex mental states is but a little closer today than was Freud's "natural science" psychology, some 90 years ago.

Genetics

The literature on early onset psychotic disorders shows little exact consensus as to the role of hereditary factors. Were modes of genetic transmission limited to strict Mendelian laws, the unequivocal appearance or nonappearance of fully developed phenotypes would allow for a relatively straightforward analysis. The complex of symptoms which, taken together, present as pervasive developmental disorders appear, however, to be neither the result of a single gene abnormality nor for that matter of any exclusive etiological factor. Current theories (such as those of Hanson and Gottesman 1976) suggest that a hereditary factor, if present, is in all likelihood polygenic or related to a dominant gene with variable penetrance. Thus, the failure to demonstrate the genetic transmission of full-syndrome early onset psychosis does not rule out a partial transmission of certain single or multiple characteristics, any of which may or may not appear in a clinically significant form. Isolated hereditary traits, which under certain conditions may contribute to the genesis of a psychotic disorder, are unlikely to resemble psychotic features when observed in the context of an otherwise healthy organism. Given the present state of the art in genetics, the failure to find a genetic component to a behavioral trait can mean either that there is none or as Hanson and Gottesman (1976) have theorized that "the operational definition of the trait is out of contact with biological realities requiring validation of our all too fallible indicators of genotype." Thus, as is so often the case, genetic factors can be included, but only rarely can they be excluded with certainty.

Pooling family pedigrees from several early studies, Hanson and Gottesman found no strong evidence to implicate genetics in the development of childhood psychoses with onset before the age of five. In contrast, psychotic disorders with onset near puberty appear in at least some cases to be genetically related to adult onset schizophrenia, representing those cases in which the full syndrome begins precociously. If a genetic factor for early onset psychoses exists at all, it is most likely a function of either a rare mutation or polygenic inheritance. The authors argue that a congenital but nongenetic factor offers a more parsimonious explanation.

Citing a 2 percent rate of autism in siblings (compared to a normal population incidence of 4.5 per 10,000) and a speech delay in approximately 25 percent of the families of autistic children as evidence for a hereditary factor, Folstein and Rutter (1978) undertook the study of a systematically collected sample of 21 pairs of same-sex twins, one or both of whom had been diagnosed as autistic by then current diagnostic criteria. Taken together, 11 monozygotic and 10 dizygotic pairs yielded 25 autistic children. Four of the 11 MZ pairs but none of the 10 DZ pairs showed concordance for autism. The authors went on to question whether nonautistic co-twins demonstrated any continuously distributed abnormal characteristics or nonpsychotic affectations. They found that in addition to the autistic twins, six nonautistic co-twins (five MZ and one DZ) exhibited some form of cognitive disability—delayed speech in three cases, IQs of 70 or below in two cases, speech articulation difficulties beyond 5 years of age in two cases, and scholastic problems requiring special schooling in two cases. All of the autistic twins met at least two of these criteria. Statistically speaking, 82 percent of the 11 MZ pairs were concordant for cognitive disorders or autism, as compared to only 10 percent of the DZ pairs. Folstein and Rutter interpreted these findings as evidence for genetic transmission with complete or partial penetrance of a form of cognitive dysfunction which includes but is not limited to autism.

The final disposition of the dysfunction may depend to a large extent on a combination of physiological as well as genetic hazards.

Exactly which autistic characteristics are inherited or genetically linked remains unclear, though Bartock et al. (1975) reported a family history of speech delay in about 25 percent of autistic families. DeMyer (1979) reported an incidence of learning plus speech difficulties approaching 20 percent among siblings of autistic children, as compared to 15 percent among siblings of normal children. The difference between the two groups did not reach statistical significance unless physical defects were combined with cognitive dysfunction, in which case the siblings of autistics tended to have a greater incidence of composite physiological and psychological abnormalities.

In summary, genetically inherited characteristics appear to be among the precipitant or predisposing factors in the genesis of some cases of pervasive developmental disorder. In certain instances genetic factors alone are sufficient to produce the entire range of symptoms, while in other cases an amalgam of genetic and congenital nonhereditary factors appear to work in tandem in the genesis of a full psychotic syndrome. Finally, there are those cases in which nongenetic biological factors alone or in interaction with environmental stressors may be implicated with no evidence for genetic transmission whatsoever. From one case to the next, genetic transmission may or may not be necessary and may or may not be sufficient to account for the full range of symptoms associated with the various psychotic syndromes.

The apparent interrelationship between (and interchangeability of) environmental, physiological, and genetic factors in the etiology of the pervasive developmental disorders is further evidence for a final common pathway phenomenon. Biopsychological systems, it would seem, do not fail in random or infinitely variable ways but tend to conform in sickness as in health to certain narrowly defined functional parameters. The convergence of essentially dissimilar types of trauma (genetic, environmental, and psychophysiological) at a common endpoint, that is, a characteristic patterning of symptoms, has implications for treatment as well as for pathogenesis. The fact that, in general, organisms respond to diverse input in characteristic ways suggests that in treating such disorders, the manner of treatment need not necessarily follow from specific causative or etiological factors either. Genetic disorders, for example, may be treatable by way of nongenetic interventions. Perhaps the therapeutic action of different treatment interventions, like the pathogenic action of different traumatic factors, converges at certain points to produce common, nonspecific effects. Genetic anomalies, congenital defects, and severe parental deficiencies, for example, may independently or in concert produce severe distortions in development that are phenomenally similar. Again, the total organism appears to decompensate stereotypically, regardless of specific etiological factors. Perhaps the converse is true as well: organisms tend to restitute in certain stereotyped or characteristic ways, regardless of specific therapeutic interventions. I am not saying that every intervention works; obviously, that is not the case. But I am suggesting the possibility that, by aiming our interventions at one level of organismic functioning, we may be able to influence processes at a totally different level of functioning; that by starting with abnormal behavior or pathological object relations, for example, we may be able to influence the course of physiological as well as psychological processes. This idea has been well documented in the case of certain psychosomatic illnesses and has been shown to have even broader implications for living systems in general.

It is clear that in at least some instances pervasive developmental disorders are the endproducts of complex congenital and constitutional defects. At some point, it may be possible to correct these defects directly with precise physiological interventions, though at present we lack the technical sophistication to do so. We need not, however, consign the deeply disturbed child to a life of chronic incapacitation. There are interventions currently available which do work and with which we have some considerable expertise. Psychopharmacology and psychophysiology will undoubtedly progress with time. We can look forward to the day when psychological illnesses will be treated with surgically precise biological interventions. This development will do nothing, however, to diminish the potency of psychological treatments. Here, too, we can expect progress: one day perhaps we will treat a broad range of physical and psychosomatic illnesses with surgically precise psychotherapeutic communications.

Chapter Five

Organic Therapies

Throughout the 40-year history of clinical psychopharmacology, pharmacological and, more generally, biological treatment interventions into psychiatric disorders of childhood have followed established practice with adult psychiatric patients (Klein 1976). Unfortunately, methodologically sound investigations into the effects of drugs on homogeneous populations of children have not kept pace with the fairly abundant literature on drug effects with adult populations. Logistical, ethical, and clinical problems encountered in the kinds of research necessary to test the efficacy of new and established drugs in the treatment of young children are myriad (Jurgensen 1979). Both psychological and physiological development must be considered in the selection of homogeneous index and control groups. An almost unfathomable array of environmental factors must be considered. Control groups must be matched within critical tolerances for factors such as chronological age, IQ, and socioeconomic status, to name but a few.

In principle, at least, demographic variables can, in most instances, be controlled with considerable precision. Real difficulties arise, however, around loosely defined diagnostic categories and the relative interchangeability with which terms such as "psychotic," "autistic," and "schizophrenic" are used in discriminating index populations. Finally, ethical problems involving informed consent are a particularly sensitive issue when applied to the use of children in potentially dangerous pharmacological studies.

The net effect of methodological and ethical obstacles to psychopharmacological research with children has been a proliferation of poorly controlled drug studies, typically incorporating small, nonhomogeneous populations. Interpretation of findings and speculation as to generalizability are often little more than rough approximations. Thus, it is not surprising to find that results are frequently irreplicable.

Psychopharmacological Treatment

Psychopharmacological interventions, now the most widely used form of biological treatment for early onset psychotic disorders, follow a long history of physical therapies, including lobotomy (Williams and Freeman 1953), insulin shock therapy (Annell 1955), electroconvulsive shock (Bender 1947), and pharmacologically induced convulsions (Krantz et al. 1957), most of which have fallen into disfavor. Controlled, double-blind psychopharmacological studies beginning in the early 1950s demonstrated the usefulness of certain psychoactive agents for rendering psychotic children more amenable to educational and therapeutic interventions. Agents studied have included antipsychotic medication, biogenic amine precursors, psychostimulants, psychedelics, antidepressants, vitamins, thyroid analogues, and lithium. While each one of these interventions has been associated with improvements in some individuals, no single group of drugs has been found clearly superior in treating all of the complex symptoms associated with the full range of early onset disorders.

Prior to the development of the phenothiazines, hypnotics and anticonvulsant medication had been in wide use in the management of psychotic children because of their sedative effects. Barbiturates in particular, however, often increased the disorganization of severely disturbed children, what some considered to be a "paradoxical" effect (Campbell 1973). Diphenhydramine (Benedryl) was found effective in treating schizophrenic children with intact cognitive functioning and is still considered by some to be a relatively safe alternative to phenthiazine treatment in certain cases (Campbell 1973).

The use of psychomotor stimulants and antidepressant medication with young psychotic children is generally contraindicated. In studies of schizophrenic and autistic children, both d-amphetamine (Dexadrine) and methylphenidate (Ritalin) have been shown to aggravate psychotic symptoms, even in low doses, regardless of hyperactivity (Campbell 1973). Psychotic children showing overall improvement on d-amphetamine (such as reduced hyperactivity and increased attention span) tended also to become increasingly withdrawn and less verbal. L-amphetamine (Cydril) has shown some promise in decreasing hyperactivity among children prone to aggressive behavior. Imipramine, a widely used antidepressant medication, was studied by Campbell et al. (1971) with a sample of ten autistic and schizophrenic children 2 to 6 years of age and showing low-average to severely retarded intelligence. The drug produced a mixture of stimulating, tranquilizing, and disorganizing effects. Five of the children in the study deteriorated behaviorally, three improved moderately, and two improved slightly. The authors concluded that the overall effect was only "infrequently therapeutic" and usually outweighed by toxic effects. Imipramine has been used successfully, however, in treating anxiety related specifically to separation issues in cases of school phobia (Klein 1975).

Major Tranquilizers

Currently, the most widely utilized and well documented psychopharmacological agents in the treatment of the childhood psychoses are the major tranquilizers. Of the phenothiazines, chlorpromazine has been found particularly useful in treating school-age children but tends to produce an excessively sedative effect when administered to younger children, irrespective of dosage (Campbell 1973). Trifluoperazine (Stelazine), one of the activating antipsychotics, has been found useful in overcoming the marked apathy and hypoactivity characteristic of many psychotic children. Fish et al. (1966) reported significant improvement in speech functioning, social contact, and motility among a group of 2 to 5-year-old psychotic children treated with trifluoperazine at a dosage of .7 milligrams per kilogram of body weight. Even in higher dosages, this drug seldom produced dystonic reactions in the young age group, though extrapyramidal symptoms have been a problem among older children.

Among the butyrophenones, trifluperidol (in doses of .5 mg per day) was found more effective than either chlorpromazine or trifluoperazine (Fish et al. 1969) in treating a population of young retarded "schizophrenic" children. Along with its effective antipsychotic properties, trifluperidol was found to be less sedating than chlorpromazine, though extrapyramidal side effects were a problem at 1.3 to 2 times the optimal dosage.

Haloperidol (Haldol), also a member of the butyrophenone series, was compared by Englehardt et al. (1973) at doses of .3 mg per kg of body weight with fluphenazine (Prolixin), one of the activating phenothiazine derivatives, and was found equally effective both qualitatively and quantitatively. In a more recent study, Campbell et al. (1982) found that in doses ranging from .5 mg a day to 3.0 mg a day, haloperidol was superior to placebo in reducing stereotyped behaviors, withdrawal, hyperactivity, "abnormal object relations," and fidgeting. However, four of the 33 schizophrenic children (ages 2.3 to 7.9 years) developed abnormal, drug-related movements. In addition to symptomatic improvement, children receiving haloperidol demonstrated an enhanced learning capacity on a computer-controlled discrimination learning task.

Thiothixene (Navane), a thioxanthene derivative, has been shown to have both stimulating and antipsychotic properties at therapeutic dosages (from 1 to 40 mg) in young schizophrenic children (Campbell 1973). However, in an early study (Fish et al. 1969) involving five 3 to 4-year-old schizophrenic youngsters, the drug was found to be less potent than trifluperidol and more frequently induced "toxic behavioral effects" such as excessive agitation and excitement.

Fenfluramine Studies

Perhaps the most intriguing work to date in the organic treatment of early onset psychoses has evolved from the biochemical study of abnormalities in serotonin metabolism (see p. 40). A recent research survey on the serotoninergic system (Gellar et al. 1982) suggested that as many as 40 percent of children diagnosed as autistic by *DMS III* criteria show elevated blood serotonin levels as compared to matched normals. In an earlier study, Ritvo et al. (1971) obtained small reductions in blood serotonin levels in four autistic children (ages 3 to 13) through the administration of l-dopa, but noted no clinical changes in the course of the illness. In a recent preliminary study, however, Gellar et al. manipulated brain serotonin levels using an anorexigenic drug, fenfluramine, which produces a longlasting but reversible decrease in brain serotonin levels in animals, with only minor side effects reported. Preliminary findings demonstrated that fenfluramine effectively reduced blood serotonin levels in each of three young autistic males. Furthermore, this reduction was accompanied by improvements in behavioral and cognitive functioning which in some cases were maintained for several weeks following administration of the drug. In each case, serial IQ scores indicated substantially improved performance, with one child nearly doubling his pretest score. Significant behavioral improvements as measured by the Ward Symptom Rating Scale corroborated staff clinical impressions. Though no formal control group was used in this rather impromptu research, the authors cite the lack of any spontaneous improvement before drug administration and the unchanged status of an untreated autistic twin as evidence for the therapeutic efficacy of fenfluramine in treating the three index cases.

A followup study by the same group (Ritvo et al. 1983) tended to corroborate earlier findings, but, again, the data base is small (14 patients) and the research methodology of questionable efficacy. Although pretest-posttest differentials across certain behavioral variables—most notably, improved motor and sensory functioning—reached levels of statistical significance, absolute changes in the children's actual behavior and performance (given the unusually tight calibration of the scales incorporated in the study) would have been extremely subtle and difficult in actual practice to discriminate from the uncontrolled effects of extraneous variables (such as maturation effects). Leventhal et al. (personal communication), one of several groups currently running fenfluramine trials, have failed to replicate the findings of Ritvo et al. What behavioral changes were obtained among Leventhal's group of autistic children following the administration of fenfluramine were minimal and did not, in Leventhal's opinion, justify risks associated with the drug, in particular, substantial weight loss. Moreover, even if fenfluramine is demonstrated to be effective in treating autistic children, its exact therapeutic action remains a mystery: biochemically, the drug is observed to produce numerous neurochemical changes, decreased blood serotonin concentration only one among them.

Chapter Six

Cognitive and Behavioral Perspectives

Forty years after its first publication, Kanner's study of "Autistic Disturbances of Affective Contact" continues to reflect much of what is currently known about the descriptive aspects of early onset psychosis. Impressions based on a sample of 11 children have been reaffirmed in the study of what, by this time, must amount to literally thousands of severely disturbed youngsters. Just as interesting, however, as those aspects which have stood the test of time are those which have not. Some of Kanner's original diagnostic criteria (such as negative neurological signs, cold obsessional parents, and so on) have fallen gracefully to the findings of subsequent research based on larger samples and relatively more sophisticated methodology. But other early impressions have remained, in spite of disconfirming evidence. Of these impressions, the "good cognitive potential" of psychotic children is perhaps most controversial.

A growing body of literature indicates that severe and sustaining impairments in cognitive development are characteristic of a majority of severely disturbed children, yet images linger of the "idiot savant," destitute of intelligence but for islets of profound and uncanny ability. Despite what is believed to be an extremely low incidence (.06) (Hill 1977), the infrequent occurrence of exceptional abilities in the context of global retardation has suggested to some the possibility of a potentially intact cognitive apparatus masked by the confounding effects of a hypothetical "basic disorder." Rimland (1964) wrote of "brightness gone awry"; Eisenberg (1968) wrote of children with "good intellectual potential" for whom a lack of affective contact and "human purpose" constitutes the primary deficit.

Cases of exceptional ability notwithstanding, the vast consensus of recent studies suggests that psychotic children, as a group, suffer pervasive and sustaining cognitive deficiencies. Lockyer and Rutter (1969), in an extensive follow-up study of a group of 63 diagnostically heterogeneous psychotic children, found that 40 percent obtained IQ scores below 50, 30 percent between 50 and 69, and 30 percent at 70 or above. Of the higher-functioning group, only 25 percent obtained scores within the average range of intelligence. In a more recent study of 135 autistic children (mean age 5.32 years), DeMyer et al. (1974) found that a scant 2.6 percent of autistic children tested obtained IQ scores above 85, while 74 percent obtained scores below 52. Like Rutter, DeMyer found a very high follow-up correlation (.70) between original test findings and retest findings six years later. Thus, global retardation for the vast majority of autistic psychotic children appears to be a stable characteristic and a key factor in outcome. Even children showing improvement in the area of social competence maintained low intelligence test scores. Neither treatment nor special education appeared to have resulted in significant increases. Overall, both authors found IQ scores among autistic children to be highly stable over time and good predictors of outcome. While social and intellectual growth were observed in some children falling within the 66 to 70 Full Scale IQ range (particularly among those with some verbal ability), children obtaining scores below 40 rarely demonstrated measurable cognitive growth and were in some instances noted to decline even further with the passage of time.

Although it is maintained by some that retardation secondary to psychosis is qualitatively different from intellectual deficits associated with other disabilities, Rutter (1974) found that IQ functions for autistic psychotic children in much the same way as for any other group of individuals: "Autistic children with low IQs are just as retarded as anyone else with low IQ and the score means the same thing." There is, however, one important difference. The test profiles of psychotic children characteristically show greater variability than what is typically found in the test records of either normals or nonpsychotic retardates (Lockyer and Rutter 1969). Significantly, psychotic children perform relatively well on tasks emphasizing visual-spatial functions or shortterm memory but do poorly on tasks involving sequencing and language skills. In a recent review of cognitive functioning in psychotic children, Prior (1979) interpreted these findings, together with data concerning specific language deficits and abnormalities in information processing, as evidence for a developmental dysfunction involving the left cerebral hemisphere. Prognosis for children so affected would depend on the degree to which the right hemisphere could take over left hemisphere functions. Even if the brain is capable of compensating in this way, however, the concentration of all cerebral functions within a single highly differentiated area may impose an upper limit upon the potential development of rerouted cognitive functions.

Taken together, the data pertaining to global cognitive functioning in psychotic children suggest that while the idiot savant may indeed be something of an anachronism, the tendency for severely disturbed children to manifest highly differential intellectual abilities is a real one. Furthermore, the pattern of cognitive variability across populations of psychotic children is also characteristic and distinguishes them from nonpsychotic retardates. Thus, while it may be true, as Rutter suggests, that a retarded psychotic child is just as limited as, for example, a retarded Down's syndrome child, the net effect is a very different one. If lay and professional opinion alike still holds tenaciously to the much-disputed notion of latent intelligence in psychotic children, this persistent belief probably reflects the seeming disparity between what these youngsters can do with at least a modicum of competency in certain circumscribed areas and what they are unable to do at all. That different lines of cognitive development should progress with relative independence, some devastated, others relatively intact, is difficult to account for and may suggest to the observer a certain latency or potential that is not so apparent in persons whose functioning is more uniformly impaired.

Before closing the door on the "myth" of cognitive potential in psychotic children, as some seem ready to do, we might think back for a moment to the results of a recent psychopharmacological study implicating serotonin metabolism in autistic psychosis (see p. 50). Among other things, Geller et al. (1982, and Ritvo et al. 1983) found that, following the administration of fenfluramine, a drug believed to reduce cerebral serotonin levels, each of three autistic children achieved significant increases on intelligence test performance. In one case Full Scale IQ was reportedly nearly doubled. Clearly, the administration of fenfluramine did not produce a sudden acceleration in the development of those cognitive structures necessary to enhance intellectual efficiency. In order to account for rapid changes in competency of this order of magnitude, we must assume the preexistence of relatively intact cognitive structures rendered inoperative by some hypothetical disease process. Put another way, the types of errors produced by autistic psychotic children appear to reflect a "microgenetic" rather than "ontogenetic" failure (Brown 1980). Unlike nonpsychotic retardates, whose developmental or maturational progress is arrested at a lower level of ontogenetic development—that is, who have failed to develop age-appropriate cognitive structures—psychotic youngsters may develop relatively intact cognitive structures which they are then, for reasons yet unknown, unable to use.

Stimulus Overselectivity

Further evidence of underlying cognitive potential among certain psychotic children comes from recent work of Lovaas et al. (1979) on the problem of stimulus overselectivity. Autistic children have difficulty responding to complex or multiple stimulus cues in discrimination learning tasks. Their behavior comes under the control of a restricted range of sensory input when they are placed in situations requiring attention to multiple stimulus dimensions. Because autistic children tend to "overselect" a limited set of stimuli from those potentially available, they may exclude relevant portions of the environment and thereby base behavior strategies on faulty, irrelevant, or insufficient information. In an initial study (Lovaas et al. 1971), autistics, nonpsychotic retardates, and normal children were taught to respond to a complex auditory-visual-tactile display. After training had established a discrimination, single cue test trials were administered in which each sensory component was presented separately to determine which aspects of the complex had gained control over the child's response. Where normal children responded to each of the components equally, the autistic children responded to only one of the salient cues. Similar results were obtained even when the stimulus complex was reduced to only two types of input. The authors interpreted these findings as evidence of the difficulty experienced by the autistic child in responding simultaneously to multiple cues presented within a complex stimulus array. Quantity it appears rather than quality of stimulus controls is the salient variable.

Stimulus overselectivity is offered by Lovaas et al. as a paradigm for understanding a range of abnormal cognitive, linguistic, and social behaviors associated with autistic and related syndromes. It is argued that almost any kind of social or emotional responding involves the simultaneous apprehension of a wide range of subtle cues. Failure to take into account any single or multiple stimulus dimension or dimensions within a social-communicational context is likely to result in the misinterpretation of complex expressive behaviors, thereby increasing the likelihood of an erroneous or inappropriate response. Limitations on the number of stimuli acquiring control over behavior would also account for the difficulty that psychotic children have in generalizing learning from one setting to another. In order for learning to transfer in this way, there must be stimulus elements in common between the old and new settings. The likelihood that generalization will take place can be expected to vary proportionately with the number of relevant stimulus elements that control a particular behavior at its inception. A child whose learning is based on overselective responding to reduced stimulus elements would be less likely to encounter relevant cues in a new, though related, environment.

In contrast to early studies indicating that reinforcement during successive discrimination training trials was effective in reducing stimulus overselectivity, Schreibman et al. (1977) demonstrated that training in the broader sense of repeated exposure, rather than contingency reinforcement, was most effective in reducing overselective attention to stimulus cues. As would have been predicted based on the overselectivity paradigm, teaching aids based on "prompt fading" techniques (introduction of additional cues to hasten stimulus discrimination, followed by the gradual removal of the cues once correct responding occurs at a high frequency) only increased response error to the extent that the child was again required to respond to a multiple cue situation. Conventional learning aids, like prompt fading techniques, create the very situation in which stimulus overselectivity is most likely to occur. In order to circumvent this obstacle to learning, Lovaas has proposed the use of "within stimulus prompts" to establish control by exaggerating the distinctive features of the correct stimulus at the start of training (rather than simply adding on additional stimuli) and maintaining this control while gradually fading in less relevant features. Other workers have demonstrated that in certain instances, overselectivity may, in fact, be modifiable. Schover and Newsome (1976), for example, trained autistic children to broaden their response to multiple cues through the overtraining of already learned discriminations. On the basis of these findings, the authors concluded that overselectivity need not be the result of a permanent or innate disability and may be amenable to treatment.

Taken in a Piagetian framework, the phenomenon of stimulus overselectivity parallels in many respects the kinds of disequilibria (errors, maladaptations, contradictions) normally found in the thinking of preoperational children. Within the context of normal development, this type of error stems from a centration on certain aspects of an object or situation to the exclusion of other equally relevant but overlooked aspects. Typically, the child at this stage in cognitive development centers on the "positive" aspects that arise from immediate perception and sensorimotor action to the neglect of "negative" aspects which tend not to be assimilated in a systematic way until the emergence of true mental operations. For tasks that lie within a child's current ontogenetic level (that is, those which can be handled given cognitive structures already available), the pointing out of contradictions typically will yield a compensating maneuver leading to a correct response. For tasks lying beyond the child's current ontogenetic level, even the provision of information relative to completing the task will not result in a correct solution. In the first instance, equilibrated cognitive structures already available to the child, though not always exploited to their fullest, are, nonetheless, capable of being drawn upon given appropriate feedback. Errors of this kind represent microgenetic failures in the evolution of a correct response rather than ontogenetic failures resulting from a developmental immaturity in the evolution of cognitive structures. Brown (1980) originally developed the concept of microgenesis to explain certain idiosyncrasies in the thinking of schizophrenic adults who, though ontogenetically mature (that is, have developed equilibrated cognitive structures) yield excessively to normal response bias errors. Given problems that are either difficult or unfamiliar enough to require a high degree of equilibration, such individuals are more likely than normals to experience difficulty monitoring and self-correcting erroneous responses. Providing appropriate feedback, however, such as negations, enables many schizophrenic persons to use higher-level knowledge structures already available in order to correct their errors. Were an actual loss of structure involved (that is, regression to a lower ontogenetic level), erroneous responses would remain irreconcilable.

Although a normal 3 or 4-year-old preoperational child has a relatively limited complement of knowledge structures and would not be expected to master the likes of complex negations, equilibration at a sensorimotor level is sufficient for solving multistimulus discrimination tasks of the type used by Lovaas in his studies of stimulus overselectivity. Normal 3 and 4-year-olds have little difficulty with this. By comparison, autistic children tend to overselect, that is, they center attention on one of many possible cues to the exclusion of other relevant stimuli. In this respect, their errors are similar in nature to those produced (though at a more highly equilibrated level) by adult schizophrenics who focus on the positive aspects of a situation while excluding equally salient negative ones. Taking this model a step further, if autistic children are ontogenetically immature and have failed to develop actual stage-appropriate cognitive structures, then no amount of feedback, reinforcement, or trial exposure should result in compensation for and correction of the original response error. This is not the case, however. The overselectivity of autistic children has, in any number of experimental cases, been modified through within-stimulus prompts (Schreibman 1975) and overtraining techniques (Schover and Newsome 1976). Much as fenfluramine alone could not have been responsible for the rapid generation of cognitive structures among the autistic 3 and 4-year-olds in Gellar et al's study, so is it unlikely that limited behavioral-educational methods of the types described by Lovaas and Schreibman can account for the rapid reequilibration demonstrated by autistic children working at a stimulus discrimination task. Both lines of research, psychopharmacological and cognitive-perceptual, imply the same conclusion from totally different points of view: cognitive arrest in at least some cases of childhood psychosis is microgenetic in nature and must be defined in terms of the equilibration or disequilibration of a response within a given developmental level.

Available evidence from various areas of research suggests that unlike persons who are developmentally arrested at a level of ontogenetic immaturity, where an actual failure in the genesis of cognitive structures has taken place and for whom no amount of reinforcement, feedback, or additional information will result in adaptation at a higher level of equilibration, certain psychotic children appear to have developed cognitive structures which they are nevertheless unable to use without the provision of special cognitive or biological conditions.

Case History of Jim

Such was clearly the case with Jim, a 2½-year-old who, in the aftermath of prolonged neglect and abuse during his first 7 months (his biological mother had given up all parental rights immediately following birth), was diagnosed as childhood onset pervasive developmental disorder, residual state and nonorganic failure-to-thrive. At 7 months he presented with poor muscle tone, chronic respiratory and gastrointestinal infections, self-abusive behaviors, and what his foster mother later described as "strange arm movements." When held or cuddled, he arched back and away and showed no particular interest in either his caregiver or inanimate objects placed in close proximity. A developmental assessment at 8 months, 10 days (Bayley Scale of Infant Development) revealed a 2½-month delay in cognitive development (MDI = 56) and a 1½-month delay in perceptual-motor development (PDI = 78). Several months following evaluation, Jim began an intensive intervention including hyperalimination, physical therapy, and guided interaction treatment with his new foster parents. The results of Jim's treatment were impressive: by 24 months, virtually the entire range of overt symptomatology was behind him. He grew quite literally by leaps and bounds and seemed to make up for lost developmental time by skipping certain substages and transitional steps. In his acquisition of speech and language, for example, single words and short sentences emerged in tandem, with little sign of the usual succession from basic to more complex linguistic modes. Jim, did not, however, acquire complex linguistic structures "overnight", without a pre-existing foundation to build on. He had, it is evident, achieved a degree of ontogenetic maturity—across at least certain developmental lines. The requisite cognitive structures were in place but, pitted against a background of chaotic and abusive caregiving, he was unable to exercise these capabilities in an effective or organized fashion. In other words, Jim was a child with virtually pure potential. Within a developmental medium conducive to the exercise and elaboration of these latent cognitive and affective potentialities, he advanced rapidly and is currently a flourishing 2½-year-old. Still, it is worth noting that when Jim's foster parents (to whom he is now extremely attached) left for a short vacation a few months ago, they returned to find a child who looked remarkably like the woefull and disorganized 8-month-old they had encountered two years earlier. In their absence he seemed to have lost his speech and had begun to enage in the very same self-abusive behaviors that had first brought him to professional attention. It is doubtful that Jim had actually undergone destructuralization of cognitive capacities previously gained during this brief but traumatic interval. Once again, it is perhaps more useful to assess the problem in terms of a temporary disequilibration, one likely to remit with the elimination of the traumatic and depotentiating interference. Predictably, Jim regained normal functioning within a few days after his parents returned, as if nothing had happened.

The implications of this distinction between ontogenetic immaturity and potentially temporary microgenetic disequilibration are manifest but simple: psychotic children are capable of change and may be responsive to growth-promoting interventions at multiple levels of biological and psychological process. Cognitive retardation is not, as Rutter implied, a unitary phenomenon. Although behavioral and functional manifestations of retardation appear morphologically similar across etiological subtypes and may (as was suggested earlier) represent a final common pathway, there is nonetheless an important distinction to be made between those children whose problem-solving errors occur in the generation of appropriate responses and those children whose failures represent an actual developmental arrest. The implications for prognosis and outcome are self-evident and clearly warrant further investigation aimed at differentiating subtypes of cognitive retardation. Kanner may have been close to the mark, after all, in ascribing "good intellectual potential" to his 11 autistic children.

Chapter Seven

Symbolic Representation

While many contemporary researchers believe that gross disturbances in language development are a primary characteristic of
most forms of infantile psychosis (Rutter 1975, 1978, Ricks and
Wing 1975, Churchill 1972), the prelinguistic aspects of early symbol formation and mental representation have received relatively
little attention in the literature. This finding is somewhat supris-
ing; most current etiological studies acknowledge that early manifestations of the pervasive developmental disorders are apparent
from birth. Thus, as Hermelin (1978) has suggested, the study of
cognitive processes in early onset psychosis begins rightfully with
the investigation of the precursory stages of symbolic representation and the formation and organization of internal imagery.

From a Piagetian point of view (Piaget and Inhelder 1969), the
development of a complex symbol system is dependent upon the
successful negotiation of all stages of sensorimotor development, in
particular those aspects leading to the attainment of an "object
concept." Mental representation begins for Piaget with the concept
of a permanent object external to and independent of the self and
having a stable existence outside of immediate perceptual awareness. For an infant of 5 months, what is out of sight is out of mind:
the object endures only as long as it is perceptible. By 18 months,
however, the adaptive infant is capable of taking into account a
wide range of invisible displacements and demonstrates an awareness that objects are conserved and continue to exist indefinitely,
even when they are no longer being perceived. The genesis of

mental symbols (signifiers) begins with imitation and the ability to differentiate objects from the actions performed on them. The sensorimotor child acquires a great deal of new information about an object by using his body in a way that represents various dimensions or properties of it, that is, through accommodation. With the gradual internalization of gross imitative behaviors, a true semiotic function emerges. Once formed, mental images are given meaning by the child through the process of assimilation and in this way acquire a personal significance intimately related to his own unique experience. As Greenspan (1981) has pointed out, however, the capacity for constructing mental representations of external objects does not at first imply a capacity for organizing them in any logical relationship to one another. For even the adaptive sensorimotor child, relationships within the external world are initially construed according to magical cause-and-effect associations. Differentiation of means and ends, intentionality, is a later acquisition.

Early mental representation tends, under even the best of circumstances, to be a precarious achievement, subject to the destabilizing effects of internal affective states. The maladjusted or constitutionally vulnerable child faced with the task of integrating an ever-expanding array of complex affective, interpersonal, and sensorimotor experiences is prone to fragmentation and may lose, either temporarily or permanently, the capacity for mental imagery and symbolization. Early representations, still tied closely at this stage to imitation, concrete behavioral schemata, and perception, are particularly susceptible to regression. In the case of pervasive developmental disturbances, where constitutional vulnerabilities may preclude adequate homeostatic regulation of internal and external stressors, a stable object is unlikely to develop in the first place. Thus, object loss under any circumstance may continue to evoke severe anxiety, leading to still further disorganization.

Hammes and Langdell (1981) have cited three precursors to the normal consolidation of symbolic representation: the child's ability to form internal images, the ability to imitate, and the ability to manipulate images and form expectancies by linking stored images with present and projected perceptions. In an ingenious research design utilizing matched samples of autistic and nonautistic retarded children (mean ages of 9.10 and 9.9 years respectively), the authors used these criteria to study imitative ability, the formation of mental images, and the development of object permanence. Results of the study indicated that, while autistic children are capable of imitating observed behavior at a rudimentary level (for example echoing and miming models exactly) and are able to form coherent internal images, they seem to lack the ability to manipulate these images in a purposeful and meaningful way. Their imitations tend to be rigid and inextricably bound to the exact characteristics of the model. Few in the autistic group demonstrated the "as if" flexibility necessary to imitate more complex or interpretative behaviors. At best, signifiers expressing any degree of abstractedness whatsoever acted for these children as concrete signs having a simple learned correspondence to a model. Similar interpretations were offered by Ricks and Wing (1975), who described the tendency of autistic children to learn symbols passively by operant conditioning rather than as an integrated aspect of an active processing of experience.

Tests designed by Hammes and Langdell to assess anticipatory behavior in the tracking of displaced objects indicated that autistic children, unlike retarded or normal ones, do not appear to be capable of predicting future events accurately and in at least this one important respect have not attained a stable concept of object permanence. In varying degrees, autistic children may remain both unpredictable and unable to predict well beyond the point in development at which a stable object concept is normally achieved. The authors concluded by relating these findings to the disjointed, poorly modulated interactions between the parents of the autistic youngster, unable to read the unpredictable signs and signals their child emits, and the autistic child, unable to find comfort in a seemingly random array of parental behaviors and communications.

Although Hammes and Langdell demonstrated the ability of the autistic child to learn by imitation, they made little note of the conditions under which this learning occurs spontaneously. Other workers (Prior 1979, Wing 1976) have commented on the infrequency with which autistic children actually initiate imitative behavior on their own. Wing, for example, pointed out that autistic children seem to learn new motoric patterns, such as riding a bicycle, most expediently if their limbs are put through the required movements by the trainer. Spontaneously acquired imitations (such as echolalia) are often mere fragments of more complex behavior patterns and have little utility in and of themselves.

Play as Symbolic Representation

The behavioral manifestations of faulty symbolization and object representation can be seen most clearly in the play of the psychotic child. Ungerer and Sigman (1981), observing the play of

16 autistic children, noted that in most instances the youngsters were capable of demonstrating a wide range of play behaviors in either structured or unstructured free play settings but that the quality of play was markedly different from that observed among normals and nonpsychotic retardates. The autistic children tended to occupy themselves excessively in developmentally immature forms of play, even where more sophisticated play motifs were well within their grasp. Object manipulation and relational play, for example (normally the precursors of more mature forms of symbolic play), were preferred by the autistic group over more functionally sophisticated activities. More than either normals or retardates, the autistic children tended to avoid symbolic doll play. The authors attributed this avoidance to a fundamental deficit in their ability to represent and transform objects in thought, independent of the actions being performed on them.

Wing et al. (1977), in a study of 108 autistic and retarded children, distinguished three subgroups based on the characteristics of their play. The first group (43 children) demonstrated flexible and varied symbolic play. All of these children had acquired language skills above the 19-month mark and none of them had been diagnosed as autistic. A second group (23 children) demonstrated only stereotyped or repetitive copying play. The third group (42 children) had no symbolic or presymbolic play. All the children in this last group had a language age below 20 months, and the majority demonstrated clear autistic or autisticlike features. The authors attributed the poverty of symbolic play among the severely delayed children to an inability to abstract concepts from experience and store these abstractions in symbolic form.

Among certain groups of psychotic children, maintenance of sameness within the environment seems to follow a more general tendency toward stereotyped thinking and behavior. Prior and Macmillan (1973) found a greater amount of stereotyped behavior among children obtaining elevated "sameness" scores on the Rimland E-2 assessment scales. Children who were able to create rich varied play patterns demonstrated greater cognitive ability than those engaged in rigid, less complex play activities. Masagatani (1973), in a study of 18 autistic children, ten of whom displayed prominent abnormal hand gestures, observed that those children with fewer abnormal movements tended also to have more spontaneous speech.

A number of workers have considered negativity, along with stereotyped behaviors and insistence on sameness, to be a mechanism used by the psychotic child in coping with a world perceived as being hopelessly unpredictable and out of control. Bettelheim (1967) interpreted negative and defiant behaviors among psychotic children as a form of passive resistance: "Living in such an unreasonable, unpredictable world, the only protection lies in doing nothing." In a more recent study, Clark and Rutter (1977) failed to find evidence of negativistic behavior (defined as the consistent avoidance of a correct response) in any of 27 autistic children. But negativity seems to be a rather difficult response to measure. Motivation, which is really the key to interpreting negativity, is not readily inferred from behavior without appropriate feedback from the subject, and this is something that many severely disturbed children are unable to give us. Frustration, withdrawal, or noncompliance may all take very different forms, yet still represent an essentially negative response. Furthermore, it would certainly be problematic under the circumstances to determine whether a child knew a correct response but willfully withheld it or was simply unable to generate an appropriate response in the first place. Defiance and ignorance are often indistinguishable.

Language

Few, perhaps, but the incurable romantic would dispute that words, not eyes, are the windows to a person's soul. Language is but one form of symbolic representation, yet a very special form. Like other cognitive abilities, speech and language develop according to their own timetable, in an invariant sequence of stages set in motion by the maturation of the central nervous system, shaped and modified through interaction with the social environment. More than other cognitive abilities, however, spoken language forms a locus for the complex representation of affect, physical patterning, cognitive imagery, metaphor, and expressions of the self. Beyond its communicative function, language has a significant influence on the codification of ongoing experience, the organization of object relations, and the representation of mental life in general (Call 1980).

The development of language begins long before the infant's first well organized verbal productions. Prelinguistic behaviors with which the infant is equipped by a long phylogenetic history are in evidence at birth and provide what Call has described as a "matrix of communicative and semiotic functions" out of which language functioning develops. Given "average expectable" conditions, the adaptive neonate will emit a range of forceful and relatively differentiated expressions (such as crying, smiling, and anticipatory gestures) that will allow the mother to feel what the child is feeling and respond in a reciprocal or complementary fashion. The infant is not simply a passive recipient of imprinting or operant learning, however, but an active organizer and initiator of interaction. The language-facilitating parent learns to distinguish between subtle gradations of expression (such as the cry of hunger and the cry for warmth) and encourages the use and expansion of verbal signals through his or her differential need-gratifying responsiveness. The infant's initiatives are in this way rewarded and lead to an enhanced sense of effectuality and self-esteem. Again, it must be emphasized that in the healthy, stage-appropriate "primal dialogue" (Spitz 1964), the infant is the initiator and architect of interaction, the mother the follower and facilitator. Together, parent and child shape and contour each other's spontaneous verbal output. Expressions signifying needs, wishes, and affects registered in the communicative nuances of each are identified, "phonematized" (Call 1980), and, finally, endowed with a shared, mutually comprehensible meaning. In this way, essentially nonmeaningful or premeaningful interactional events are rendered significant and become prototypes for the later acquisition of true symbolic motifs.

Having acquired an object concept and an increasing capacity for organizing internal representations (18 to 30 months), adaptive youngsters begin to elaborate on their symbolic modes (Greenspan 1981). The range, depth, and richness of gestures, vocalizations, and expressions are seen to undergo continual refinement, differentiation, and integration in the evolution of a complex linguistic function. The adaptive infant will go beyond mere description of animate and inanimate phenomena and will begin to represent personal interactions as well. Advances in language development, including the use of personal pronouns and action oriented verbs, will be paralleled by advances in social development as language becomes increasingly instrumental in interpersonal interactions.

For the adaptive child, the acquisition of verbal communication will be a stable one that will not backslide or regress under stress. In contrast, the less adaptive youngster will be prone to lose or give up early linguistic functioning under the stress of illness or trauma. What language develops (if any) is likely to stagnate at a descriptive level and will not be elaborated as an instrumental expressive motif. In either case, much will depend on the growth-promoting characteristics of the environment in fostering the child's use of this new representational capacity and in helping him to cope with stress by encouraging reengagement in the symbolic mode following disruptions. Regardless of the outcome, constructive or destructive, the child's impact on the environment must be acknowledged and clearly defined. Growth-inhibiting caregivers (Greenspan 1981) may undermine or discourage representation and verbalization by misinterpreting or distorting the child's symbolic communications or by matching the child's regressive behaviors with regressive behaviors of their own.

Expressive Abnormalities

Delays and distortions in language behavior are viewed by many as a primary diagnostic characteristic of early onset psychotic disorders (for example, Rutter 1978, Rutter et al. 1967, Wing 1971). Even for the minority of pervasively disordered children who make some spontaneous progress in the acquisition of language, the learning process is not only slow, but deviant (Ricks and Wing 1975). In contrast to the developmentally adaptive youngster, who acquires language through an active, evocative reciprocation between parent and child, the pervasively disordered child seems to acquire the use of words passively, in an operant fashion. What language develops is often rote, stereotyped, and isolated from the modifying influences of social experience. Verbal fragments taken out of context are imitated or echoed relentlessly. Whole phrases may be treated as individual symbols for persons, objects, or events, but are rarely reintegrated conceptually as the basis for generating new and creative linguistic forms. Shapiro et al. (1970), in a linguistic evaluation of eight schizophrenic children, found that the psychotic youngsters spoke as often as normal controls but were retarded in the length and expansiveness of their utterances. Exact echoing of phrases or words without regard for context was found to be a distinguishing characteristic of psychotic speech patterns. The unusual production of "congruent echoes" (full repetition of modeled speech patterns with no grammatical or creative transformation) among the schizophrenic children were regarded by the authors as an odd linguistic variation in which the spectrum of imitative sounds is limited to more rigid patterning than is the case in normal development. Follow-up studies on the same group of children suggested that styles of speech production among psychotic children tend to show continuity and stability over time.

The documentation and description of specific linguistic deficits in psychotic disorders is well represented in the literature and has generated a number of useful diagnostic criteria for the differentiation of language disorders associated with psychotic and non-psychotic syndromes. Comparatively few studies, however, have analyzed systematically the various components of language behavior—phonology, syntax, semantics, and pragmatics—each of which may, to some extent, develop independently. In a recent research review of linguistic functioning in autistic children, Tager-Flusberg (1981) found a majority of studies indicating that phonological and syntactical development follow the same course among autistic as normal children (though at a delayed rate), while the development of the semantic and pragmatic aspects of language among autistic children may be qualitatively deficient in a way that is unique to this population. Frequency distributions of speech sounds taken from the autistic sample were found to be comparable to those of nonpsychotic retarded children. In both cases, the classes of phonemes used least frequently were those that are normally acquired latest in childhood, suggesting a delay in speech acquisition rather than a specific distortion in phonetic production per se (Bertolucci et al. 1976). Several writers have commented on the peculiar voice quality of linguistically impaired psychotic children (Ricks and Wing 1975, Simmons and Baltaxe 1975). Certain groups of autistic children seem unable to modify the intonation pattern of utterances they have heard other persons use. Thus, voice stress and pitch may sound strangely incongruous with content and context.

A consensus of studies indicates that autistic children are similar to other language disordered groups in the syntactical properties of language use (Tager-Flusberg 1981). In both groups, delays in grammar and coding are typically related to developmental level, as are deficits in linguistic production and receptive language functioning. Bartak et al. (1975), in a comparison of developmental aphasic and autistic children, found both groups comparable in mean length of utterance, though the autistic children performed significantly worse on tests of comprehension.

Both syntactic and phonological functioning in autistic children typically are delayed but otherwise fall along a normal developmental continuum. In contrast, there is evidence in the research literature to suggest that autistic children have specific abnormalities in the processing of semantic aspects of language (Tager-Flusberg 1981). Meaning tends not to be used by autistic children as an organizing factor. Hermelin and O'Connor (1967) found that, unlike normal children who use categorical clustering as a mnemonic device for remembering sequences of words from different semantic categories (such as blue-three-red-five, and so on), autistic children repeat sequences in the exact order presented. They do not actively reorganize words according to set. Tager-Flusberg (1981) observed that autistic children tended to use word order rather than a semantically based strategy for decoding simple sentences. The author noted that this tendency could not be attributed to cognitive delay alone, because the use of word order is a relatively advanced syntactic strategy, however inappropriate it may be to the completion of the task. There is as yet no exact consensus as to the nature of the semantic difficulties found among autistic children, though most workers seem to agree that deficits in certain aspects of semantic processing may be tied to cognitive impairments involving complex conceptualization.

Perhaps the most profound, yet least well studied, language deficit among psychotic children is manifest in the way in which linguistic communication is used to effect behavior: the pragmatic aspect of communication (Watzlawick et al. 1967). Several studies report that autistic children differ significantly from other disordered groups in terms of reduced frequency of verbal output and communicative behavior in general (Bartak et al. 1975, Prior 1979). Baltaxe (1977) described three patterns of impairment deduced from language samples of five autistic adolescents: impairments in speaker-hearer relationships, impairments in rules of conduct governing dialogue, and impairments in differentiating old from new information.

Unlike the semantic and syntactic aspects of communication which develop in conjunction with verbal language competency during the second year, the pragmatic aspects of communications are apparent from birth in the early dialogues between parent and infant. Though most pervasive disorders are not diagnosed until after the second or third year, it is not uncommon for mothers of psychotic children to report that "something felt wrong" from the first days following birth. As neonates, psychotic children often fail to exhibit anticipatory gestures and may show little response to their mothers' voices (Wing 1971). With the differentiation of affective signals, some psychotic children are able to smile, laugh, cry, show anger, or fuss, but do so only in violent extremes. Subtle gradations of pleasure, displeasure, anger, embarrassment, and annoyance are seldom expressed (Wing 1975). About 50 percent of children with early onset psychoses never develop speech and show only the grossest differentiation of affect and need states.

Receptive Abnormalities

Receptive abnormalities among psychotic children often parallel deficits in expressive communication. Understanding of facial expressions and expressive movements develops very slowly for most. Perhaps the most difficult aspect of raising a psychotic child is his problem in understanding complex behavioral-vocal cues through which other people express emotion. The child's parents may experience this problem as a pervasive lack of empathy or an inability on the part of the child to reciprocate or complement emotional overtures. In fact, the inability of the psychotic child to respond to complex interpersonal cues may reflect what some believe to be a more general defect in cognitive processing—stimulus overselectivity. Responding to common affective expressions involves attending to multiple cues in a constantly changing stimulus complex, the very type of situation in which the psychotic child, by virtue of this special handicap, is unable to respond. Overselective responding to interpersonal signs and signals will invariably lead to the child's receiving only a part of the intended communication, and in most cases the isolated elements of complex social behavior are insufficient for making accurate interpersonal inferences.

An infant whose expressive signals are garbled, poorly differentiated, and inconsistent, in a word, unreadable, is frustrated over and over again by ineffectual communication. He is likely to be temperamental in disposition and difficult to console, demanding but insatiable. As the architect of interaction, the child leads in communication, but the lead is nearly impossible for the mother to follow. Across an unbridgeable gap, the child's feelings seem not to be her own. Neither is able to decipher or reflect the response of the other. In an atmosphere of tension, anxiety, and utter helplessness, mother withdraws and baby withdraws, each feeling only mounting tension and, perhaps, anger. There is a sympathetic response but no real empathy; mother cannot decipher where her infant needs to go.

The infant who can neither understand nor be understood by a caregiver is likely to experience the world described by Bettelheim as "utterly destructive." The caregiver who can neither understand nor be understood by her infant is likely to feel herself inadequate, her child utterly unreachable. Neither is gratified and the dyad fails. What was perhaps a genotypically vulnerable infant will adapt as a phenotypically psychotic child. Probably, neither hereditary predisposition nor congenital defect "caused" the psychosis. There are children, a majority of pervasively disordered children it is likely, for whom any number of vulnerabilities, single or in concert, alternate and interact in the genesis of the psychotic disturbance. The fact of the disorder may well involve prenatal constitutional factors. The specific form of the disorder, however, evolves around early modes of relatedness in which affect, cognition, and self are shaped and organized.

Chapter Eight

Behavioral Treatment of the Psychotic Child

Within the fields of child psychology and psychiatry (much as within the growing child) we can discern a number of developmental lines. Research pertaining to description, diagnosis, dynamics, and treatment are interrelated in practice, though they often seem to progress independently on a conceptual level. Fortunately, those who evaluate and treat disturbed children have not been paralyzed by ambiguities in the literature and seem, along with their patients, to have prospered despite considerable controversy over what exactly is being treated and how. Thus it comes as little surprise that each of the aforementioned research reviews demonstrates slow but steady progress in surmising the mechanisms underlying psychotic phenomena and treating psychotic disorders while the conditions themselves remain poorly defined.

From a behavioral point of view (Lovaas 1979), the problem in defining the pervasive developmental disorders as distinct pathological syndromes is endemic to clinical models which assume an underlying disease entity or process of which abnormal behaviors are mere symptomatic expressions. In order to construct a disease model, Lovaas contended, we must first identify either an internal process (psychodynamic or organic) that has gone awry or some type of hypothetical disease agent which has infiltrated an otherwise healthy organism. Once identified, the pathological agent or process must be eradicated in order for the organism to resume its normal development. The problem, maintains Lovaas, is very simply that the disease model has failed in both the identification and the treatment of the psychotic child. To begin with, autism (the manifestation of pervasive developmental disorder most frequently referred to in the behavioral literature) may not exist as a disease entity. Even if we could identify a homogeneous group of autistic children, it would be impossible to verify that autism as such was responsible for their behavior. Causality is equally difficult to assess within this mode. Both the child's behavior and any hypothetical organic or psychodynamic factors may covary with a third, possibly unknown, variable. Finally, Lovaas insists, even if a physiological or psychological abnormality were identified, we could not, given the present state of the art in psychophysiology and psychotherapy, prescribe an effective treatment.

The alternative to a disease model, Lovaas believes, is a behavioral model based on learning theory in which no assumptions are made about antecedent conditions. Treatment focuses on the development of procedures for helping psychotic children eliminate pathological behaviors and develop healthy ones in their place. Diagnostic evaluation becomes a process of analyzing the kinds of behavior a child has available and determining how certain specifiable conditions in the child's environment influence these behaviors.

Ferster

The first systematic attempt at understanding the behavior of psychotic children from a behavioral point of view was Ferster's pioneering study (1961), "Positive Reinforcement and Behavior Deficits of Autistic Children." Ferster's theory of childhood psychosis was plainly psychogenic. Intermittent reinforcement of the autistic child's abnormal behaviors, he maintained, could produce the manifest behavioral deficits commonly associated with the disorder "The general principles of behavior applied to the specific situation presumably present during the child's developmental period will lead to hypotheses as to specific factors in the autistic child's home life which could produce the severe changes in frequency as well as form of his behavior" (1961, p. 437). Behavior, Ferster believed, had to be analyzed in terms of its functional consequences (operants) in order to determine what specific effects the child's performance had on the environment and how these effects, in turn, maintained the autistic performance. From this point of view, the major difference between autistic and normal children, outside of a narrower range of performance, is the frequency with which various types of behavior available to the child are actually exercised. Autistic children, Ferster tried to demonstrate, emit lower rates of behavior and are therefore less likely than normal children to come under the formative influence of social or environmental controls. The behaviors which persevere in the child's behavioral repertoire are frequently aggressive in nature, because the aversive consequences they produce are often found to be most effective in controlling and manipulating the social environment. Less effective though potentially more adaptive behaviors are weakened because of the intermittent reinforcement and extinction schedules produced by the parents' inconsistent responsiveness. Ferster cited three factors within the parental environment: overall disturbances in the parental behavioral repertoire (for example, a reduction in total behavioral output secondary to depression); prepotent activities that take precedence over the child; and escape from the child because of his aversiveness, which may reduce potential reinforcement of the total behavioral output, thereby resulting in severe behavioral deficits. A vicious circle is set into motion in which a low level of behavior output further impedes the expansion of the child's repertoire as fewer and fewer behaviors are brought under effective stimulus control.

A short while after Ferster's paper was published, Ferster and DeMyer (1962) reported on a series of experiments with autistic children who were exposed to a simple but controlled environment in which they could engage in simple lever pulling or match-to-sample tasks for desired reinforcers. Though of little practical consequence, these early studies demonstrated that given certain programmed environmental contingencies, psychotic children could learn new behaviors in much the same way as normal children do. Therein lay the promise that by perfecting educational techniques for teaching more appropriate behavior, rather than searching for a hypothetical disease entity, it might be possible to enhance and enlarge upon the overall functioning of the severely disturbed, behaviorally deficit youngster.

Lovaas

Lovaas, perhaps the principal exponent of the behavioral treatment of early onset psychotic disorders (Lovaas et al. 1974), began with Ferster's original finding of behavioral deficits among autistic children and promoted a treatment methodology designed to strengthen those adaptive behaviors already represented in the child's repertoire while gradually shaping absent behaviors through successive approximation. Undesirable or maladaptive behaviors (such as self-stimulation, self-mutilation, and atavistic behaviors), he believed, could be extinguished by withholding the reinforcers that maintained them (such as parental attention maintaining tantrums) or through the systematic application of response-contingent aversive stimuli (such as electric shock). In this way, Lovaas maintained, the child would develop a more adaptive behavioral repertoire at the same time as his environment acquired meaning as a function of perceived reward and punishment attributes.

Lovaas currently proposes two behavioral paradigms for modifying the development of the psychotic child. In the first, treatment focuses on facilitating the child's acquisition of social reinforcements rather than on building specific behaviors as such. By establishing a normal hierarchy of secondary social reinforcers, such as praise, smiles, and hugs, persons within the child's everyday environment stand better equipped to build and modify behaviors utilizing the kinds of rewards or incentives to which children normally learn to respond.

A second, cumbersome approach involves building specific behaviors directly, by utilizing already effective primary reinforcers such as food or desirable toys. When this procedure is used to extinguish existing inappropriate behaviors, the therapist may rely on any number of strategies, including contingent reinforcement withdrawal (in which the child is denied adult attention during the performance of undesirable behaviors), contingent aversive stimulation (such as electric shock), or reinforcement of behaviors incompatible with inappropriate behavior patterns. This methodology has been incorporated in the elimination of self-destructive, self-stimulating, and aggressive behaviors. Where desired behaviors such as language are absent in the child's behavioral repertoire, these may be acquired through successive approximations based on the performance of an adult model. Verbal imitation is defined for the purposes of this model as a discrimination task in which the child's response comes to resemble its stimulus, the adult's verbal response (Lovaas 1977).

Although the use of primary reinforcers such as food and toys is somewhat easier to operationalize than the use of secondary social reinforcers, there are a number of serious drawbacks to this approach in terms of diminished response generalization. In using primary reinforcers, we must construct special environments creating conditions that may have little efficacy in the child's life outside the clinical setting. For this reason, a number of behavioral programs have shifted emphasis to parent training in an attempt to extend the child's useful application of newly acquired behavior patterns to the home environment (Koegel et al. 1973).

Since the mid 1970s, behavioral interventions have been widely applied, with some success, to the elimination of a considerable range of problematic behaviors and behavioral deficits among psychotic children. Particularly promising results have been obtained in the reduction of self-stimulating and self-abusive behaviors through the use of timeout procedures (Solnick et al. 1977), overcorrection methods (Foxx and Azrin 1973), and electric shock (Lovaas et al. 1974). Frankel et al. (1978) found that certain self-stimulating responses could be extinguished by simply eliminating the element of sensory reinforcement. The auditory feedback from plate spinning, for example, was eliminated by installing carpeting over an area where one child was noted to engage in this activity. Harris and Wolchik (1979) found that significant reductions in self-stimulating behavior were often accompanied by increases in more appropriate play with toys.

Despite the encouraging results of behavioral interventions when applied in vitro, in carefully controlled clinical settings, long-term follow-up studies show wide variations among psychotic children in terms of the maintenance of treatment gains (Lovaas et al. 1973). Much seems to depend on the post-therapeutic environment. Children whose parents have been trained to carry out behavior therapy on their own generally continue to improve, while those who are institutionalized following initial treatment often regress.

Even the staunchest supporters of behavioral intervention are hesitant to talk about cure. Lovaas, for example, has stated that constitutional or "structural" pathology may well put an upper limit on what some psychotic children are capable of learning, regardless of intervention. There may also be serious limitations to the kinds of behavior that can be built or modified to any truly productive end. For example, little has thus far been achieved in "teaching" emotional responses. Regardless of progress in cognitive development, most psychotic children continue to manifest difficulties in the interpretation of their own feelings and the feelings of others. Similarly, when relied upon for their own motivation or initiative to perform, few will spontaneously incorporate learned behaviors in flexible or creative applications. In most cases the locus of control remains outside the child and is wholly a function of reinforcement contingencies.

In this regard, I well remember a 3-year-old autistic girl being treated behaviorally at a local therapeutic day school. Through the methodical administration of response-contingent reinforcements, Julie had been "trained," so her therapist claimed, to ask for food when she was hungry, evidence, I was told, of the intrinsic modifiability of motivation through behavioral means. What I saw in the lunchroom that afternoon, however, looked quite different from the intentional, internally motivated command of a hungry little girl awaiting her lunch. Indeed, Julie did ask for crackers, one right after another. Each time she was given one, however, she looked it over confusedly, threw it on the floor, and immediately demanded another one in its place. Clearly, she had learned to ask for food and had even come to associate the request with the school lunchroom. Still, her behavior had no connection with her internal state and reflected neither the need nor the desire for something she could actually eat. If the behavior was, in fact, motivated, hunger had little or nothing to do with the motivation.

Some early workers in the behavioral field believed that one day key or pivotal response patterns could be isolated which, when modified, would trigger broadbased changes throughout the child's personality organization and across multiple lines of cognitive, affective, and social development. To date, no such patterns have been identified. The wider implications of this failure to isolate pivotal responses bring into question, for me at least, the philosophy of behavioral intervention in the broader sense. In a paper entitled "The Behavioral Modification Approach," Lovaas (1974) stated: "A behavioral approach to autism has not addressed itself to the child or to autism as an entity, whatever that means . . . [these] children present certain immediate problems which we can attempt to ameliorate on the basis of what we know today." Following a stimulus-intervening variable-response model, the "total" child is positioned somewhere within the proverbial "black box" of unknowable intervening variables. Technically speaking, the child's responses as measurable units of behavior are the medium within which intervention takes place. Although some will argue that treating behaviors rather than persons compromises the essential cohesiveness of experience from which human subjectivity derives its meaning, an equally cogent criticism may be lodged against the behavioral model in terms of contradictions within the theory itself. A growing body of behavioral theorists, it will be recalled, subscribe to Lovaas's belief that the primary deficits in social, cognitive, and linguistic functioning characteristic of certain groups of psychotic children may be explained in terms of stimulus overselectivity—a tendency to respond to limited, often irrelevant stimulus cues in the environment without learning or discriminat-

ing other equally relevant aspects. Where normal children apprehend complex, integrated wholes, psychotic children focus on isolated parts. The point of my criticism should be clear: behavior
therapists treat psychotic children as psychotic children treat
the world at large; both overselect isolated elements of a complex
whole.

While no one would go as far as to attribute the treatment
philosophy of behavior analysis to a perceptual abnormality, it is
nonetheless paradoxical that a therapy whose goal is to facilitate
perceptual integration regards its patients from the point of view
of isolated behaviors. It would seem particularly important in a
treatment model such as behavior modification, in which imitation
is a central concept, to begin by treating children who fail to
perceive totalities in a milieu in which they themselves are regarded as total human beings. This may be one instance in which
we should not "fight fire with fire" or, more to the point, overselectivity with overselectivity.

Chapter Nine

A Psychoanalytic Perspective

Up to this point, we have considered the pervasive developmental disorders of childhood as a function of anatomical, biochemical, and behavioral phenomena, the tangible aspects of the disease process. In each of these areas, we know a great deal more about psychotic children than, in all likelihood, they will ever know or understand about themselves: how they look, how they learn, how their neurons fire, the relative dimensions of their right and left anterior horns, and so on. These are the kinds of phenomena with which we work most comfortably as natural scientists: things that can be perceived directly or surmised inferentially with the proper instrumentation. But what do we know about the way in which psychotic children experience themselves, their relationships with other people, and their interactions within the world at large? Although it is unrealistic to talk about meaning in this context—most would agree that severely disturbed children in the first and second years of life lack the cognitive structuralization necessary for complex symbolic representation and self-reflection—there is nonetheless a prestructural subjectivity, a quality of experiencing at the most rudimentary levels of psychic organization. Regardless of specific etiological factors, the "inner life" of the psychotic child will reflect defects or deficiencies as these occur at any level of physiological or psychological organization. Whether "bad blood," bad parenting, or both are culpable may not be as important to understanding the phenomenology of the psychotic child's development as the manifestations of these pathogenic factors in the child's subjective experience of significant persons and events during the early years of life. Kernberg (1980) has noted in this regard that irrespective of the source or origin of the psychotic syndrome, whether a function of genetics, congenital factors, or the response of an essentially healthy organism to parental or familial psychopathology, the phenomenal outcomes will be a pathologically distorted subjective world.

How, then, do we plant ourselves at a vantage point within the psychic organization of the prestructural psychotic child? We can isolate physiological processes, perceptual styles, and behavioral manifestations, but how are these experienced by the child within a phase-specific developmental context? What are the subjective concomitants? Simply put, what is it like to be a psychotic child?

Traditionally, problems involving the phenomenology of mental events have fallen within the domain of psychoanalytic investigation, though here, too, questions of vantage point and primacy are often a source of controversy. Data derived from introspection, empathy, and direct observation frequently yield strikingly different renderings of intrapsychic processes, each with important clinical and theoretical implications. However, it is not my purpose to critique psychoanalytic models but to examine the development of psychoanalytic theory with respect to early deficits and distortions in the formation of psychic structure and the relationship of these abnormalities to the pervasive developmental disorders.

By 1937, Freud had recognized a group of recalcitrant psychoanalytic patients among whom "unfavorable modifications of the ego" were unreconcilable in terms of a classical drive-defense model of infantile neurosis:

> The factors which are prejudicial to analysis and may cause it to be so long drawn out as to be really interminable are a constitutional strength of instinct and an unfavorable modification of the ego in the defensive conflict. . . . One is tempted to make the first factor, strength of the instincts, responsible for the second—the modification of the ego—but the latter has its own etiology and indeed it must be admitted that our knowledge of these relations is as yet imperfect. (1937, p. 238)

In spite of Freud's admonition, a conflict model of early psychological development and psychopathology has until recently been retained by most psychoanalytically oriented clinicians. Toplin (1980), in a critique of conflict theories, noted that such analysts as Melanie Klein, Karen Horney, and H. S. Sullivan, despite theoretical differences, all shared a common emphasis on the defensive splitting of objects, infantile impulses connected with "good" and "bad" object representations, and intrapsychic conflict, as core concepts in both normal and pathological development. Klein in particular has been criticized for extending the structuralization of object relations to stages in development prior to the point at which most cognitive theorists place the capacity for complex mental representation. Gedo and Goldberg (1973), among others, have commented on the inconsistency of applying a tripartite structural model based on the resolution of the oedipal conflict to preoedipal disturbances of the first three years of life.

Today, many object relations theorists continue to recognize a variety of structural or prestructural organizations which predate the final consolidation and integration of distinct id, ego, and superego organizations during the oedipal period. While these early structures lack the synthetic and integrative capabilities of their more developmentally sophisticated counterparts, they are nonetheless believed to be sufficiently differentiated to accommodate rudimentary representations of the most elemental units of experience.

Kernberg

Otto Kernberg (1976) has defined object relations theory as "the general theory of the structures of the mind which preserve interpersonal experiences and the mutual influences between these intrapsychic structures and the overall vicissitudes of expression of instinctual needs in the psychosocial environment" (1976, p. 56). As a "special approach" within psychoanalytic metapsychology and clinical psychoanalysis, Kernberg's object relations theory stresses the construction of "bipolar units" (object and self-images) linked by affect and reflecting early parent–infant dyadic and triadic relationships during preoedipal and oedipal stages and the development of progressively more differentiated interpersonal relationships throughout the life cycle.

Early development according to Kernberg's object relations theory begins with fused self- and object images split defensively according to "good-gratifying" and "bad-frustrating" characteristics. During the first months of life, part-object representations are stored separately because of the primitive ego's inability to integrate incompatible aspects into composite wholes. Eventually, however, the separateness of part-objects is maintained defensively in order to protect positive valenced from negative valenced introjects. The earliest ego state is consolidated from a complex mosaic of part-object introjects in which "good internal objects" (fused self- and object-images) and "good external objects" constitute a primitive defensive organization while negative introjects are objectified in the external world where they are identified projectively as alien ("not me") to the self. Only later, under the influence of maturing ego functions and the differentiation of external reality from the world of internal psychic representations, does a tripartite organization emerge in which the ego is organized around positive introjects; a positive libido-invested aspect of reality is acknowledged as external reality, leading to interactions through which self and object representations are further differentiated; and, finally, an "entity of bad external objects" is acknowledged representing both realistically frustrating or threatening external objects and the projected negative early introjections (Kernberg 1971, p. 36).

Normally, splitting processes begin during the 3rd and 4th months of life, peak between the 6th and 12th months, then gradually disappear during the 2nd year. Positive and negative self- and object images are consolidated and repression is established as the central defensive operation of the ego. By contrast, the pathological object relations of the psychotic child are such that the inner representational world remains fragmented, with little or no integration of part-objects into self- or whole object representations (P. Kernberg 1980). In cases of extremely early onset such as the autistic disturbances, it is doubtful that undifferentiated self and object representations necessary for a normal symbiotic relationship with the mother would have developed in the first place. Kernberg was insistent, however, that these deficits do not mean that psychotic children are bereft of intrapsychic structure. Primitive forms of defense mechanisms waged against extremely primitive conflicts, she maintained, are still detectable from the 1st year of life. These are not intersystemic conflicts between ego and superego, but intrasystemic conflicts involving various incompatible and disassociated self- and object representations of an extremely primitive nature.

Mahler

It is probably a truism that any simple explanation of human nature is likely to be either inaccurate or incomplete. In this respect, certainly, no one would fault Kernberg, yet his theory of developmental psychopathology is strikingly cumbersome at times and difficult to apply firsthand to clinical observations. Mahler's model of early development in infantile psychosis is also an object-relations theory, but a theory that is informed by the direct obser-

vation of mother–infant interaction as well as by genetic reconstructions of the 1st years of life. Mahler (1968, 1980) likened the
psychotic child to the very young infant insofar as neither of them
seems to have been born psychologically in the sense of being tuned
in to the outside world. Unlike the normal infant, however, the
psychotic child will not achieve psychological birth and the capacity for becoming a separate individual with a cohesive sense of self
and identity. Although constitutional factors may be a prerequisite
for psychotic illness, the course of the disorder unfolds within the
relationship between parent and child. "The psychotic infant,"
wrote Mahler, "seems to lack, or fails to develop in earliest ex-
trauterine life, the capacity to perceive and therefore to utilize the
mothering agent for the maintenance of his homeostasis; nor can he
release her later on" (1968, p. 32).

The psychological birth of Mahler's infant begins with the
"Normal Autistic Phase" (birth to 1 month), during which the
neonate is capable of perceiving little beyond internal stimuli originating within his own body. Homeostatic regulation, the primary
developmental task of this stage, is maintained through an initially
passive, ultimately active stimulus barrier to external stimuli, and
through affective and motor discharge patterns organized around
mutual cuing and signalling within the parent–child interaction.
Serving in the capacity of "external executive ego," the caregiving
partner augments the neonate's limited capacity for binding instinctual energy and delaying of discharge and in so doing regu-
lates against overwhelming internal stimuli and "organismic distress."

During the "Normal Symbiotic Phase" (1st to 5th months), the
infant demonstrates a rudimentary capacity for apprehending, during periods of intense need, that gratifications are dependent on a
source outside of the bodily self. The infant moves from the point of
perceiving objects as indistinguishable from one another to acknowledging a specific symbiotic partner who is differentiated
from others. The shift from proprioceptive-enteroceptive cathexis
to sensory-perceptual cathexis of the periphery is the major developmental task of this stage. Gradually, outward directed perceptual activity augments the infant's near complete absorption with
internal stimuli. "Hatching," as Mahler termed this redistribution
of attention, begins the separation-individuation phase proper
(from the 5th to the 36th month), during which the infant differentiates from psychological symbiosis with his mother into a relationship in which he experiences himself and mother as separate and
individual entities linked by a strong libidinal bond. Given optimal

holding behavior on the part of the mother, the infant will "hatch" from the symbiotic orbit, separate physically from his former symbiotic partner, and, at an intrapsychic level, differentiate self-representations from the hitherto fused symbiotic self/object representations.

The separation-individuation process represents two simultaneous and intertwined developmental tracks culminating in distinct, internalized self- and object representations. Separation refers to a physical disengagement from the mother, a foraging out and away from the orbit of symbiotic dual unity and into the external world at large. Individuation, which complements this increasingly independent behavior, involves the evolution of autonomous intrapsychic structure. Together, these complementary processes evolve over the course of four subphases. During the "Differentiation Subphase" (from the 5th to the 9th month), the infant's initiatives are characterized by efforts at separating physically from the mother. There is a new look of alertness, perceptiveness, and goal directedness as the child experiences active pleasure in the use of his own body and the manipulation of the environment as a source of stimulation. The "Practicing Subphase" of the separation-individuation process (from the 10th to the 16th month) begins with the infant's earliest locomotor excursions away from the mother and culminates with free upright walking. Contributing to the infant's first awareness of separateness are rapid bodily differentiations from the mother, leading to boundary formation, the enhancement of a specific libidinal bond to the mother, and the maturation of autonomous ego functions in close proximity to the mother. Thus begins the awakening of what Mahler likened to a "love affair with the world," a sense of profound elation associated with the exercise of autonomous functioning and escape from the regressive pull towards reengulfment in the symbiosis.

With Mahler's third subphase, "rapprochement" (from the 16th to the 24th month), the toddler becomes more fully aware of separateness and the limitations and vulnerabilities incumbent upon independent functioning. Primitive omnipotent fantasies collapse, threatening a loss of self-esteem as the child realizes that his wish is not mother's command. At the same time, however, there is increasing pleasure in autonomous functioning. Thus, the child of this stage faces a conflict between his desire to maintain proximity to mother and his "compulsion" to move away from her on his own.

The rapprochement crisis is resolved with the advent of libidinal object constancy, Mahler's fourth subphase (from the 24th to the 36th month), at the point at which the child is capable of representing an internal image of the mothering figure which produces a sense of comfort and security much as the actual mother had in the past. Given the "good enough" presence of the actual mother, both good and bad, self- and object representations, which had split under the conflictual ambivalence of the rapprochement crisis, undergo consolidation. Gradually, given favorable growth-enhancing conditions, the toddler is able to function separately and independently.

Underlying the child's individuation and identity formation is a progressive structuralization of the ego and neutralization of the drives (especially aggressive drives). In order for this to occur, two conditions must be met: internal and external stimuli must be kept within tolerable limits because inundation from any source is prone to overwhelm the premature ego, thereby precluding structuralization, and, until such time as the child is capable of organizing his own inner experience, the symbiotic partner must be available in the capacity of buffer against inner and outer stimuli, organizing these for the infant in such a way as to facilitate boundary formation ("inner vs. outer") and sensory perception (Mahler 1968).

Clearly, the developmental sequence leading to separate, autonomous functioning is not managed singlehandedly by the infant. From birth the neonate is enmeshed in a complex parent–child interaction out of which autonomous functions evolve only gradually. The infant is initially ill-equipped to go it on his own and manages to do so only with the optimal resolution of painful conflict and ambivalence. In those instances of pervasive developmental disorder described by Mahler as the "infantile psychoses," the symbiotic relationship between mother and child is either distorted gravely or missing altogether. The core disturbance in infantile psychosis is a "deficiency or defect in the child's intrapsychic utilization of the mothering partner during the symbiotic phase and subsequent inability to internalize the representation of the mothering object for polarization" (1968, p. 32). In the absence of the normal polarization or splitting of objects, differentiation of the self from symbiotic fusion does not occur. In both symbiotic and autistic manifestation alike, the child fails to perceive the symbiotic partner's need-satisfying ministrations as coming from the outside to relieve tensions on the inside. Rather, there is a delusion on the part of the child of participation in an omnipotent mother–child unit. In the case of the predominantly autistic psychosis, the mother, as a representation of the outside world, seems never to have been perceived emotionally by the infant and remains a part-object regarded indiscriminately from inanimate objects. It appears in this instance that the child is unable to sustain any affective awareness of other human beings whatsoever.

For the predominantly symbiotic child, the maternal representation remains undifferentiated or is regressively fused with the self. When, by virtue of maturational growth in locomotor development, symbiotic fusion is threatened, restitutive attempts are made in order to regain the former state of dual unity: "The child behaves as though he has magical control over the object which he does not distinguish from himself" (Mahler, 1968, p. 226). In the behavior of the child towards the symbiotic partner, we can observe an amalgam of alternating clinging and distancing from which Mahler infers both a wish for fusion with the object and a dread of reengulfment. Thus, the clinical picture of infantile psychosis may change over time as the child alternates between delusional-autistic modes aimed at shutting out potential sources of sensory perception and delusional-symbiotic modes aimed at restoring the original omnipotent oneness with the symbiotic partner.

The contribution of maternal psychopathology to infantile psychosis varies markedly from one instance to the next and may, as recent studies have demonstrated, be absent altogether in the majority of cases. As was mentioned in an earlier section, certain children seem to present a hereditary or constitutional anlage of inherently defective tension-regulating mechanisms in the face of which even the most responsive parenting is insufficient. On the other hand, however, there are cases in which the emotional unavailability of the need-satisfying parent may strain the vulnerable neonate's tenuous proclivities towards contact with the environment just as there are parents whose intrusiveness and intolerance of the child's autonomous functioning obstructs developmental expansion beyond the symbiotic orbit.

Mahler, Kernberg, Klein, and other object-relations theorists share in common a view of psychological development that derives from Freud's early theory of the psychoneuroses a concept of psychic functioning based on antagonistic or incompatible relationships between intrapsychic structures. In each instance, conflict and trauma are the "motors" of growth. "Mahler's baby" (as Tolpin [1980] characterized Mahler's psychologically yet-to-be-born infant) is "closed off in an autistic orbit. . . . symbiotically merged or fused with a hallucinated object, pre-object, or part-object, dangerously split by drives and defenses which make objects good and bad, prematurely separated, and traumatically deflated and disillusioned because of normal physical and mental growth" (p. 53).

In order to reach the developmental position of autonomy and individuation, the child in Mahler's model must first resolve a primitive psychic conflict between positively and negatively valenced self- and object representations. Consolidation of incompatible part-objects will occur only if the real mother can counteract the pathogenic effects of these split, "all good or all bad" introjects by her continuing libidinal availability. The importance of the mother for the child's development, in Mahler's theory, relates primarily to her ability to satisfy basic bodily needs. Adequate attention to need-satisfaction forms the base upon which mature object relations are established (Cohler 1980). How this process of need-gratification evolves and what makes the "good enough mother" good enough remain, however, ambiguous.

Kohut

For Kohut (1971, 1977, 1984) the important aspect of "good enough mothering" goes beyond the dependable gratification of appetitive needs. The primary caregivers as self-objects (objects whose functions are experienced as a part of or in the service of the self and its maintenance and restoration) act in the place of self-sustaining and self-regulating psychic structures yet to be formed. The normal infant, far from experiencing either incompleteness or conflict, experiences himself as a reasonably coherent being, an independent center of initiative with continuity over time and space, with urges to achieve his own purposes, and with feelings of competence and effectiveness, all by virtue of ongoing and expectable ties with psychologically nourishing self-objects. When surrounded by a normally responsive human environment, normal young children are vigorously assertive and demanding of the kinds of responses they automatically expect, responses which reaffirm their subjective experience of wholeness and solidity and quell the sense of fragmentation that comes with momentary disequilibrium.

The initial danger in the early stages of self-consolidation does not, as in the genesis of the psychoneuroses or the defensive splitting of whole objects into part-object representations, arise from conflict or fears around libidinal and aggressive impulses but from threats to the cohesiveness of the self. Threats to self-cohesion (experienced as "disintegration anxiety") in their most primitive form occur when the child's self-objects either fail to apprehend and respond to his needs for experiencing what Kohut described as "the firming confirming delight in the proud display of his body and phase-appropriate achievements" or fail to provide an image of "calm strength and limitless power with which he can merge when his equilibrium is disturbed" (the "idealized parent imago"). Normally, as the child grows in the awareness of his own expanding capabilities, he realizes that the abilities and capabilities of his parent, once perceived as boundless, are in fact limited and fallible. Optimal phase-appropriate failures and frustrations on the part of the self-object, however, are not experienced as devastating losses. If these disappointments are tolerable and of a small order of magnitude, they will gradually bring about growth and structuralization by the bit-by-bit (transmuting) internalization of soothing and regulating functions once provided by the parent. Over time, the child becomes progressively less dependent on the mirroring and approval of self-objects for the maintenance of self-esteem and self-directedness and is increasingly able to live up to his own goals, ideals, and ambitions.

In most classical formulations of conflict psychopathology, danger from libidinal and aggressive impulses generates anxiety which results in regression to an earlier level of psychosexual organization. Typically there is a rejection of reactivated pregenital impulses, a heightening of defensive operations, and the appearance of compromise symptom formations. In contrast, preoedipal structural deficiencies occur when the child's self-objects fail to meet his innate endowment halfway by providing the transitional precursors of psychic structure which normally undergo internalization and allow the child to maintain an autonomous sense of esteem, vitality, and cohesiveness (Tolpin 1978). Threats to self-cohesion (the danger of fragmentation or the loss of vitality) occur as a consequence of traumatically frustrating empathic failures on the part of the primary caregivers in their role as mirroring and idealized self-objects—what Cohler (1980) described as an "asymmetry" between what the parents can provide and what is optimal for the child at a given point in development. Infants who, because of parental psychopathology, suffer massive deprivation (as opposed to optimal, structure-promoting frustrations) cannot internalize a self-soothing function they have never experienced. Psychological growth that is enhanced by minor breaks in empathy is severely disrupted by pervasive gaps in phase-appropriate responding. Children who fail to internalize the tension-regulating, vitalizing, and confirming functions of the self-objects are prone throughout life to seek relationships in which psychic structure can be borrowed, in what amounts to a reedition of the original, frustrating interaction of self and self-object. Efforts at replacing missing self-object functions needed to overcome feelings of emotional emptiness and loss of vitality may appear symptomatically in pseudophobias, excessive self-stimulation, narcissistic rage, and indiscriminate sexualization of interpersonal relations.

Although self-psychology has not as yet produced a theory of the infantile psychoses per se, both the model of structural deficit psychopathology and the observational method of "vicarious introspection" (empathy) provide powerful tools for understanding the phenomenology and psychic reality of early onset psychotic states. Empathy as a "value-neutral tool of depth psychological observation" (Tolpin and Kohut 1980) may be a singular means of tracking the inner experience of children who have failed to achieve a capacity for conceptualization or verbal communication, a way of knowing what they cannot tell us directly.

Broadly conceived, the early onset psychoses represent a massive failure in the bit-by-bit internalization of intrapsychic structure. To the extent to which developmental needs for self-confirmation, regulation, and affirmation go unfulfilled in traumatic proportions, structural deficits are incurred and the child's inner experience of wholeness and cohesiveness is compromised. Again, the exact etiology of the psychotic disorder is difficult to attribute to either parental psychopathology or to specific vulnerabilities in the infant. In all likelihood, the contributions of caregiver and child are relative and complementary. For a child who is constitutionally vulnerable, whose temperament strains even the "good enough" mother's ability to soothe, regulate, and confirm, even minute frustrations are likely to be experienced as intolerable deprivations. To the extent to which disintegrative anxiety precludes the internalization of self-soothing and self-regulating functions, the child is prone to remain dependent upon the external regulating functions of the actual self-object. Disruptions in the delusional merger of the psychotic child with the self-object result in fragmentation or depletion of the precariously organized cohesive self. This theory is borne out clinically as well as theoretically. Children manifesting severe disturbances of the self are observed to react intensely to separations, exhibiting violent inconsolable rage, clinging, and excessive demandingness. No amount of frustration, however fleeting or minute, is optimal. What the normal child needs in order to grow, to become the master of his or her own drives, emotions, and ambitions, the psychotic child is unable to tolerate under any circumstances.

Chapter Ten

Psychoanalytic and Psychotherapeutic Treatment of the Psychotic Child

Of the three major theorists discussed in the previous chapter, only Mahler has presented a systematic approach to the treatment of psychotic children based on psychoanalytic principles (Mahler 1968, 1976). Moving from theory to therapy with a consistent emphasis on the importance of disturbances in early mother–child interaction, Mahler has developed a "tripartite design" in which mother, child, and therapist work together in establishing a "corrective symbiotic experience." Broadly conceived, the treatment goals of the tripartite design are threefold: restoration or establishment of a well integrated body image and sense of "entity and identity," simultaneous development of object relations, and restoration of missing or distorted maturational and developmental ego functions. In order to facilitate the renegotiation of early developmental stages, the child must first progress through absent or disturbed phases of development with the therapist serving as a more readily utilizable auxiliary ego than the primary caregiver may have been during the original developmental sequence. A relationship is offered in which the child is gradually enticed into reliving a more fully gratifying, albeit regressive, "symbiotic parasitic relationship" with the substitute mother. At the same time, the child's biological parent is trained to assume the therapist's role in maintaining the corrective experience outside the treatment setting.

Mahler describes two stages in the tripartite treatment process. In the first, the therapist must establish some form of indirect contact and primitive communication with the psychotic child, who is initially unable to experience direct relations with another person. The therapist must carefully establish a presence allowing it to be experienced as something positive without the implicit or explicit demand that the child acknowledge the existence of the therapist as a person. Rather than impose on the child by directing the interaction, the therapist follows the child's lead, making it possible for the child to accept gradually the presence of the therapist as soothing and to anticipate interpersonal contact as something to be desired. More than a mother substitute, the therapist represents what Mahler refers to as a "mothering principle," an auxiliary stimulus barrier, protecting the infant against excessive stimulation from the environment and drawing his attention away from threatening internal stimuli. Gradually, as the therapist is recognized as a source of comfort and gratification, a separate and responsive other, the mother is led into the same kind of relationship with her child. This, the reestablishment and working through of symbiotic ties to the original maternal object, is the goal of the tripartite design. In order for the transition from substitute-mother to therapist-mother to progress smoothly, the mother as well as the child must undergo considerable preparation. Before the mother can be drawn into a relationship with either the therapist or her child, however, it is first necessary that the mother be "fed," often both literally and figuratively, in order to compensate in some measure for the emotional starvation of her own childhood. Ultimately, it is the mother's identification with the therapist that makes it possible for her to circumvent the panic and uncertainty that frequently occur when the child turns to her, perhaps for the first time, in a way that had previously been disrupted by the psychosis.

During the second phase of treatment, the child begins to invest in the therapist as a more differentiated and whole human object. Gains in object relations established during the first phase lead to the child's reliving and, eventually, understanding and reintegrating early traumatic experiences that impeded growth in the original developmental sequence. Again, the therapist serves as a bridge between psychotic preoccupations and the reinvestment of the mother. We look at this stage for a greater differentiation of self and object, evidence of enhanced ego control, the ascendancy of secondary process thinking, and the acquisition of speech.

It is the consensus among our clinical perspectives that early onset psychosis is, in all likelihood, a diverse and varied phenomenon. Still, many treatment models seem to pose what amounts to a general, nonspecific therapeutic methodology for treating what amounts to an "average expectable" psychotic child. In contrast, Mahler discriminates within the tripartite format a number of specific technical considerations according to the predominantly symbiotic or autistic characteristics of the child's disturbance. In the treatment of the predominantly autistic child, it is first necessary that the child establish contact with a human love object. To this end, the child must be lured gradually into what is described as "quasi-accidental tangential contact with the human object." Any attempt at hastening this process, however, may result in "symbiotic panic" and regression, which Mahler likens to a catatonic state. Luring the child into an affective relationship may begin with interactions around inanimate objects or pleasurable stimuli. Optimally, over a protracted course of treatment, the child may develop genuine affective contact with the therapist-mother substitute. While this contact may in some instances lead to rapid growth across many developmental lines, the prognosis for the autistic child remains guarded. Initial signs of progress are often followed by a plateau of intractably arrested growth.

Treatment of the predominantly symbiotic child begins with a problem diametrically opposed to that encountered in work with the pathologically detached autistic youngster. Children whose psychological functioning is characterized by symbiotic mechanisms respond to any perception of separateness with panic and violent behavioral disorganization. Pushed prematurely into separation, the symbiotic child may regress still further by turning to autistic defenses in an effort to forestall the loss of whatever precarious sense of self he may already have established. Thus, in facilitating a corrective symbiotic experience, the therapist must take care to allow the child to test reality slowly and in small increments. As the child begins the process of experimentation, testing himself as a separate entity, the therapist provides "continued ego infusions" with support, direction, and encouragement. Once panic reactions subside, the symbiotic child may benefit from a special therapeutic milieu offering diversified substitute relationships in place of the original parasitic fusion with the mother. Gratifying strides in reexperiencing and reliving, leading to expanded development, are possible with this approach, though cure in the sense of autonomous functioning and independent living may be an unrealistic goal in many cases.

Mahler emphasized that reexperiencing within the corrective symbiotic relationship is not the same thing as the normal phase-appropriate experiencing of separation and individuation within the original somato/psychic matrix of the primal mother–infant dyad. Where the normal developmental sequence leading to autonomous functioning has been missed, ego development may remain disturbed irremediably. In this case, the child's need for "borrowed infusions of ego strength" is likely to persist for a lifetime.

As a group, object-relations theorists seem to agree that the corrective reexperiencing of distorted or deficit developmental phases is fundamental to the treatment of early psychotic disorders. Conceptually at least, the notion of a developmental second chance has found a much wider acceptance among child psychotherapists than Alexander's "corrective emotional experience" found among psychoanalysts working principly with adults, many of whom have long regarded noninterpretive, extraanalytic parameters as problematic, if not heretical (see p. 299). Even if we accept the general conceptual format, however, it is difficult to pinpoint in something as nebulous as a human relationship (whether it is the original interaction or the corrective reedition) how we go about "correcting" and what exactly is "corrected." Concerning these questions, we can find as many theories as we find writers on the subject. Mahler's tripartite design, which is certainly the most comprehensive, links a conceptual metapsychological theory to clinical practice with an eloquent simplicity that makes it easy to overlook controversial aspects. Any number of case studies incorporating a tripartite design format and demonstrating varying degrees of therapeutic success are reported in the literature (such as Furer 1964, Elkisch 1971, Benjamin 1971, Kupferberg 1971, Mahler 1976, Resch et al. 1981). Subsequent object-relations-based therapies, while differing on points of technical emphasis and theoretical justification, have, by and large, maintained the format of Mahler's original treatment model.

Alpert

Alpert's "corrective object-relations technique" (1964) was among the first corrective experience models applied to the treatment of early infantile autism. While Alpert emphasized the importance of tailoring treatment to the needs of the individual child, the aim of treatment was always the same: remediation of the pathogenic effects of maternal deficiency through the establishment of a symbiotic-dependent relationship with a constant and consistent need-gratifying object. Initially, the child is induced to regress to an "anaclitic oral incorporative level" (how this is accomplished remains unclear), at which point, Alpert maintained, the child is maximally educable through an incorporation of and identification with the therapist. Gradually, through the therapist's participation in the child's stereotyped and repetitive games, new variations are developed. The child's activity becomes less stereotyped and begins to take on a meaning which can be verbalized and elaborated, thereby creating a bridge between primary and secondary process thinking. The therapist becomes in this capacity a psychic organizer, helping the child piece together meaningless fragments of disconnected activity into meaningful derivatives. Rendered conscious and coherent, early traumatic events are more readily mastered and assimilated within the child's emerging personality organization.

Given our present understanding of the wide range of biological as well as environmental factors that may contribute to a psychotic outcome, few today would be as confident as Alpert in treating early infantile autism as a distinct disease entity attributable to a single etiological factor.

Wieland and Rudnick

A short time after Alpert's initial studies (1954), Weiland and Rudnik (1961) noted that, while some autistic children appeared to respond to a corrective object-relations therapy by progressing to a working object relationship, many others, perhaps a majority, failed to respond at all. An intermediate group was observed to exhibit some changes but developed only what the authors called a "pseudo-object relationship" in which they appeared nearly unaware of the existence of human beings as a separate class of objects. For such children, other persons existed only in the most instrumental sense.

In view of the wide variation among autistic children in treatment response, Weiland and Rudnick proposed a distinction between at least two forms of autistic psychoses, each calling for specific treatment considerations. In one group, symptoms may develop primarily as a defense against traumatic and overwhelming experiences with destructive primary objects. For these children, object relations have become associated with a potential for danger. In the second group, however, symptoms may be related to a lack of exposure to the primary object or the absence of crucial experiences during "critical" developmental periods ("critical" in an ethological sense) and a consequent failure to become imprinted on human beings with appropriate reciprocal responses. Unlike children in the first group, those in the second would not be expected to develop defenses against the apprehension of objects, having been unable to recognize human beings in the first place. For these children, therefore, failure to develop appropriate techniques of relating, rather than defensive withdrawal, is responsible for alienation from the world of early psychosocial experiences.

Children who have already developed rudimentary object relations and secondarily defend themselves against involvement with human beings would be more likely, Weiland and Rudnick believed, to respond to a therapeutically corrective life experience than children who, having developed no early object relations, have little foundation for interpersonal relating and would most likely be limited to the establishment of need-gratifying interactions with little or no distinct awareness of human beings as a separate class of objects. If the intensely needful life experiences necessary for object-relatedness cannot be recreated, then there is only one therapeutic solution for children repesenting this second group of disorders: to facilitate the best possible adjustment by offering them as many experiences as possible in which need-satisfaction coincidentally includes other persons. On the other hand, the authors suggested, if the conditions necessary to facilitate imprinting or primary object cathexis can in fact be recreated beyond infancy, it might be feasible to reinduce the state of helpless dependency in which early forms of bonding normally occur during infancy. In this case, the optimal therapeutic program should be organized to recreate an intensely needful situation in which all gratifications are offered by a single person who can erect those barriers necessary to make it impossible for the child to achieve these gratifications autistically—in isolation from other human beings. Once the child has established a primitive but well differentiated need-gratifying relationship with a therapist, the treatment is then gradually transferred to the original primary objects, typically the parents.

Des Lauriers

Most object-relations theorists would agree that in order to treat the disturbed child through the corrective experiencing or reexperiencing of deficient developmental phases, conditions surrounding the original developmental situation must be made clear. Des Lauriers (1967), in contrast, suggested a "structural understanding" of childhood schizophrenia focusing on what the condition "intrinsically is" without attempting to pinpoint the factors—heredity, physiology, society, or environment—that may have caused it. The therapist, according to Des Lauriers, must accept as a starting point that his is not the task of tracing systematically the origins or causal factors involved in the disturbance. What is most salient from the standpoint of treatment is an inability on the part of the psychotic child to establish stable interpersonal relationships within which he might otherwise experience the satisfaction of his needs and the maturation of his personality. Relatedness to others presupposes the child's having already experienced himself as separate from others. There can be no integrated reality sense until he has experienced himself as real by defining the boundaries of his own identity. This experience of separateness and differentiation of self from others, Des Lauriers maintained, is consistently found lacking in the schizophrenic child. The therapist's task, therefore, is to facilitate for the child a restoration of those conditions necessary to induce cognizance of external reality and an investment in human relations. In order to stimulate ego functioning and development, those kinds of experiences must be emphasized which make the sense of bodily limits and self-other differentiation inevitable. Ego development for Des Lauriers begins with the emergence of body ego.

In establishing contact with the child, the therapist must seek to establish a presence by creating a distinct sensory impression. The emphasis here is on developing a physical rapport conducive to immediate and varied sensory experiences, with relatively less importance attached to symbolic or linguistic communication. Communication in any form requires separateness and differentiation between communicators. In particular, physical communication, modeled after the mutual stimulation of mother and child, has the additional effect of enhancing body definition and boundary formation. Growth-facilitating interactions of this type are accomplished very naturally by offering the child a multiplicity of age-appropriate sensory experiences. Initially at least, linguistic communication between therapist and child is important not as much for its symbolic content as for its usefulness in creating within the child both an awareness of his own separateness and a need to be heard.

The child of whom Des Lauriers wrote emerges from an undifferentiated autistic self-object unity in response to bodily sensations stimulated through contact with a caregiving object, typically the mother. Gradually, a sense of boundary ("body ego") is defined by impinging sensory impressions perceived as emanating from a source outside the self. With repeated stimulation, this source is brought into focus as an object apart from the self yet eminently reachable, responsive but with a will of its own. Reality begins for the infant as a sociobiological reality and only later embraces non-human aspects of the external world at large.

For other object-relations theorists, most notably D. W. Winnicott (1951), full apprehension of reality begins not with a focal awareness of distinct human entities but with a series of preobject and transitional phenomena out of which the relationship between what is "objectively perceived and subjectively conceived" is defined. The child must first delineate the broad parameters of inner and outer reality before differentiating those aspects that are uniquely personal and interpersonal. Awareness of separate self and object entities does not become a salient developmental issue until the child has first differentiated between inner and outer experiences. An important part of this process is negotiated through the transitional object, for Winnicott an intermediate area of experiencing to which both internal and external reality contribute: "it is an area which is not challenged because no claim is made on its behalf except that it shall exist as a resting place for the individual engaged in the perpetual human task of keeping inner and outer reality separate yet related" (Winnicott 1951, p. 230).

Fisher (1975), who focused on the role of transitional phenomena in the corrective therapeutic experience of an autistic child, believed that prior to the transitional stage proper, in which the child attempts to integrate and tolerate the separate existence of human others, there occurs a gradual differentiating out, from within a "reality matrix of mother-himself," a more or less diffuse awareness of an "out-there subsystem" of neutral shared events. The capacity for experiencing a separate interpersonal realm of self-other presupposes a transitional world of unchallenged, freely interchangeable, inner-world/outer-world experiences which, in turn, presupposes the child's having first had some solid interaction with various aspects of the world around him. Fisher maintained that it is this earliest awareness of the explorable world of things and people "out there" that remains deficient or distorted in the development of the autistic child. Optimally, well before the process of separation proper has even begun, the child's attention is drawn by the allure of an interesting, challenging, and potentially gratifying external world. Here, from among myriad enticing and intriguing objects, a special, transitional object is found, one which will ultimately bridge the gap between self and other. For the autistic child, Fisher maintained, all of this has yet to occur.

From this point of view, the task of the therapist, prior to the establishment of a corrective symbiotic relationship, is to help make outer reality in the broadest possible sense a relevant aspect of the child's experience. Fisher conceptualized this process as helping the child to establish a suitable field beyond his inner fantasy life in which a playful, masterful interchange and experience with real objects can unfold—a personal corner of external reality in which the child can operate with curiosity and abandon. This is not yet a transitional field between internal and external worlds (there is to begin with no external world to which the child can relate), but rather a "shared public space" created together by child and therapist "to which the child can travel and from which [the child] can return." Gradually, the child will fashion from this stronghold in the external world a true transitional object, bridging inner and outer reality and facilitating free commerce between the two.

With recent advances in the study of early parent–child interaction, other writers have also become attuned to the pre-object aspects of child development and their implications for the treatment of severe disturbances of the first years of life. Resch et al. (1981) have described the treatment of a 2-year-old autistic girl employing a modified tripartite design. By working with child and mother together at an early biosensory stage prior to the development of psychological defenses or differentiation from the mother, the authors sought to organize the precursors of psychic structure and establish the groundwork for what might ultimately lead to a balanced symbiosis. Given the child's primitive cognitive, affective, and social characteristics, the therapist decided not to begin treating the mother and child at a dynamic level of object relations (that is, by addressing the symbolic meaning of the interaction). Instead, treatment focused on the biological-perceptual level of the child's maturation where impaired sensory regulations were believed to have prevented the development of a normal symbiosis with the mother.

Areas targeted for intervention included the child's use of perception, attention, stimulus thresholds, stimulus-modulating mechanisms, pacing, synchrony, and sensorimotor integration. Rather than utilize mother–child play in its social-reciprocal sense, therapy began with baby play in which the mother acted as facilitator and mediator of sensory thresholds, sensory reception, and sensory processing. By safeguarding the optimal regulation and processing of inner and outer stimuli, mother and therapist created a matrix out of which the child could safely recover inanimate and ultimately animate, human objects. Mother's ability to make herself a part of the child's action schemata had the effect of reinforcing the child's own sense of instrumentality, thereby enabling her to differentiate from both her toys and her mother. In every instance, the therapist worked towards relating the child more directly to the mother and towards specifying mother as a uniquely important person.

Bettelheim

Differences in therapy, theory, and technique aside, most of the theorists described thus far would agree that restoration of the psychotic child to parental care is an important aspect of the treatment process. For some, this means a reintroduction of the primary caregiver at a point in the child's development where phase-appropriate investment in a gratifying, growth-facilitating relationship becomes a realistic possibility, perhaps for the first time. Others choose to work with the parent and child together, from the start, towards the amelioration of pathological interactions that have made it difficult in the past for one or both participants to attain healthy, independent function. Finally, there are those, following Bettelheim, who maintain that the prospects for treating the psychotic child on an outpatient basis or in conjunction with the child's parents are of dubious therapeutic value for everyone involved. Why, Bettelheim argued (1967), should we undertake to help the disturbed youngster through the very person who impeded development in the first place? Everything that is needed to treat the psychotic child, he maintained, exists latently within the child; infantile autism as an illness is a way of reacting to a total life experience by a total human being. By involving parents in the treatment of the disturbed child, we once more fail to regard the child as an autonomous human being and thereby perpetuate the very conditions under which development was derailed during the original primal interaction.

The goal of treatment for Bettelheim is to create for the child a world that is totally different from the one abandoned in despair, a world the child can enter unconditionally and without demands. Because the autistic child responds to all forms of relatedness as "utterly destructive and inescapable," treatment must work towards creating an awareness that other positive forms of relating exist:

> Because of the one single relationship that propelled him out of a position of love and ambivalence with overwhelming force he became . . . glued to hate. It is our task to help him move from this position of extreme hate and destruction towards that human ambivalence in which normal relationships exist. (1967, p. 91)

Treatment is a slow and all-encompassing process. Because the autistic child has ceased to expect need-gratification from the environment, the therapist must provide an alternative of "potentially positive valence" long before it can be expected to awaken any positive interest. Years of interaction, with the therapist offering himself as a steady, ever-present object, may be necessary before the autistic child can begin to fathom the possibility of a relationship different from the "all-pervasive" one he has known. Only when the child has recognized certain aspects of reality as having positive value is there justification for his abandoning autistic withdrawal as a primary means of coping.

The process of reexperiencing in Bettelheim's model is one laden with confrontations and distrust. The therapist, however, must at all times meet the child's defiance with encouragement and understanding and prove to him that nothing will be forced or imposed upon him—that he is in control over, rather than subservient to, his environment. Assertion and opposition are part and parcel of the autistic child's struggle to experience himself as an autonomous, self-determining human being and must not be thwarted or curtailed prematurely.

Criticisms of Bettelheim's work are well known and have become something of a pastime among reviewers of psychiatric literature. While allowing himself much in the way of poetic license, Bettelheim offers few empirically demonstrable principles that might serve as guidelines in transferring the Orthogenic School model to other treatment programs. Equations of mental health with an optimistic outlook on life and mental illness with a volitional withdrawal from reality are at best incomplete, at worst inconsistent with current research data. In summarizing a review of Bettelheim's *The Empty Fortress*, Scholper (1976) was moved to comment: "It is repeatedly the failure to meet scientific gains that enables the author to approach the artistic."

Each of the foregoing therapeutic models is based on an assumption that central to the treatment of childhood psychosis is the child's corrective experiencing or reexperiencing of key developmental phases. The emphasis here is squarely on the facilitation of a particular quality of experience in which the therapist's role is primarily that of the empathically attuned participant-observer. The child is offered a relationship that is "good enough," neither so frustrating as to coerce the impression that satisfaction of needs in relationship to another person is unattainable, nor so gratifying as to maintain the omnipotent delusion that "my wish is your command." Optimally, the experience is representative of the best that can be anticipated in a reality of reasonably responsive human relations. What the therapist cannot or will not provide for the child, the child will learn to provide autonomously, without the therapist's help: tolerable frustrations that can be mastered by the child independent of the caregiver-therapist's intervention form the basis for self-regulation and the consolidation of stable intrapsychic structure.

Other therapists, perhaps more solidly grounded in the mainstream of traditional psychoanalytic psychotherapy, have followed treatment models based either on a broadening of the ego through the interpretation of unconscious conflict and defense (that is, "expressive" psychotherapy) or on a strengthening of the ego through the suppression of unconscious material and the fortification of defensive operations. While neither approach has been demonstrated to produce consistent therapeutic results, the concepts of suppressive and expressive treatment have proven useful in examining the therapeutic action of various technical maneuvers aimed at facilitating growth at different levels of personality organization.

Escalona

Escalona (1964) in a comparison of psychoanalytically oriented treatment models for psychotic children defined the expressive mode in terms of its aim of facilitating, through interpretation, the full awareness of previously unconscious material with the eventual restoration of normal ego functioning. Fantasies are seen as meaningful creations and are interpreted in context with the child's reality experience. The relationship between affects and their sources as well as between symptoms and their deeper meanings are explored. Suppressive psychotherapy, in contrast, proceeds from a recognition of the fact that the psychotic child, by definition, shows an extreme weakness in ego functioning and a failure to repress psychic experiences which typically remain unconscious during the course of normal development. In those cases where the ego is judged to be too weak to assimilate and reconcile impulses, needs, and conflicts, treatment may aim at protecting the child from the impact of instinctual forces by discouraging the expression and acting out of fantasies and offering as much gratification as possible in more realistic pursuits.

Escalona stresses that both forms of treatment have advantages and disadvantages; in either case there are inherent compromises. Expressive psychotherapy may succeed in working

through and "curing" specific symptoms. However, while temporary overall improvement may result, the author notes that the
improvement is seldom maintained. The functioning of the personality as a whole is rarely altered to a significant degree. Suppressive treatment may bring about clinical improvements in terms of
increased control and conformity, but the underlying psychotic
process remains untouched. The most favorable outcome in this
case is what Escalona describes as a "pseudoadjustment" in which
apparent clinical gains are maintained as long as the child is not
subjected to unduly stressful or provocative situations.

Ekstein

Ekstein (1966, 1971), perhaps the most outspoken advocate of
the interpretive method as applied to the treatment of psychotic
and borderline children, rejected the notion of suppressive psychotherapy as contrary to the ultimate aim of any psychoanalytic
psychotherapy: restoration of the continuity between primitive and
advanced psychic organizations. It impressed Ekstein as equally
erroneous, however, that the same psychoanalytic technique used
in treating neurotic children is often applied indiscriminately and
without modification to the treatment of psychotic children as well,
an artifact, perhaps, of Freud's unification of neurotic and psychotic processes under a single conceptual framework. What is
most important (perhaps of paramount importance in the case of
the psychotic youngster) is that the therapist join the child in the
child's own world. The psychotic child who is dominated by primary process thinking, poorly controlled impulses, and unstable
self- and object-representations offers the therapist verbal associations or other symbolic representational productions and a range of
transference reactions much as any other patient does. The therapist, in turn, must meet the child's regressive primary process
response with his own capacity for controlled regression and secondary process functioning:

> He must match the patient's intrapsychic functioning, essentially
> foreign to him, with his own intrapsychic functioning which is not
> foreign. . . . The therapist is to know the patient and his mind so
> well as to know his strange and foreign thoughts, to understand
> him on his own level of thinking. (1971, p. 65)

Having entered the child's world, the therapist must gauge his
responsiveness in such a way as to make himself available to the
child while at the same time maintaining his self-identity. Like

the "good enough mother," the therapist must meet empathically the child's simultaneous needs for both regressive and growth-promoting stimulation.

How the therapist structures communication is particularly important in light of the psychotic child's sensitivity to intrusion and loss of psychological boundary. As an interpreter of intrapsychic events, the therapist functions in the capacity of "psychological mother," using empathy and understanding to estimate distance from and closeness to the patient's inner state. Optimal contact, according to Ekstein, is restored under those conditions in which the therapist conveys an understanding of the child's material while at the same time avoiding a complete communion that would threaten the child's fragile sense of self with the frightening experiences of diffusion or reengulfment. Where interpretations are offered, they are couched in the context of the child's own metaphors. In this way the therapist "permits the outer world to enter the patient's inner world without demanding that [the patient] cope with a foreign object [that cannot be mastered]." The goal of interpretation must always remain the same, however: restoration of the continuity in psychic organization "destroyed by deadlock struggle" between impulses on the side of the id and adaptation on the side of the ego. Technical modifications aside, Ekstein has maintained a conflict model of psychotic process.

In joining the psychotic child's private world of experience, Ekstein was acutely sensitive to his patient's authority and control. As a foreigner hoping to be assimilated into the child's inner life, the therapist must do as the child does to preserve the integrity of personal symbols and meanings while bringing coherence to those experiences that seem to defy understanding. Not all tread so lightly, however. Goldfarb (1970) took issue with the "undue fascination" some therapists have shown with the psychotic child's bizarre behaviors and primitive verbal productions. According to Goldfarb, the primary disability among severely disturbed youngsters is a failure to acquire those communicational techniques necessary in order to bridge the gap between self and others. Consequently, the psychotic child requires therapeutically a continuous flow of "clarifying experiences" designed to help articulate, discriminate, and schematize levels of internal and external experience.

Goldfarb's method, a combination of educational and psychoanalytic principles, assumes an active and intrusive posture on the part of the therapist, who must respond to the child's verbal ambiguity by confronting unclear responses and encouraging improved clarity. Once ambiguous speech patterns are examined, conflictual elements (which the ambiguity was meant to hide) may be uncovered, interpreted, and reintegrated into the child's conscious mental life.

Despite certain technical modifications, both Ekstein's and Goldfarb's use of the interpretive mode as a vehicle for altering the balance between conscious and unconscious elements of the personality assume a level of intrapsychic structuralization which many theorists agree is lacking for most psychotic children, particularly those whose illness dates back to the first years of life. The ability to assimilate interpretive statements intended to alter defenses, resurrect memories, and facilitate connections between dissociated fantasy and affect by virtue of their content presupposes a capacity for mental representation and complex conceptualization that far exceeds the limited cognitive-affective resources available to the most severely disturbed youngsters. Thus, the value of therapeutic communication to the psychotic child would seem in most instances to lie not in the specific content of verbalization but in the process of verbalization itself. The "interpretation that changes" in this case is one that facilitates the development of new intrapsychic structure more than just the modification of structures already extant. Structural conflicts cannot be analyzed and interpreted effectively before underlying structural deficiencies have been overcome (Harley and Sabot 1980). Put another way, we cannot address conflict between structures where structures do not already exist. The psychotic child who is able to experience intrapsychic conflict is the child who stands the best chance of recovery, for here the raw materials for a relatively differentiated and integrated personality organization are already in place.

Tustin (1972) conceptualized the therapeutic action of interpretation in terms of the therapist's providing the psychotic child with an auxiliary mental apparatus which enables him to sustain tension and delay action until such time as he can do so on his own: "By using the therapist's mind as an auxiliary interpretive agent, somatic processes of immediate discharge gradually become transformed into mental states." The child's inability to conceptualize and communicate on his own only adds to the pain of autistic isolation. Thus, the therapist must act for him in this capacity until he can begin to use the kinds of evocative symbolic expressions which will enable him to give form and substance to the "nameless and invisible terrors which arise from the depths of the mind."

The fact of interpretation, aside from its specific content or meaning, also introduces an important element of interactional pragmatics into the treatment relationship by establishing that spoken language is the commonly accepted mode of communication between human beings. The child begins to experience himself as both listener and speaker. Finally and perhaps most importantly, the therapeutic communication indicates to the child that someone is trying to get through to him, is sustaining the frustration of his lack of response without anger or intimidation, and will patiently await his readiness to move ahead. When treated with respect, patience, and care, the child too may come to experience himself as a human being, separate from but intimately connected to others, self-contained but eminently reachable and worthy of being understood.

Synthesis

The literature of psychoanalytic child psychology is replete with methods and models for the conceptualization and treatment of early onset psychotic disorders. To interpret, not to interpret; to express, to suppress; to confront, to support; to touch, to talk—the alternatives are many. Clearly, no single model can lay claim to be the definitive therapeutic approach to this problem. The range of treatment modalities covered under the auspices of psychoanalytic psychotherapy is as diverse as are the manifestations of the syndrome itself. Nonetheless, the literature as a whole is reasonably coherent. There is a good deal of overlap between even the most divergent points of view.

To conclude this chapter, perhaps we can cull from the various points of view those elements of the treatment process that are central to psychoanalytic psychotherapy in general and of specific relevance to the treatment of the pervasively disordered child.

All of our theorists would agree that the primary agent of change in the psychoanalytic treatment of pervasive developmental disorders is the relationship between child and therapist. When the relationship is oriented towards the corrective experiencing or reexperiencing of early developmental phases, the therapist functions as either a need-satisfying object (a source of emotional supply) or as an auxiliary ego, safeguarding the child from overwhelming internal and external stimuli. Differentiation and structuring of the child's primitive personality organization emerge within a matrix of phase-appropriate therapist-child interactions. Like the "good enough mother," the therapist maintains an empathically attuned responsiveness to the child's needs that results in an optimal blend of gratification and frustration which leads, in turn, to the gradual internalization of self-regulating intrapsychic structure. Because of the psychotic child's limited capacity for direct communication, the therapist must rely heavily upon guided empathic observation, controlled regression, and countertransference reactions as indices of the child's inner experience.

Anyone who has had the opportunity to work with psychotic children (including most of the theorists reviewed above) will attest to the virtual impossibility of therapeutic passivity. Helping the child to overcome confusion, structure experience, and establish contact with reality necessitates active emotional and physical participation on the part of the therapist. Much of the therapist-patient dialogue may be transacted nonverbally, but interpretive interventions aimed at reconciling conflict, altering defenses, explicating transference reactions, and building connections between fragmented remnants of experience are often effective means of bringing coherence to the child's moment-to-moment experience and facilitating longterm personality growth. Several writers have commented on the importance of formal as opposed to content aspects of the therapist's communications. For many psychotic children, the medium is truly the message: language gradually takes on an organizing function (often prior to its semantic function) and establishes the spoken word as an important instrument in the conduct of human relations.

Complementing Mahler's child whom "every mother knows" is the mother whom every child knows. What comes most naturally to the "good enough mother" is the standard against which most of our therapists gauge their technique and measure the efficacy of their results. While there is some disagreement as to the process level of developmental experiencing to which the therapist most effectively addresses his interventions, the mode of intervention is typically conceived in terms of a reparenting experience. What mothers do normally to foster their children's sense of separateness, autonomy, esteem, and self-worth provides the basis for most forms of psychotherapy aimed at facilitating independent functioning.

Finally, the consensus suggests that in most instances treatment of the child alone, excluding the parents, is insufficient, particularly if the aim of treatment is to restore the child to the original family unit. Any number of unresolved psychopathological reactions around issues of autonomy and separation brought into the parenting situation from the parents' own childhood experiences may influence both the course and symptomatic manifestations of early infantile disturbances, even where the role of constitutional factors is clearly indicated.

The success of psychoanalytic methods in the treatment of pervasive developmental disorders has probably fallen short of original expectations. Reported cures are rare, and progress short of cure means many things to many people. Thus, it is disappointing but not surprising to find that dynamic psychotherapy as applied to the treatment of the childhood psychoses has fallen into disfavor since the halcyon days of psychoanalysis in the 1940s and 1950s. The current review shows a steep decline in relevant publications beginning around the mid 1960s. The reasons for this decline probably have much to do with the availability of cheaper, less protracted therapeutic alternatives. Psychotherapy is a long process; behavior therapy is relatively brief; goals set in advance of intervention are defined clearly and the criteria for success are fairly straightforward. Furthermore, psychotherapy is exorbitantly expensive, whereas psychopharmacology is relatively inexpensive and may make life easier (at least more immediately) for everyone involved in the child's care. In either case, however, the child's experience of the treatment process can only be inferred.

Psychotherapy conducted within an intensive interpersonal relationship between patient and therapist remains the only method currently available that allows the treatment process to reach the child at the child's level of experiencing. Far from diminishing the importance of behavior and physiology, the empathic understanding of human experience can only expand our ability to measure and understand effects at any level of organismic functioning as these are registered or reflected in subjective awareness. Furthermore, there is much evidence to suggest that psychophysiology as a unified system representing a continuum of psychological and physiological events is responsive to input originating at either level of process, psyche to soma or soma to psyche. A frightening story will make a person's skin crawl; a warm word of affection will cause a person's heart to race. That the right words can quell the psychotic youngster's fear of annihilation remains to be seen, but, hypothetically at least, the pathway is there.

Until biological science generates a model of the central nervous system that allows for precise, focal interventions, are we not better off beginning with the psyche, in which the subjective concomitants of psychophysiological events are potentially accessible through empathy in a form that is readily apprehended by the skilled psychological observer, than with the soma, where the exact relationship between physiological events and subjective awareness remains elusive? For the time being, psychoanalytic methods remain our sole means of access to that element of the psychophysiological continuum that is uniquely human: the experience of meaning. Perhaps it is still too soon to give up lying on the couch for the laying on of hands.

Chapter Eleven

Summary and Conclusions

The foregoing review examines the pervasive developmental disorders of childhood from a variety of clinical and theoretical perspectives. We have tried to look at severely disturbed children as they look at themselves, as well as from points of view of which they are unlikely ever to be aware. Problems of mind and body and of nature versus nurture have been treated as artifacts of study which in reality exist along a continuum of interrelated phenomena, neither independent nor mutually exclusive. We have assumed that what occurs on one level of organismic (systems) functioning is likely to resonate throughout all levels. Where there is trauma, injury, or deformity of the body, there are likely to be parallel processes echoing these abnormalities in subjective awareness. Where trauma, insult, or injury begin in the subjective experience of the person, we would expect equally to find reflections or registrations of this in the physiological substrate. I believe that, on balance, our study of the collected literature on pervasive developmental disorders would support this. Those theoretical interpretations which have proven most cogent and enduring are rarely incompatible with one another. In many cases, the most convincing cross-validations have occurred between disciplines rather than within them.

Are we any closer then to the definition and description of the pervasively disordered child? Description probably, definition probably not. I do not think there is any question but that the designation "early onset psychosis" is generic in the broadest sense of the word. Even such terms as "autistic," "symbiotic," and "schizophrenic" seem to be inadequate classifications for what are on closer inspection a truly diverse range of phenomena. The same could probably be said for etiology and causation as well. In all likelihood "psychosis," not unlike "fever" and "infection," represents a general, nonspecific psychophysiological response on the part of a total organism to any of a number of massive biological or psychological pathogenic influences. Thus, while it is likely that none of our major theoretical perspectives is entirely wrong in ascribing a causative influence to various constitutional, congenital, or environmental factors, no single theory or perspective can claim to be comprehensive. To the extent that pervasive developmental disorders represent a final common pathway phenomenon, any truly comprehensive theory must consider the possibility of relatively few symptomatic outcomes resulting from a vast array of potentially traumatic factors.

In order to define the "average expectable" pervasively disordered child, we must describe a child who, in all likelihood, does not exist in nature. For summary purposes, however, it may be useful to construct a montage representing the most salient features of each theoretical position. Although it is highly unlikely, given the present state of the art, that the interaction of physiological, biochemical, genetic, cognitive, behavioral, and psychodynamic lines could be traced neatly for a given child, any one or several of these factors have been demonstrated to account for the kinds of pathological phenomena encountered among various groups of pervasively disordered children. For illustrative purposes we will consider that our hypothetical pervasively disordered youngster has been evaluated fully from each of our five points of view.

The child who, for purposes of illustration, has been brought into our office may have been considered a late bloomer by his parents and pediatrician; perhaps a bit aloof, unresponsive to affection, and difficult to console when upset. By 12 to 18 months, however, when most toddlers begin to speak and take their first tentative steps away from mother, our youngster is mute and intolerant of any changes in routine. At times he cannot bear mother's absence and panics with every move that threatens an impending separation. At other times, however, he seems to be oblivious to contact and is emotionally impenetrable; mother's presence is ignored, a matter of seeming indifference. More than mercurial, the child is nearly inscrutable. Mother's intuitions about him seem never to be correct. Try as she will, she is unable to make sense of his confused, often contradictory communications. Nothing seems to satisfy him. "Perhaps," mother worries, "he is retarded, or brain damaged, or deaf-mute. Something is clearly wrong, but it's not an emotional problem—he's too young!"

Were our hypothetical child to undergo a hypothetical diagnostic evaluation of physiological as well as psychological signs, what might we expect to find?

Beginning with an EEG examination, we might detect focal abnormalities in the direction of hyperarousal or hyperreactivity. This may be a child who, because of innately limited homeostatic regulating capacities, is unable, given even the best maternal care, to tolerate changes in stimulus quality or intensity. We might speculate at this point that these unusual sensitivities are tied to a focal brainstem abnormality within the reticular activating system. Further structural analysis of the central nervous system might also reveal morphological asymmetries of the parieto-occipital region or bilateral dysfunction of the temporal lobes. In all likelihood, however, we would find few if any positive neurological signs; many practitioners believe that such abnormalities are the exception, not the rule.

Perhaps the dysfunction is invisible down to a cellular level of neuronal transmission and neurochemical metabolism. An assay of chemical transmitter substances might reveal an excess concentration of brain serotonin, a neuro-transmitter substance implicated by some in the regulation of neuronal growth. Finally, were we able to examine our patient at a subcellular level, we might look for evidence of a hereditary abnormality, though it is unlikely that we would find either a single gene or a polygenic constellation for the full pervasive developmental syndrome. Genetic transmission of single or multiple characteristics (typically related to cognitive functioning) may or may not, depending on other constitutional and environmental factors, manifest itself as a psychotic disturbance. We would not be at all surprised, for example, to find an unusually high incidence of nonpsychotic speech and learning defects among first-degree relatives.

At a behavioral level, many of our pervasively disordered child's peculiar, seemingly senseless activities become comprehensible as restitutive or compensatory mechanisms. Insistence on sameness, endless repetition, and stereotyped behaviors may serve a gating or barrier function in the modulation of potentially overwhelming stimuli. Even the child's cognitive style, an overselective focusing on isolated cues, seems calculated to limit the flow of sensory input.

Most apparent to everyone is our child's intellectual impairment and delayed cognitive development. If our patient is like most pervasively disordered children, he is likely to show mild to severe retardation. He will be as handicapped by his limitations as any child whose intellectual functioning falls within the retarded range. Unlike the retarded child, however, our pervasively disordered youngster is likely to evidence areas of relative intactness; probably not the circumscribed genius of the idiot savant, but a few activities at which he demonstrates a special aptitude. Given appropriate feedback on response errors, our patient is also more likely than a retarded youngster to adjust his response and successfully negotiate tasks he had previously failed. Parents and clinicians alike may sense a potential, a latent capacity for higher-level functioning.

The inner, representational world of our patient is a world of frozen, disconnected fragments locked into rote, stereotyped, and repetitive patterns. He is able to evoke mental images, yet unable to manipulate them in any creative or meaningful fashion. His language registers pervasive defects in semiotic functioning. Verbal communication is stereotyped; he can reproduce phonetic sounds but is unable to organize them into novel generative forms. Our pervasively disordered child does not respond to the full range of gestures and communicative nuances available in social interaction, and his own poorly informed communications are ineffective at influencing the behavior of others. Faced with a potentially devastating influx of unmodulated stimuli, he has shut down receptive channels to the point where only fragmentary input is filtered through, processed, and stored. Based on only the most disconnected impressions, his responses are incoherent.

Each of the foregoing diagnostic vignettes could conceivably have been drawn from the data of direct observation. Understanding the subjective experience of our hypothetical child, however, requires that we momentarily place ourselves within the child's frame of reference, transpose his self-awareness into our own, and learn as much as we can about what it is like both to be this child and to be with this child. Mother's first impressions of a youngster who seems aloof and inaccessible represent, clinically speaking, the core disturbance of infantile psychosis (austistic type). The severely disordered child is able neither to utilize caregivers as sources of comfort and need-satisfaction nor to internalize their homeostatic regulating functions. Even the most minute phase-appropriate frustrations, the type which normally lead to the gradual consolidation of internalized personality structure, are tolerated poorly. In place of developing his own capacities for self regulation, our patient remains dependent upon mother herself, with whom he maintains a delusion of symbiotic fusion. What precarious semblance of self the child is able to preserve will diminish gradually as those early forms of mother–child interaction which bolster his sense of wholeness and omnipotence become increasingly difficult to sustain.

How will we treat our patient? There are many alternatives, none of them clearly optimal. We can provide medication, which may render the child easier to handle and free his capacity to utilize latent cognitive structures masked or debilitated by the psychotic process. We can employ a varity of classical and operant conditioning strategies in the hope of gradually shaping a repertoire of more adaptive, socially appropriate behaviors. Finally, we have the option of treating the child as a whole person who, by virtue of constitutional or experiential deficits, was unable from the first months of life to negotiate the complex sequence of developmental phases leading to autonomous, independent functioning. We can offer the child a second chance to become a person in the way in which young children normally develop into vital human beings, through a complex, ever-changing interpersonal relationship that is neither perfectly responsive nor hopelessly frustrating. In the optimal growth-promoting interaction, "good enough" is best. Providing this experience for the pervasively disturbed child is the art and science of psychotherapy.

PART TWO

Talk Therapy for Children Who Don't Talk

Chapter Twelve

A Developmental Approach to Normative Assessment

A group of six or seven children (participants in the University of Chicago's Parent–Infant Development Service) amuse themselves, alone or in pairs, with an assortment of toys, games, and building blocks. Each child is joined by a therapist who follows closely the movement of activity, changing expressions, and the broad spectrum of feelings that emerge over the course of the hour-long session. Feelings are identified and connections are drawn among fragments of loosely organized play. One 3-year-old boy who has difficulty discriminating various emotions and connecting them to expressions that will allow other people to know what he is feeling is told that he needn't smile when he's angry. A 3-year-old girl who has recently begun sleeping by herself for the first time fills a toy bed with dolls, then covers them over with a blanket, as her therapist wonders aloud about frightening bedtime mysteries and the comforts of having a mother to sleep with. At the end of the session, the mothers of the children return from their own group. The room fills quickly with skepticism as the mothers see grown men and women talking to babies. One mother's taunt captures the sentiments of all: "Are you people crazy? They don't understand a word you're saying!"

Several hours later, that same day, another 3½-year-old girl sits quietly with her mother (from whom she is unable to separate) in a therapist's office. The room is silent except for the child's heavy breathing as she preoccupies herself with a felt tipped pen from the therapist's pocket. With monotonous regularity the pen cap is alternately removed and replaced. The therapist follows closely, noting on occasion how "things that come apart go back together again." The child, Kathy, seems oblivious to the therapist's quiet commentary; mother is sure that her daughter doesn't understand a word of it. Suddenly, however, the repetitious play desists. Kathy looks over to acknowledge the therapist as if for the first time that day. For a moment she seems deeply absorbed in something, though mother again denies that there is any connection to the therapist's words. Once more the question is raised: "Why talk like that to Kathy, as if she can understand a word of it?" The therapist responds "because that is where she needs to go."

Knowing where a child needs to go is the aim of psychotherapy, what every mother knows and what every therapist strives for. It is being with the child, knowing what the child needs, is experiencing, and knowing the child's inner state. It is being one step ahead of the child, knowing what comes next developmentally and is just out of reach. Understanding of this nature is informed by many sources: some of them personal, delving into the distant past, present life circumstances, and furture aspirations; some of them impersonal and scientific, representing the cumulative knowledge of child development. In the case of relatively healthy and adaptive youngsters, 2-years-old and older, the task of understanding is facilitated by what the children themselves can tell us. With the development of linguistic and representational capacities, youngsters are able to share, in a common idiom, much about themselves that is not directly observable. As therapists we can assert an influence, concretely or symbolically, utilizing the full complement of cognitive and affective channels available within a developmental matrix of increasing social and maturational competencies. In the case of the pervasively disordered youngster, however, or even the relatively adaptive prelinguistic, prerepresentational infant, the task of tracking and responding to complex mental states not directly observable can be a formidable one. How do we know where these children need to go developmentally?

To a large extent, our understanding of immature, psychotic, and developmentally delayed youngsters is a function of knowledge derived from the study of developmental stages and lines of development. About children in general, the average expectable children, we can say much with regard to developmental expectancies, the kinds of experiences, states, and capacities that are typical of various phases in the life cycle. Within certain broad parameters, we know from where most children are coming and where they are likely to be headed. In this respect our knowing is normatively based.

Greenspan

It should be clear from the review of the literature in the first section that no single theory of developmental psychopathology is sufficient to account for the diverse manifestations of the various disorders of early childhood. The closest theoretical approximations we can devise represent composite models based on the synthesis of behavioral, biological, and psychodynamic positions. In conceptualizing severe developmental disturbances among very young children, some of them scarcely past delivery, we (the Parent-Infant Development Service) often find it useful to organize clinical findings within the framework a developmental structuralist classification of adaptive and pathological personality organizations (Greenspan 1981, 1981b). Unlike many other developmental schemata, which focus on narrowly defined lines of social, cognitive, psychosexual, or physiological development, the developmental structuralist model offers an integrative, clinically useful theory of assessment and intervention encompassing the full gamut of physical, neurological, cognitive, affective, intrapsychic, and interpersonal lines as these develop throughout the first four years of life, each in the context of the progressive organization and differentiation of experience.

Greenspan's developmental structuralist approach focuses on the child's individual and normative capacities for processing, organizing, and differentiating experiences at each stage in the early years of life. It is a dynamic model in which key biological and psychological events take on an ever-changing meaning and significance depending on the point in development at which they occur and the manner in which they are represented in awareness. Experience, the subjective manifestation of somatopsychological events at all levels of organismic functioning, represents a final common pathway for the multiple and diverse determinants of behavior and can be studied in relation to any or all lines of development.

Proponents of the developmental structuralist approach talk a lot about levels of somato-psychological organization, the relative adaptiveness with which the developing human organism processes and integrates new experiences. With each thrust forward in development, the child is expected to organize an ever-broadening and diversified range of experiences into complex patterns. The relative efficiency and effectiveness with which the child accomplishes this task can be evaluated according to the age- or phase-appropriateness of salient developmental experiences, the range and depth of experiencing, the stability of behavioral and emotional patterns in face of stress and disruption, and the personal uniqueness with which experiences are organized and the extent to which individual differences are integrated adaptively. The degree to which the child is able to integrate a full range of phase- and age-appropriate experiences into stable stress-resilient patterns determines his readiness to progress to the more complex experiential realm of the next developmental stage. The consolidation of durable and resilient adaptive structures at each phase and stage provides the foundations for successive developmental advances. Like other stage theories, the developmental structural model is epigenetic. The critical tasks of each developmental phase must be successfully negotiated at the proper time and in the proper sequence in order to assure adaptive personality consolidation across all developmental lines.

For each of Greenspan's developmental stages there are certain core experiences and phase-specific tasks which determine the stability and contour of the stage and provide the field within which the child's unique organizational capabilities unfold. The primary developmental task of the newborn infant during the first "somatic" level of organization (birth to 3 months) is to establish the capacity for maintaining equilibrium in face of potentially overwhelming internal and external stimulation. The adaptive infant of this stage, bolstered by the primary caregiver's auxiliary stimulus-barrier function, habituates easily to moderate changes in sensory input and readily regains composure after mild disruptions. The child is responsive to the caregiver's comforting ministrations, but is capable of some self-soothing in its absence. By contrast, the maladaptive infant at this stage is unable to regulate internal states and is prone to hyperexcitability (overstimulation) at one extreme, hypoexcitability (withdrawal or apathy) at the other.

Complementing the infant's innate homeostatic mechanisms is the auxiliary stimulus–regulating function of the caregiving environment. The growth-promoting environment stimulates interest by supporting sensorimotor schemata and providing the infant with a broad but well-modulated range of rich, evocative sensory experiences. The maladaptive caregiver, in contrast, does not support the infant's interest in the outer world and may even undermine, through over or understimulation, the balanced internal equilibrium that is necessary before attention can be turned outside of and away from the body.

Assessment of this early stage of development is based on the degree to which the infant takes an active interest in the outside world and is able to integrate sensorimotor schemata across multiple sensory modalities. Where, owing to either unusually vulnerable sensory thresholds or a dissynchronous partnership with the stimulus-regulating caregiver, infants are overloaded, they may recoil from further stimulation by drawing interest or attention away from the external world. Intervention in this case aims at augmenting the limited stimulus-filtering capacities of the infant and mother–infant dyad by identifying unusual sensitivities and fostering the necessary protective measures. What is offered the infant will be offered to the caregiver as well. By establishing a regular and predictable structure for the infant's caregivers (paralleling the protective regulating measures provided for the infant), the therapist builds an experiential base upon which they can draw in the provision of a safe, predictable, and regulated environment for the infant.

Once having established and maintained solid contact with the external world in general, the infant must begin to focus on that part of the environment that is specifically human and interpersonal. The principal task of this second stage in development, "attachment" (2 to 7 months), is the engagement of a special relationship with the primary caregiver, a rich multisensory engagement that will serve as a basis for the later differentiation of self from nonself. The adaptive infant undergoing this first attachment relationship is deeply invested in the newly differentiated caregiver who is recognized as a source of comfort and gratification. We can observe at this point the emergence of a wide range of affective signals, some relaxed and relatively diffuse, others sharp and unmistakably demanding. The adaptive caregiver woos and courts the infant's "falling in love" and rewards each early signal with appropriate gratifications. Both participants in the dyad are comfortable together across the broad spectrum of human emotions.

The infant who at this stage has yet to achieve a balanced homeostasis, whose interest in the external world is limited, is unlikely to develop the specialized interest in other persons that marks the successful negotiation of this first human attachment. The shifting, often intense emotional stimulation of parent–child interaction inundates the child's limited sensory thresholds, making even tentative engagements painful or unbearable at times. The attuned, empathic caregiver recognizes the child's vulnerability and modulates the tone and intensity of his overtures. Other dyads, however, will not engender this degree of sensitivity or flexibility. The unresponsive, growth-inhibiting caregiver responds to the infant's withdrawal as rejection and counters with rejections in kind.

The strength and resiliency of early parent–child attachments are assessed in terms of the range, depth, and phase-appropriateness of feelings expressed and experienced by both members of the dyad. Does the attachment show resiliency in face of stress? Are synchrony and relatedness maintained in spite of mounting frustrations? We look at this stage not only for stability, however, but range. Both parent and infant should begin to incorporate an ever-expanding repertoire of clear, powerful, and well-differentiated signals.

Failures during the attachment stage are rarely one-sided. Although there are some lopsided relationships, in which a constitutionally or congenitally vulnerable infant is unable to invest in even the most sensitive and responsive caregiver, in many other cases there are family histories of attachment difficulties. Behind every uninvested infant there is likely to be a parent who has experienced similar difficulties in interpersonal relatedness. Often, in the dyadic treatment of early attachment disorders, there appears to be a parallel between the therapist's work with the parent and the parent's capacity for supporting a solid attachment relationship with the infant. Where the primary caregiver becomes capable of experiencing a deep affective investment in relationship to a clinical worker, similar capacities often become available in the parent–child relationship as well.

Once a secure parent–infant attachment is established, a gradual process of differentiation occurs in the affective, behavioral, and somatic realms of experience. Although there is, as yet, no capacity for complex mental representation, the infant undergoing "somato-psychological differentiation" (3 to 10 months) experiences a dawning awareness of things mental and things physical. Basic schemes of causality are also established during this stage, setting the groundwork for accurate reality testing. A shift from magical cause-and-effect relationships to more complex differentiation of means and ends heralds a rapid advance in the adaptive infant's capacity for intentional behavior. Optimally, the infant at this stage will begin to perceive himself as a causal agent, capable of influencing events involving both inanimate objects and interpersonal relationships. The maladaptive infant, undermined by a foundation of flimsy attachments and precarious internal regulation, withdraws from situations in which he must function independently and persists in demanding that caregivers gratify needs and wishes automatically. At best, the infant's assertions are negativistic and reinforced by their aggressive and maladaptive consequences. Magical cause-and-effect associations remain unchallenged.

The growth-promoting caregiver at the stage of somato-psychological differentiation, solidly invested in a supportive and gratifying attachment with the infant, reads and responds differentially to behavioral, somatic, and affective communications. A multitude of new opportunities are created in which the infant can cause things to happen as the result of his own initiatives. Indications of personal style or expressive uniqueness are recognized and reinforced. The growth-inhibiting caregiver may respond to the infant's assertions inconsistently or not at all. Certain responses, those that are agreeable or nonthreatening, may be confirmed and reflected, while signals and expressions that evoke discomfort or anxiety are discouraged or ignored entirely. As a result, the child's self-experience is also erratic and inconsistent. Some feelings, behaviors, and expressions are confirmed and responded to, acquiring the weight of reality. Other self-expressions, however, seem to evoke fear, anxiety, or nonresponsiveness; here the child's sense of initiative and causality, of having made an impact, is uncertain.

Uncorrected disorders during the stage of somato-psychological differentiation may lead to disturbances in reality testing, cognitive organization, perception of communication, regulation and perception of affect, and the interpretation of affect, action, and thought. Thus, it is extremely important for purposes of assessment to gauge the adequacy of those behaviors, communications, and expressions through which the child produces effects on the environment and makes his intentions known. Optimal responsiveness on the part of both infant and caregiver at this stage will show an increased depth and range of expression, greater consistency over time, increased resilience to stress, and a gradually evolving personal style of action and expression. The adaptive child truly becomes the child of a particular parent during this stage, the adaptive parent, the parent of a particular child.

The basic treatment strategy for disturbances appearing for the first time during somato-psychological differentiation aims at facilitating the acquisition of those behavioral and communicational raw materials necessary for optimal, contingent interaction. Where specific sensory, behavioral, or expressive modalities are weak or underdeveloped, either or both members of the dyad are offered repetitive, pleasurable, and gradually more intensive stimulation in the area of the underutilized capacity. Where specific developmental difficulties or conflicts inhibit the caregiver's sensitivity to certain of the infant's signals, these may become the focus of exploration and working through. As the caregiver is made aware of the blind spots in her or his own development and is helped to differentiate fantasy from reality, she or he is enabled to facilitate parallel developmental progress in the child's emerging capacity for reality testing.

A toddler entering the stage of "behavioral organization, initiative, and internalization" (9 to 24 months) demonstrates an enhanced capacity for differentiating means from ends, self from nonself, and significant others from the wider interpersonal sphere. A more thoughtful youngster now, the child is freer from the immediacy of impulse and more willing to experiment with new possibilities for detour, substitution, and delay of discharge. Cognitively, sensorimotor schemata from earlier stages are combined to form new and creative goal-directed behaviors. The range of potential variations is enlarged still further as the child, with an increasing capacity for imitation, learns how to learn from the example of others.

For the first time, the child of this stage is capable of internalization at a rudimentary level. Objects can be maintained in awareness beyond the duration of their actual physical presence, fleetingly at first, then for progressively longer periods of time. With the maturation and development of distal modes of communication—looks, gestures, and complex vocalizations—the child can begin to gain distance from mother without losing contact altogether. She can be reached when out of sight and remembered when out of mind.

The growth-promoting environment at this stage encourages the toddler's growing autonomy and independence. Responsive caregivers follow their child's lead and support initiatives, but are available as needed, when only the real thing will do. Wherever possible, the child is helped to organize beyond his immediate abilities and is given at least a glimpse of the next step ahead. This is contrasted by the overprotective caregiver, who, frightened by the child's pulling away, may attempt to restrict signs of independent functioning and behavioral initiative. While firm limit-setting in the context of a stable attachment relationship is quite appropriate at this stage, overcontrol will undermine or discourage the child's first tentative steps towards independent functioning.

Disturbances during the stage of behavioral organization may compromise the child's development of a rich, stable internal psychological life. Behaviors appear fragmented or stereotyped and remain tied to concrete external cues. Affectively charged object representations which normally undergo consolidation during this period may remain polarized or split. In place of the normal phase-appropriate assertiveness and expansiveness that come with new locomotor and communicational capabilities, the maladaptive child is clinging, obstinate, and negativistic; interpersonal relatedness is temperamental and aggressive.

Interventions aimed at correcting disturbances at this stage encourage organization and integration of behavior at a representational level while attempting to illuminate the source of limitations both within the formative environment and within the child. The child's leads are followed and supported and opportunities are created for experimentation with new modes of affective expression and new behaviors. Where the child is unable to maintain an organized state, limits are set and external structures are offered which can be used until inner controls are consolidated more fully. Interpersonally, the child's use of distal modes of communication is encouraged in order to facilitate a gradual distancing from caregivers and an increasing reliance on the soothing-regulating function of internalized mental representations.

The advent of mental representation is a quantum leap forward in the child's experiencing of self, others, and physical objects as permanent and persisting entities. With the "Capacity for organizing internal representations" (18 to 30 months) the adaptive toddler exercises a new ability to form and arrange complex mental images and symbols into organized units of internal experience. For the first time, the child is freed from the actual to ponder the imagined. Children can pretend, plan, and learn to use one object to represent another. They can momentarily leave themselves behind to imagine they are someone or something other than who or what they really are. The possibilities for experimentation are now limitless as evidenced by a proliferation of new behaviors and abilities. Language and new words abound, play takes on a symbolic quality, and every so often the child reports a dream. A penchant for naming and describing gradually evolves into the instrumental use of complex signs and symbols in action-interaction sequences.

For the maladaptive child of this stage, mental images, to the extent that they occur at all, are precarious and unstable. Under stress, the ability to represent internally may be lost entirely, with the child reverting to an unyielding dependence on actual persons and things. What language use has been acquired, if any, is likely to stagnate at a descriptive level and will not be applied instrumentally to the representation and manipulation of complex interactions. The maladaptive child's behavior is impulsive and disorganized, his diffuse affective expressions labile and unpredictable, and he is unable to plan or conceive in advance of action.

The optimal growth-promoting environment at this stage meets the child's developing representational capacity with an increasing reliance upon symbolic rather than concrete responding. The child is engaged through words and symbolic play forms, and verbal language is offered as the preferred modality for conducting interpersonal interactions. Where the child uses representational forms spontaneously, the optimal caregiver acknowledges the impact of this new acquisition on the environment. Where there are setbacks or regressions, reengagement in the symbolic mode is encouraged. In contrast, the growth-inhibiting environment may undermine the child's representational capacity by misreading or distorting symbolic communications or by supporting certain modes of representation to the exclusion of others. Expressions of unique personal style and autonomy, perceived by certain caregivers as a rejection on the part of the child or as an assault on a comforting symbiotic unity, may be poorly tolerated. Separation-individuation, it should be kept in mind, is a two-way street.

Adaptive symbolic capabilities are evaluated in terms of the range of experiences that can be represented, the depth and richness of representations, the stability of representations in face of stress, and the uniqueness and creativity with which representations are generated and manipulated by the child. Where there are disturbances in the utilization of symbolic motifs, both parent and child must be assessed first for earlier, unresolved conflicts around attachment and separation, self-regulation, and somato-psychological differentiation. Developmental crises originating in earlier stages of development often come to a head when the child is faced for the first time with the prospect of relying upon his own inner resources, independent of the caregiver's support. Each of the modalities developed up to this point for negotiating interactions with persons and inanimate objects must be renegotiated at this stage on a symbolic level. To this end, the child must learn that words and symbolizations create an impact on the world equal to and in many instances exceeding that of concrete behaviors. Notions of causality must also be realigned to accommodate cause-and-effect relationships on a symbolic level.

The inner world of mental representation and symbolization emerges as a new reality for the developing toddler. Gradually, the child's rudimentary sensorimotor capabilities are filled out with rich, ever-expanding stores of mental content that can be manipulated in thought much as actual objects are manipulated in action. Mental representations are not actual objects, however, and as much as we may take this for granted, the distinction is not immediately apparent to a toddler of 2½ or 3. Thus, the child's developmental task during the stage of "representation, differentiation, and consolidation" (30 to 48 months) is the differentiation of means-ends relationships at the level of mental representation. The adaptive youngster of this stage is able to organize and differentiate imagery according to such categories as self and non-self, reality and non-reality, and animate and inanimate. Magical thinking in the primary process mode is gradually supplanted by logical secondary process thought as viable cause-and-effect relationships are increasingly distinguished from wishful imagination. The child no longer assumes that other persons automatically feel what he feels or are omnisciently attuned to his undeclared needs. Consequences, the child realizes, are intimately connected with the acting self as causal agent. For the first time, perhaps, the child is aware of the extent to which he is responsible for and in control over events going on around him.

The maladaptive child of this stage may demonstrate some capacity for representation, yet be unable to differentiate fantasy from reality or self from non-self. Primary process continues to predominate and there is little cognizance of cause-and-effect relationships. Unlike the adaptive child, who is able to maintain the representational mode in face of stress and can, in a controlled way, suspend secondary process thinking, the maladaptive child loses reality orientation entirely when strong feelings or vivid fantasies are evoked. Oftentimes, things imagined assume a frightening reality. Where his emotions are stirred, he is unsure what he is feeling or who, for that matter, is actually doing the feeling. He continues to engage in disorganizing outbursts and tantrums.

The optimal caregiver during the stage of representation, differentiation, and consolidation facilitates the child's movement in the direction of reality orientation by highlighting the distinction between what is real and what is imagined, what belongs to the self and what does not. In situations where intense feelings are involved, the child is helped to maintain integration and self-esteem by the caregiver's stable and dependable presence. When the fragile differentiation of internal mental representations is threatened by stress or anxiety, the optimal caregiver steps in to set limits and restore equilibrium in a way that facilitates the structuralization of inner controls. Finally, the growth-promoting caregiver prepares the child to move to the next, higher developmental level at which exclusive dyadic interactions are broadened to include triadic (oedipal) relationships as well.

Differential responding on the part of the growth-promoting environment to subtle gradations in the child's representational and expressive capabilities assumes caregivers who have themselves successfully negotiated this developmental stage. When, in contrast, the caregivers are unable to distinguish between reality and fantasy, self and non-self, they are likely to misread or respond noncontingently to the child's symbolic communications, treat the youngster's expressions as if they were their own, or impart distorted meanings to them that undercut or confuse the child's actual intentions. Where the child suffers momentary lapses in reality-testing in face of stress or strong emotions, caregivers may also lapse into regression, further undermining the child's ability to reconstitute. Regressive behaviors on the part of the child meet with the parents' own regressive responding.

By the time children are 3 or 4-years-old, therapists can work with them psychotherapeutically in much the same way that they would work with the adult parents. In either case, the aim is to correct gross distortions in mental representation and reality-testing. Growth-inhibiting caregivers can be helped to modify their perception of and response to the child's communications so as to facilitate reality oriented feedback. At the same time, the child is offered a relationship in which his communications are understood and attended to and in which he is encouraged to put feelings, fantasies, and concerns into words. Optimally, both parent and child are helped simultaneously to achieve a more developmentally appropriate personality organization and reality sense.

Starts, stops, progress, setbacks—all of the imponderable variations of development notwithstanding, we know something about the average expectable child, where he is headed or ought to be headed and the general characteristics of his growth. We can sit down and play or talk with him and learn a great deal about the ways in which he is like other children his age, as well as the ways in which he is different; we have good operational norms with which to work. The same can be said of the immature, delayed, or pervasively disordered youngster. Development does not deviate in totally random ways either. Here, too, there is a degree of predictability. Anyone who has worked with young children, however, understands that the problems encountered in evaluation and treatment do not end with normative data or even the individual child as a separate, autonomous entity. We have not only to concern ourselves with the developing child but also developing caregivers, developing environments, and developing parent–child interactions as well, each having a distinct formative influence on the child's psychological growth. Even adaptive youngsters cannot be evaluated or treated as wholly independent entities until such time as they are, in fact, relatively individuated human beings capable of some degree of autonomous functioning and self-regulation, certainly not before the 2nd or 3rd year. Particularly in the case of the severely disordered youngster who has not yet achieved autonomous psychological being, whose mental functioning still includes the organizing and regulating capacities of actual (as opposed to internalized) caregivers, data acquired from the assessment of caregiving environments and parent–child interaction is indispensable. What is intrapsychic for the older child or adult is intersystemic for the immature or developmentally disordered youngster. Until such time as object relations are fully internalized, organized, and differentiated, the mental life of the child encompasses a network of real relationships within a diverse environment of actual persons, places, and things. More so, perhaps, than at any subsequent stage, psychic reality is a shared reality.

Given the complex interaction of individuals and environments, realities and representations that constitute the primitive psychological organization of early childhood, how do we come to know the specific child in so intimate a way as to assert a potentially corrective influence over the entire course of his development? In theory, at least, we could isolate, then reconstruct in great detail each element of the child's composite experience as one might reconstruct an ancient architectural site or piece of pottery. In practice, however, we find that often the pieces are not all there and that inference and extrapolation become the better part of clinical judgement (Spence 1982, 1983). It is virtually impossible and highly impractical in any event to track every combination and permutation of each of the child's significant relationships and interactions. Moreover, at a certain point, the accumulation of minutiae obscures rather than enhances understanding. Most often we learn something about background, history, and presenting problems, and then allow our theories to fill in the gaps. We are still left, however, with the problem of the particular child and his particular difficulties in growing up. How can we ever be certain of reaching that peculiarly troubled youngster sitting in the office, and reach him at his own level of experiencing?

Knowing the child and knowing where the child needs to go is a function not of the minute reconstruction of total relationships and environments as much as the focused reconstruction of those aspects that are salient to the child's immediate experience at a given point in development. We needn't know everything, we need only know something of what the child knows in the way in which he knows it. Our understanding is always relative; it cannot and for that matter should not be complete. Complete understanding, as I will point out later, would undermine rather than facilitate growth. What we are capable of knowing intimately and usefully about the specific child are those aspects of his experience that are consonant with our own experiences, past and present. Some of these experiences are universal yet highly personal; others are generated anew within the treatment relationship. As therapists in touch with fantasies and feeling states representing the sum total of our own developmental experience, we enter this relationship equipped with the perspective of hindsight and maturity; we have already been where the child is going. Understanding alone is obviously not enough, however; this is the stuff of sympathy. Insight, in order to be useful, allows us to anticipate outcomes and facilitate growth. Understanding is strategic when it helps children take things a step further developmentally than they are able to take on their own and in a way that takes account of their unique endowments, strivings, and disposition. This is knowing in the empathic mode.

Chapter Thirteen

Sources of Knowing in the Empathic Mode: A Model of Psychotherapy and Parent–Child Interaction

The capacity for human empathy is universal and as old as mankind. Most people seem to have it, everyone seems to need it, and some of the least successful and most successful personalities of our time, we are told, never got enough of it. Why, then, the sudden resurgence of interest? It is a curious thing perhaps, but certainly not the first time science has happened upon a ubiquitous human experience with the kind of enthusiasm usually reserved for new discoveries. Psychoanalysis in particular has had more than its share of revivals. The nocturnal dream, for example, was as common a topic in Pharaoh's court as in Freud's study, yet centuries passed before the "royal road to the unconscious" was recognized as such. Since time immemorial, mothers, lovers, and even small children have described in rapturous detail an uncanny knack for knowing the other as the self. Our language is replete with idioms designed to get this point across: "I know what you must be going through; I can feel for you; it must be difficult . . ." or painful or frightening or pleasant. It is only a relatively recent advent, however, going back to the late 1950s, that Kohut proclaimed empathy an "irreplaceable tool," one that "defines the field of depth psychology" and differentiates things merely physical from things psychological (Kohut 1959, 1971, 1977, 1984). Why is this happening now?

There is certainly some truth to the adage "everything in its time." Freud's interest in dreams and the unconscious was cultured in a harshly repressive 19th century Viennese society in which people invested an extraordinary amount of energy in keeping unknown things already known, often with the now-familiar neurotic consequences. More than half a century later, Kohut's interest in empathy, introspection, and disorders of the self emerged in a culture which, in the view of contemporary social observers, is more preoccupied with admiration, exhibitionism, and self-importance than with the prohibition of forbidden sexual fantasies. If empathy per se is not on many people's minds today, being empathized with certainly is. A great deal of energy is invested by a great many people in obtaining this kind of response.

In light of this recent interest, it is not surprising to find that empathy, as a psychological process, has gained a new respectability and seems at long last to have been delivered over from the realm of the mystical or occult into the hands of science. Considerable debate persists as to the nature of empathy—whether it represents an irreducible eighth sense or is simply a specialized organization of the other seven—but few today would dispute either the fact of human empathy as an indigenous form of perception, understanding, and responsiveness or its centrality in the early development of the self. As a psychological process, empathy appears to be a remarkable, uniquely human capacity for apprehending the experience of the other as an experience of the self.

Most contemporary theorists are in essential agreement about the nature of the empathic response and the conditions under which it is likely to occur (Bachrach 1976, Basch 1983, Buie 1981, Kohut 1959, 1971, 1977, 1984, Schafer, 1959, Shapiro 1974). As a mode of understanding, empathy involves a "knowing," comprehending, or perceiving of the inner subjective experience of another person or persons. Although some theorists have conceptualized empathy as a special form of merging, fusion, or partial identification, it is generally acknowledged that some awareness of separation between self and object is maintained throughout the empathic process and that it is a momentary or transient state, never complete and always relative. Neither sensory awareness nor affective evocation are, in and of themselves, sufficient to account for empathy as a mode of perception. Empathy is simultaneously a perceptual and an intrapsychic process consolidating both immediate sensory impressions and the collective personal and interpersonal experiences gathered over a lifetime.

As mentioned above, the exact status of empathy is still unresolved as either an innate, structurally irreducible sensory modality or a specific organization of mental and sensory functions which may be used in the empathic mode but are not limited to this application alone.

For Kohut, empathy is a basic human endowment not unlike vision, audition, or olifaction, which, in the hands of the psychoanalytic clinician, is tuned and sharpened into an observational tool. As a specific mode of cognition ("vicarious introspection") attuned to the perception of complex psychological phenomena, empathy from an operational standpoint literally defines the field of observation germane to depth psychology. The empathic accessibility of an action having conscious or unconscious intent renders it psychological as opposed to physical, behavioral, social, or somatic. "Knowing" in this sense is the resultant of perception combined with reflection—an intermingling of sensation, fantasy, meaning, and feeling—and leads to our apprehending another person's inner experience as if it were our own. What allows empathy to occur at all, Kohut believed, is the commonality of certain core experiences, some of which are developmentally or constitutionally endowed, others of which accrue throughout the lifespan in the form of cultural, social, and material experiences.

Other theorists, more in line with traditional thinking, have been reluctant to embrace Kohut's notion of a specialized response mode adapted peculiarly to nurture and support a distinct line of development (that is, the narcissistic line). Buie (1981), among others of Kohut's recent critics, regarded empathy as a capacity that evolves with increasing neurophysiological maturation and interpersonal interaction throughout the course of development. From this point of view, empathy depends not on an irreducible innate endowment but rather on the sensory perception of behavioral cues provided by the object and reflecting some aspect of the object's inner state. Within the mind of the empathizer (that is, intrapsychically), Buie believed, these behavioral cues are compared with any number of referents which could be expressed by similar behaviors. The empathizer then infers that the inner experience of the object is qualitatively similar to that associated with these referents. Referents may be conceptual models built up over time of what another person is like; self-experiential models based on impulses, affects, and bodily feelings evoked during the empathic interchange; imaginative models deduced from internally constructed fantasy; or resonant sympathetic response models duplicating, "by contagion," an affective response within the empathizer that is similar to that being experienced by the object.

Clearly, empathy has its limitations; it is, after all, an inferential process, an approximate fit between certain perceptual cues offered consciously or unconsciously by the sender and a complex array of experiential referents activated within the receiver. The accuracy of the empathic response is subject not only to the clarity of communicative symbols (such as behavior, appearance, and expressions) but also to the capacity of the empathic observer to receive, process, and integrate the full range of sensory information made available by the object. Finally, and most importantly, the communication of a complex experiential state assumes that all participants in the empathic interaction attribute an equivalent meaning and valence to the experience being shared and ascribe a certain agreed-upon significance to the symbolic motifs through which the experience is conveyed. Each must share with the other both a medium of communication and a common interpretation of meaning. Simply put, the efficiency and accuracy of the empathic response depends upon the degree to which both the empathic observer and the empathically observed are alike and share certain experiences in common. "The reliability of empathy," Kohut wrote, "decreases the more dissimilar the observer is from the observed."

In the final analysis it is the degree of commonality between observer and observed that determines the limitations of empathy. Common sense dictates (as did Kohut) that psychological understanding is facilitated between persons sharing similar cultural backgrounds, whose language, appearance, and expressions are to some extent mutual. Following this line of reasoning a step further, we can imagine that there are certain core human experiences which almost everyone has undergone and for which the capacity for empathy is universal. Tension regulation, attachment, separation, to name but a few of these early prototypes, belong literally to every person and are a part of the greater human developmental tradition. Only with physical maturation and social and psychological development does human experience acquire the countless idiosyncrasies of a specific culture or society. Thus, we can expect the capacity for empathic responding to vary proportionately with the distance of the experience being responded to from a core developmental prototype. Experiences that are analogous to or in some way approximate early mental states should be most accessible to empathy, whereas experiences generated entirely out of later life circumstances and reflecting the unique conditions of the specific individual's background should be least accessible.

Curiously, these early core developmental experiences, the common heritage of all human beings, are the ones Kohut insisted fall beyond the reaches of empathic understanding. Regarding the early interactional exchange between mother and child (a form of exchange relegated to a social-psychological as opposed to depth-psychological frame of reference), he wrote: "some psychological processes (tension, tension release of the newborn) are almost beyond empathy and the adaptation that takes place may be said to lie closer to the movement of water as it interacts with rocks and gravity" (that is, to purely physical action) (Kohut 1959, pp. 468–469).

Kohut suggests here that what is distant chronologically is distant experientially as well; that the peculiar subjective awareness of tension release in the newborn is irretrievably remote and lost for all time. Clearly, primitive mental states dating back to the first months of life are irretrievable to the extent that memory function in the neonate is extremely limited. I believe, however, that it would be a mistake to overlook the continuity of experience over time and the tendency for human beings to organize experiences according to early developmental prototypes (a phenomenon which Kohut himself acknowledged as the "telescoping of analogous experiences"). People respond to certain types of evocative situations in characteristic ways (and here, again, we could make a good case for a final common pathway). Painful losses or separations occurring in later life, for example, though represented at a relatively more organized and differentiated level than the same experiences would be had they occurred earlier in the life cycle, are, nonetheless, organized according to the same developmental prototypes. In both infant and adult, the quality of grief that accompanies loss (if not its intensity) is similar. The experience of the one is really not so different from that of the other.

The early mental states of the neonate, infant, and toddler are from a clinical standpoint no more distant from the empathic observer than are comparable states occurring later in life among adults engaged in comparable situations. Far from being "beyond empathy," these core developmental prototypes may be the very source of empathy, the irreducible basis for commonality among all persons. *How* the infant experiences these states is probably lost forever. This, I think, we would all acknowledge. *What* the infant experiences, however, is revived continuously and recapitulated at progressively more advanced developmental levels and continues to resonate throughout the life cycle. Mental states and experiences undergone by children at a very young age are uniquely common to all persons and are therefore the most likely rather than the least likely referents for empathic understanding even between people years apart in age and cultures apart in background.

There is still another, perhaps more important, point to be made about the sources of commonality between persons of different age, stage, and background and the relationship of these sources to the process of empathic understanding. I believe in this regard that many writers, Kohut among them, underestimate the capacity of human beings for evoking commonality and for creating it in its absence. Throughout life, people bring with them expectations, transferences, wishes, opinions, and attitudes that play an important role in making familiar situations out of situations that are otherwise unfamiliar in their experience. Perhaps the best example of this process, and one germane to the present work, is the relationship between parents and young children. We will consider the possibilty that the empathically responsive mother does not simply await the passage of time to develop experiences in common with her infant but creates together with her child a developmental context with which she is already familiar and within which she can respond empathically.

Parent–Child Empathy

For the "good enough mother" who is constitutionally sound, whose own early needs for nurturance, regulation, attachment, and self-confirmation were met in such a way as to facilitate growth, and whose own parent(s) provided a developmental context of optimally frustrating and gratifying responsiveness, maternal empathy should be both natural and inevitable. To begin with, she will create together with her child a commonality, an environment with which she is already familiar by virtue of her own experiences and to which the child can adapt by virtue of his constitutional readiness and potentiality. The developmental context which the mother creates for her child will be the one she knows best, the developmental context of her own childhood (modified, of course, by learning and life experience). By recapitulating an environment informed by and infused with her own experience, she lays a foundation for the kind of commonality between herself and her infant that is necessary in order for empathic identification, fusion, or referential matching to occur. The context she will have created is a context that is familiar to her and one in which she can knowingly share, a context born of her own aspirations, wishes, intentions, meanings and values.

A mother's knowing where her child needs to go developmentally is a function of where she herself once needed to go, how her own poorly-differentiated strivings were deciphered, organized, and focused as salient experiential events through the empathic responding of her own caregivers. Again, the most likely and most adaptive developmental environment a caregiver can create for her child is an environment informed and defined by her own experience, the only experience with which she is thoroughly familiar and therefore the only experience within which she can be optimally responsive. Simply put, the good enough mother selects, constructs, and organizes the very conditions in which she can be "good enough."

Although the mother imparts specific meaning and significance to the infant and the infant's surroundings, the infant is by no means an inactive participant. The child, after all, presents the raw materials and potentialities from which the specific caregiver shapes and contours the particular child whom she knows as her own and to whom she must adapt. Mahler (1981) summarized this interaction in terms of the process of separation and individuation: "we must say that it is the specific unconscious need of the mother that activates, out of the infant's infinite potentialities, those that in particular create for each mother 'the child' who reflects her own unique and individual needs." Through a form of mutual cuing the mother imparts to her infant what Mahler described as a "mirroring frame of reference" to which the infant as a primtive self adjusts automatically, becoming in the process a child thoroughly familiar and accessible to his caregiver and his caregiver alone.

We can add to this that the original reference point for the mother's "mirroring frame of reference" is a complex amalgam of experiences stretching as far back as her own early development and as far forward as her wishes, aspirations, and fantasies will carry her. This is the basis for the selection of cues and the way in which a mother finds among her child's limitless potentials those nascent characteristics that are familiar to her experience and to which she can respond empathically.

Children bring more, however, than random behaviors into the developmental environment that they create with their caregivers; they bring an innate constitutional endowment to which their caregivers must adapt. Biology and genetics serve a dual prupose in regulating an optimal balance of similarity and dissimilarity between parent and child. Each helps to ensure that the particular child is equipped constitutionally to thrive within the developmental environment that the particular caregiver is able to provide while at the same time creating enough variability so that the fit is only approximate and thereby growth-promoting. The optimal confluence between caregiver and child is not perfect, it is only "good enough." Were it possible by virtue of constitutional and experiential factors for caregivers actually to know their children as well as they knew themselves—if, that is to say, they were perfectly empathic and need-gratifying—growth would never occur. Psychological development evolves out of a matrix of optimal gratifications and optimal growth-promoting frustrations that are intrinsically tension-producing. Parental responsiveness will enhance growth as long as there is room for the child to internalize gradually aspects of the need-gratifying and tension-regulating parental function as intrapsychic structure. Ultimately, the child must follow his own needs as mother once followed them; they must be empathic with himself.

To summarize, despite similarities and commonalities between parent and child, empathy is only relative and never perfect. This is guaranteed both by the child's constitutional endowment and by his unique style of integrating and organizing new experiences. He is not a carbon copy of his caregivers, though they share enough in common to make attuned "good enough" responding a likely outcome. This, of course, is how it should be: optimal responding produces tension and promotes growth.

Parent and child facilitate each other's growth; the empathic responsiveness of the parent makes this possible. A developmental environment is created that will be neither strange nor alien from what has been experienced in the past and wished for or aspired to in the future. The child, because of biological similarities and inherent constitutional variability, brings to this environment a uniqueness to which the child and the caregiver must adapt and, most importantly, to which both are uniquely suited to adapt. An approximate fit creates an inherent tension; it promotes growth. A perfect fit is delusional, and inhibits growth; it allows no room for separateness or variability.

The illusion or delusion (as the case may be) of perfect empathy, of perfectly synchronous mutual regulation of mother and child, inhibits growth and conspires with inertia to keep the child fused in symbiotic oneness. The caregiver whose own sense of separateness and autonomy is tenuous or distorted will not be able to sustain a simultaneous foothold within her own self-identity and the primitive pre-self organization of her child. She will merge with her child so completely, with his neediness, helplessness, and dependency, that she will be unable to facilitate growth within the interaction, either her child's or her own. She may project aspects of herself onto her child, then respond to the child as if the child's needs were identical to her own. Rather than recapitulate a responsive, growth-promoting developmental environment (an environment which she herself may never have experienced), she will recreate a growth-inhibiting environment based on her own early developmental situation.

The parent who is not "good enough," whose own early experience was one of rigid, nonresponsive, mechanical, or regressive caregiving, will approximate unwittingly a similar experience for her child. She, like the optimal growth-promoting caregiver, can bring to the developmental environment only that which is familiar to her and already known. When her experience has been one of misunderstanding, poor regulation, and faulty attachment, and one in which her own strivings to express unique constitutional endowments were thwarted, this, too, is likely to pervade the environment she creates for her child. This is an environment to which no innate constitutional potentially or genetic variability can equip a human infant to adapt. These are the children we see in our offices and clinics.

The optimal therapist, like the optimal caregiver, also creates a developmental context within which the child is knowable from the vantage point of empathy. By virtue of background, formative experiences, self-analysis, and training, the therapist will orchestrate, together with the child, a sense of the familiar and an environment to which both can adapt. Like the "good enough" caregiver, the therapist will exercise an active and creative empathy based on his or her distant past, present experiences, and future aspirations.

In addition, the therapist has access to a reliable system of checks and balances with which to evaluate rightness of response and the validity of interpretations. What the therapist first apprehends in the empathic mode with respect to the specific child is weighed against a knowledge of child development, reflecting what is known about children in general. Where there are discrepancies between what is learned empathically and what is known developmentally, the therapist will examine process within the treatment relationship, within the developmental environment created in common by himself and the child. A new object relationship is forged, one relatively conflict-free and built on solid developmental foundations. The child, in a manner that is expressive of his unique constitutional endowment, will lead the interaction; the therapist will observe, mirror, follow, focus, and contain (Roth 1982). From the unique vantage point of the creative empathic observer, the therapist will determine where the child needs to go, facilitate what the child wants to do, and expand in any direction in which the child seems to be moving.

The goal of psychotherapy for the immature or developmentally disordered child is to facilitate the consolidation of stable, self-regulating intrapsychic structures, and the consolidation of coherent internal object relations. We would be much gratified (to take Freud's old adage a step backwards) if we could replace a dread of self-annihilation with common neurotic suffering. Conflict among the children with whom we work will follow from structure, structure modification from structure building (Weiss 1981). The consolidation of intrapsychic structure will occur in treatment as it occurs normally in the developmental sequence. The child's needs for nurturance, attachment, containment, confirmation, reality testing, and regulation are responded to optimally but not perfectly. We do not strive for an illusion of complete symbiotic knowing, nor do we seek to gratify the child's needs with unerring regularity. Moderate frustrations within an overall context of relative empathic responsiveness will lead to the gradual internalizations through which the soothing, firming, self-regulating functions of the caregiver-therapist are structuralized within the child's emerging personality organization. How do we facilitate "optimal frustrations"? To a large extent this process will take care of itself. The child's innate constitutional differences will ensure that we are not perfectly responsive. The therapist, for his part, will facilitate a developmental context in which empathy, identification, and internalization can take place, but will respect and reinforce the child's sense of boundary and separateness.

As Pine (1976) pointed out, treatment of the severely disturbed child emphasizes certain of the "silent features"—safety and identification with the therapist—which have traditionally been relegated to the background of psychoanalytically oriented treatment. New capacities are modeled after the therapist's example. These are practiced first within the therapeutic relationship, then in other relationships outside the treatment hour. Gradually these capacities become a part of a child's psychic repertoire as the child takes in and makes his own that which is given by the therapist. This is most likely to occur in a "context of safety," an environment like the average expectable environment of normal development that is reasonably stable, trustworthy, and empathic to the child's psychic reality.

The therapist-child interaction parallels but does not substitute for the parent–child interaction. The therapist facilitates a form of experience for the child with which he can be empathic in a way the original caregiver could not within the experience he or she was able to provide. Obviously, the therapist cannot reconstitute the exact content or context that might have been provided by the child's original caregiver were that person less impaired in the parental role, nor would this be desirable. The therapist can, however, provide a different and uniquely personal developmental context in which it is possible, based on personal formative experiences, training, and knowledge of child development, to act as a more optimally responsive, growth-promoting, caregiving figure. The child's need is for a specific kind of object relationship but not necessarily a specific object relationship as such. We do not attempt to recreate the exact conditions of the original developmental sequence. Rather, we create anew a developmental environment that reflects the formative experiences of both child and therapist and within which the child can move ahead to a more phase- and age-appropriate adaptation.

The reader who is familiar with the current research in parent psychopathology and early onset psychoses is likely to object at this point to my apparent vilification of the "caregiving environment." Regardless of what we call it, when we speak of primary caregivers, growth-inhibiting and growth-facilitating environments, developmental contexts, and so on, we are, in most instances, referring to mother and father and, more often than not, to mother in particular. Any implication here of culpability flies in the face of what is known about the relationship between parental psychopathology and early onset pyschosis. Most studies indicate that, in most instances, the primary caregivers of severely disturbed children are no more pathological than any other parents. They are, perhaps, somewhat more anxious, it is true, but who, under the circumstances, would not be? Although I do not believe that I have portrayed quite the ruthlessly narcissistic mother of early psychoanalytic lore, I have, at the very least, depicted a kind of parent who, because of constitutional deficiencies or early formative experiences, is ill-equipped to facilitate the development of his or her particular child. My emphasis here on the particular child is crucial, for if we are going to talk about psychological deficiencies in the parental personality, deficiencies which limit the capacity for growth-promoting empathic responding, we are justified in doing so only within the context of a specific caregiver-child relationship.

Given a constitutionally healthy youngster, one who by virtue of sound biology and genetics is relatively less vulnerable to specific developmental stressors than our constitutionally predisposed child, even the moderately limited or psychopathological parent might be "good enough." We will see this illustrated graphically in the current case study. Kathy is a grossly disturbed youngster whose pathology seems to dovetail with certain of her mother's characterological deformities, while Kathy's older sister, Carol, is a relatively adaptive child whose constitutional strengths seem to have carried her despite her mother's psychological difficulties.

All parents have their inherent limitations, but most parents can adapt, given a fairly broad range of variability, to the specific needs of their children. There are children, however, to whom a particular parent cannot adapt and other children to whom no parent can adapt. The youngster who is able to meet the caregiver halfway in regulating internal states, whose innate stimulus barrier is sufficient to maintain homeostasis under most circumstances, is unlikely to make excessive demands. Even caregivers whose own capacities for tension regulation are precarious may be able to adapt, provided they are not overtaxed. Given a child who is unable to maintain even minimal homeostasis, however, whose inner states shift rapidly and chaotically, the same caregiver might fail to provide adequate auxiliary functioning. In the first instance, the caregiver is "good enough." In the second instance, the same caregiver is inadequate and, within the context of the interaction, psychopathological. Similarly, there are some children who seem literally to reach out to their caregivers, drawing them into solid attachments. Not even the characteristically aloof or withdrawn parent could help but be seduced. A less assertive infant, however, might not stimulate the interest and investment of his reticent caregiver. In this context the caregiver's disinclination appears pathological.

It is easy to imagine similar scenarios around issues of separation, mental representation, reality testing, and so on. A child whose first foraging steps away from mother's side are bold and assertive will manage to achieve autonomous functioning even where the parent finds it difficult to disengage. In contrast, the same parent, given an infant who is less surefooted than his developmentally adaptive counterpart, may, by virtue of unresolved separation issues, inhibit or discourage independent functioning. A child whose cognitive development and sensory maturation are relatively sound may achieve the capacity for complex mental representation and symbolization even if the caregivers are prone to concreteness, where a less well-endowed youngster will find it difficult to transcend the parents' example. In each instance, the caregiver's capacity for facilitating growth is relative to the particular child's constitutional adaptiveness. Particular parents are pathological within the developmental environment created together with their particular child. The parents' ability to empathize is relative to the child's ability to make himself understood. The parent's ability to regulate is relative to the child's ability to gate and habituate to incoming stimuli. The parent's ability to follow is relative to the child's ability to lead. The parent's ability to limit is relative to the child's ability to substitute for and delay gratification. In each instance there is complementarity. Pathology is defined by the interaction.

Not all parents of psychotic children are psychopathological. Some parents of psychotic children are psychopathological relative to their particular child. When this is the case, treatment of the child alone is insufficient. Our patient is not yet an autonomous self-regulating human being. When we speak of the "self," personality, or ego of the immature or severely disordered child, we are speaking of a system that includes both internal psychological processes and external reality relations. Both elements, internal object relations and "real" object relationships, must be acknowledged in the treatment process. Thus, we treat the child, but we also treat the parent and the parent–child interaction as well as those elements of the larger family system, social network and physical environment to which we, as clinicians, have access.

How then do we treat the parents of the developmentally disordered child? Much as we treat the child. Together, the child's caregiver and the caregiver's therapist create a developmental environment, a context of familiarity and safety within which the therapist can respond empathically to the parent's needs for nurturance, attachment, regulation, confirmation, and reality testing, in order to facilitate personality growth and structuralization. Helping the caregiver to develop, by way of the gradual internalization of intrapsychic structure, capacities for self-regulation, attachment, and internal representation will, in turn, allow the caregiver to offer this same kind of experience to the child. The therapist's availability, then, provides a model or example for identification and learning.

The parent whose early developmental experience was marked by rigid, regressive, or nonresponsive interaction is given a chance to establish with the therapist what Fraiberg (1980) described as a "solid tradition of mothering." Where it is successful, intervention helps to correct what might otherwise have become a perpetual cascade of gaps or deficiencies, transmitted by selective maternal responding from one generation to the next.

In treating the child's caregivers, our emphasis is not only on making history but on repeating it as well. As in all therapeutic relationships, the parent will bring into the treatment hour certain attitudes, ideas, beliefs, wishes, and fantasies. Some of these will be examined in their own right, others as they unfold in the transference relationship. As the parent strives to create a context of familiarity or commonality, an environment that is consonant and consistent with her earlier experiences, she will recapitulate within the therapeutic hours salient aspects of her own developmental experience. What unfolds within the therapeutic relationship will represent an amalgam of the parent's past experiences, present experiences, and future aspirations; the developmental environment created for the parent by her own caregivers; and the developmental environment created by the parent together with her own child. The significance which the therapist holds for the parent will change over time depending upon which of these aspects is most significant at a given moment. At certain intervals, the therapist will be regarded as if he were the caregiver's particular child, at other intervals as if he were the parent himself, with the parent assuming, momentarily, the role or identity of the parent's own caregivers from the past. In other words, during the course of treatment, the therapist will be put in a position, transferentially, to experience both the developmental environment created by the caregiving parent with her particular child and the developmental environment created for the parent by her own caregivers somewhere in the distant past. In either case, however, the therapeutic relationship is only a reedition. The therapist is neither the patient's parent nor the patient's child and will not respond in ways that might be anticipated on the basis of past caregiving or carereceiving experiences. By virtue of formative experiences, training, and self-analysis, the therapist will introduce a different kind of responsiveness and availability than may have been forthcoming in the original developmental situations. In this respect, the aim of treatment is the same for both parent and child: the building of self-regulating intrapsychic structures. By creating with the parent a new kind of object relationship, one that is empathically responsive, optimally gratifying, and optimally frustrating, the therapist's soothing, regulating, confirming, and reality-testing functions may be internalized by the parent through a process of gradual accretion. Once these functions have been structuralized within the parent's personality organization and are made a part of the parent's self and self-experience, they are available to become a part of the developmental environment which the parent, as caregiver, creates together with the child.

Unlike the immature or developmentally disordered child

whose personality organization and sense of self show little cohesiveness, the adult caregiver, even in cases of relatively severe psychopathology, enters treatment with a comparatively stable, well-differentiated personality. With this structuralization comes the capacity for internalization of experiences, organization of drives, affects, and defenses, and of course the capacity for intrapsychic conflict. For this reason, our model of intervention takes into account two distinct aims in the treatment of adult caregivers. The therapist seeks to facilitate growth-promoting experiences aimed at the building of intrapsychic structure. At the same time, however, the therapist intervenes at the level of existing intrapsychic structures. Here the aim of treatment is structure modification and the resolution of intrapsychic conflict by way of interpretation and working-through. Caregiver and therapist undertake to examine connections between past experiences with significant persons in the parent's life and the current parenting experience, what Fraiberg (1980) has aptly described as the "eliminating of old ghosts from the parental past." Examination of transference reactions opens the pathway for insight into early ambivalent feelings revived in the parenting situation. During the course of treatment, both caregiver and child are liberated from distortions, displaced affects, and conflicts, which may obscure the reality of the present parent–child relationship.

Only a minority of parents of severely disabled children show clear signs of psychopathology. More typically, we find parents who function adequately in most areas of life or who appear to decompensate only within the context of certain emotionally charged relationships. For this reason we try, wherever possible, to treat the parent within the particular context in which these specialized maladaptive patterns of relating are most likely to occur. In many instances, the problematic context is lost in the distant past of the parent's own childhood and may resurface only derivatively in dreams, fantasies, and transference reactions. Pathological reactions evoked within the parent–child relationship, however, are current and ongoing; the therapist can observe and influence these directly. This, then, the parent–child interaction, is our third "patient" in the treatment of the pervasively disordered child. Here again, as therapists, we have several points of access and influence. Developmentally speaking, we know something about the ways in which most parents and children interact and the ways in which these interactions tend to change throughout the course of development. Phenomenologically, from the vantage point of the creative empathic observer, we learn something about the parent–child interaction, how it is experienced, and where it needs to go developmentally in order to facilitate the growth of both participants.

The aim of interaction treatment (Roth 1982a) is to enhance the quality of relationship between parent and child, to reduce interactional problems, to increase the amount of pleasure derived by both parent and child in being together, and to enhance the parent's trust in the child's capacities for adaptation, mastery, communication, and learning. Simply stated, interaction treatment seeks to give parent and child the chance to develop and practice new ways of relating to each other. It acknowledges the primacy of the child's original developmental environment and promotes the growth of the significant caregiver as therapist of her own child. The professional therapist functions as facilitator, role model, and resource person, but does not intrude upon the interaction or pose as a surrogate or substitute for either parent or child. With the parent, in the role of parent-therapist, the professional therapist maintains a treatment alliance and intervenes empathically at those points at which parental feelings, thoughts, or behaviors threaten to disrupt the treatment process. With the child, the professional therapist uses his knowledge of development to enhance and moderate phase- and age-appropriate interests and behaviors. Together, child, parent, and therapist forge a new kind of object relationship, one that is reciprocally gratifying and which rewards and reinforces interactions that stimulate developmentally appropriate responsiveness. New modes of communication are shaped and receptivity is sharpened. For both parent and child, work within the interaction enhances the capacity for clear communication and heightens the potential for growth-promoting, mutually gratifying exchange.

Chapter Fourteen

Is "Knowing" Enough?

Whether an innate, eighth sense or a specialized organization of the other seven, empathy is a uniquely human endowment for observing, organizing, and understanding uniquely human events. It is a special sensibility, a mode of processing and integrating the immediate data of sensory, motor, and affective channels with the cumulative experiences of a lifetime, all within milliseconds. Perhaps no other medium of personal or interpersonal exchange operates as efficiently. At its most refined, freed from the distortions of conflict, preconception, transference, and sensory impairment and unencumbered by the limitations of inexact linguistic or representational transformations, the empathic mode of observation and understanding provides as accurate a rendering of private, subjective events as is possible between two human beings.

Empathy is used by different persons in different capacities, yet its object always remains the same: the facilitation of a relationship between two persons functioning at different levels of psychological organization. For a mother, it is a means of knowing her particular child, of creating a world that is common, familiar, and comprehensible to both. For a psychotherapist, empathy is a means of understanding intimately the subjective mental state of another person with whom he does not share the specific developmental background of mother and child, but with whom he shares certain core developmental experiences common to all persons throughout the life cycle. The therapist's creative empathy, combined with a knowledge of developmental theory, facilitates the direct assessment of the ways in which a particular individual is like other persons and the ways in which the person is uniquely different; the ways in which growth has progressed unabated and the points at which there has been conflict and stagnation.

For mothers and therapists alike, empathy is a means of tracking and translating the mental state of another human being functioning at a different level of psychological organization who, though physically and psychologically separate, shares certain meanings and experiences in common. At this level, "knowing" something about the other person and knowing it in the way in which the other person knows it about himself is the object of the empathic mode. I believe, however, and I think that most theorists would agree, that "knowing," in and of itself, is insufficient to account for the empathic process. More than simple awareness or understanding, empathy implies a certain quality of responsiveness. As Roth has suggested (personal communication) empathy is active and operational and not a passive resonating or sympathetic responding.

In the case of a young child, the result of empathic observation is an understanding and anticipation of what the child is going to do, the meaning of this potential action in terms of the present context, and the significance of the action in terms of the child's overall development. At this first stage in the empathic process, we are talking about a type of surveillance, a gathering, interpreting, and integrating of impressions which leads to what we have so often referred to as empathic knowing. Empathic responding, however, the second stage in the empathic process, involves movement from a receptive mode to a mode of active engagement and interaction. Here, the object is to use what is known empathically to help the child move to a higher level of organization and differentiation, to a higher developmental level. At this point, we shift from following, observing, and reflecting to expanding, arousing, coaxing, and facilitating. The child first shows us of what he is capable, where his particular interests lie, and how he is inclined to order his experience in such a way as to reflect his own unique personal interests, inclinations and capabilities. How this information is used by the empathic observer, whether parent or therapist, to help the child take his strivings, ambitions, and pursuits a step further is what completes the process of empathy. Knowing where the child needs to go informs the empathic response, but empathy completed involves an active interpersonal engagement aimed at enhancing the effectiveness of the child's strivings. The process begins with receptivity and understanding, moves towards active responsiveness and intervention, then culminates in reassessment and, where necessary, adjustment.

Before concluding this section, let us return for a moment to the opening vignette: a psychotherapist speaking gently but insistently to a 3½-year-old girl who, for all the world, understands not a word. The child's mother, who looked on incredulously at this exchange, was assured that this was the direction Kathy needed to move in if she were to become a developmentally competent little girl and one day a mature young woman. Certainly, there could have been no disputing this goal. Language is, after all, the principal modality through which human beings communicate and something Kathy would have to master if she were to make her own way in life. But how did the therapist know that Kathy was able to speak and, even more importantly, that she was ready to do so?

For one thing, it is known that the development of verbal language begins somewhere between the end of the 1st year and the middle of the 2nd year of life for most children. This is the general case; it is normative. Neurological impairments notwithstanding, most children by the age of 3½ are fairly fluent in their native tongue. Nonetheless there are some children who, because of constitutional, maturational, emotional, or developmental disturbances, never acquire the capacity for fully serviceable speech. Moreover, as the developmental clock ticks on beyond the optimal normative period for language development, the odds that normal language mastery will ever be achieved diminished rapidly. Thus, the therapist's knowing that Kathy might be able to speak represented, in part, a normative probability—the likelihood that a child who showed no demonstrable neurological abnormalities and who was equipped physiologically and maturationally would make this important acquisition. That Kathy was ready to speak, however, required the assessment of an entirely different kind of information. It involved knowing in the empathic mode.

Kathy's therapist identified within his patient both a striving to communicate and a frustration at not being able to do so. Clearly, this had not always been the case. For many months before, Kathy seemed to relate to her therapist, as to her mother, as though he were nonexistent or simply an extension of her own poorly differentiated self. Gradually, however, Kathy began to regard the therapist as a special and distinct kind of object, an object like herself in certain respects, but different in many respects also, a being separate from herself yet connected. At the same time, Kathy resolved something of her own independent entity. With the dawning of separateness, however, came the need to establish contact, to bridge the gap between self and other.

The therapist's empathic understanding of Kathy's first glimmerings of self-awareness and the implications of this awareness for her relations with other persons in her life led to a clinical judgment of the child's readiness to move a step further and begin the struggle to speak. What, we might ask, did the therapist see? How did he know it was time? Most importantly, how did he hope to get through to a child functioning at so vastly different a development and experiential level?

Clearly, therapist and child were extremely different human beings, and yet Kathy's struggle to separate, to become an independent entity, is a struggle that is shared by all who have achieved an autonomous psychological being. It is simply a part of growing up, no less for Kathy's therapist than for Kathy herself. It is something that both shared in common and therefore something capable of being understood and responded to empathically. That the therapist understood seems clear. His reflection and following of Kathy's movement throughout the therapeutic hours was closely synchronized with and often anticipated the direction and outcome of her play. But what did Kathy understand, and how much of the therapist's response was she able to use? Certainly, she was responsive to the tone and timing of his communications, if not their exact content. More important, however, was the act of responding itself; the therapist's communications offered responses that Kathy could make her own and use as a bridge to the next developmental level.

The therapist's words were as a lifeline to Kathy as she began to distance and define herself within the context of the treatment relationship. They offered the possibility of genuine interpersonal relatedness in place of fusion and the assurance that being separate did not mean being alone. Kathy had begun to achieve a sense of self; now the therapist would begin to treat her as one. She would no longer be gratified omnisciently, as though wish and wish fulfillment were indivisible. Now she would have to say what she wanted so that the therapist could help her to get it for herself. It would have been easier, perhaps, and certainly more consistent with Kathy's expectations to have persisted in fulfilling her needs automatically, to have colluded with her in the omnipotent, symbiotic delusion. But this would have continued to inhibit growth. Instead, the therapist's response was growth-promoting; it helped open up possibilities for gratification at a more adaptive, age-appropriate developmental level and provided the tools with which this might occur.

Understanding built on developmental theory indicated the likelihood that Kathy was able to speak. Empathic observation indicated her readiness. In the end, however, the therapist's empathic responsiveness opened this awareness for Kathy and gave her the means and wherewithal to begin the struggle on her own.

Chapter Fifteen

The Psychotherapeutic Process: An Introduction

Is it impossible to imagine the preconceptual world of the infant, toddler, or developmentally preindividuated child? No sooner does the empathic observer watch himself watching, so to speak, the world through the child's eyes, than he has already lost the essence of the experience he is trying to understand. This is the paradox of working psychotherapeutically with preconceptual, preindividuated children, human beings who quite literally live for the moment.

It is the quality of moments and their backgrounds, as Pine (1981) has described them, to which the therapist, working within the context of those earliest and most primitive mental states, channels his empathic receptivity—the rise, fall, and flux of affect, the direction and redirection of interest, the flickering connection of cause and effect, action and reaction, and the oscillating attraction of alternatives. Each dawning and fleeting awareness is filtered through a gradual succession of developmental stages, tasks, and phases. Looked at from a clinical point of view, the task of the therapist is to facilitate patterning and sustain and to draw repetition in place of rediscovery. Once the therapist has ascertained receptively the quality of the child's moment, an empathic response must frame the event as a coherent unit of experience, reflect its dominant affect and level of intensity, impart to the event a concrete or metaphoric significance and context (which may or may not be accessible to the child), facilitate an elaboration of the event in the direction in which the child seems to be moving, and, finally, open the possibility of variation, extension, or departure. This is quite a task, and one which would be virtually impossible to perform were each of these steps consciously deliberated in the formulation of every intervention. Moments, as we know, are quickly lost, and even the best-tuned interpretation can be uselessly out of sync with the child's experience if its timing is imperfect.

Fortunately, however, certain among these response criteria may occur relatively automatically as long as the therapist's initial empathic reception is accurate. The child's affect, for example, may instantaneously evoke an identical or complementary quality and intensity of affect in the therapist (Basch 1976, 1983), as may fluctuations in the child's state of need, interest, and level of activation. Data concerning these aspects of the child's experience may immediately inform the therapist's response. Other aspects of the therapist's intervention—those which effect an elaboration of the child's experience—may also follow directly from the therapist's receptivity without conscious deliberation. These aspects, however, will encompass a different dimension of the therapist's reflective process. At this stage in the generation of response, the therapist, based on his own accumulated past and present experiences, collaborates with the child in creating a new expression or manifestation of the child's striving based on a shared attribution of meaning. In the process of reaching consensus as to the meaning, direction, and extension of a particular event, therapist and child expand both the depth and richness of the child's experience and pave the way for the therapist's continuing empathic receptivity by broadening the base of shared, subjectively mutual events.

By noting shifts, rhythms, disruptions, and reorganizations in the child's activity, letting the child know in other words that he has had an effect, the therapist is lending efficacy, substance, and support to the action. He is punctuating what must otherwise remain a continuous and undifferentiated experience, an experience of which there can as yet be no awareness. Simply put, the therapist has confirmed for the child that something of the child's own creation has happened, that it has made an impact, that it is real. During moments of special intensity, when affect, energy, or interest are on the rise, the therapist's simple notation, this time with an emphasis and intensity that mirrors the child's excitement, not only marks an experiential event but sets off the event as one which has special value for the child. Here again, the therapist is simply following or tracking the course of the child's experience and confirming that something has indeed taken place.

That the therapist's description, identification, and punctuation of the child's experience occurs in an interpretive or verbal-linguistic motif underscores my belief that psychotherapeutic intervention with the preindividuated, preconceptual child is a process of translation and retrieval, one not altogether different from interventions sharing a similar rationale in the treatment of later childhood or adult psychopathology. In order to follow the movement of the child's experience, the therapist must organize the data of empathic receptivity into a lexicon with which he is fully conversant, even though the child may not understand a word. Moreover, the therapist's words, his use of spoken language as a primary means of communication, will also give the child a developmental direction; words will be familiar once the child is ready to use them.

The therapist's notation, punctuation, and differentiation of the child's experience represents only one aspect of the process through which the preindividuated child begins to organize the diverse components of experience into coherent, replicable, and internally representable mental events. In order for these events to become meaningful, moments and intensities (the temporal and energetic aspects of experience) must be linked with content and context (the representational and associational aspects of experience). This linkage occurs in the growth-promoting therapeutic situation because the therapist marks off temporal and energetic aspects (such as a gale of boisterous laughter, which is of limited duration but high intensity) by the articulation, reflection, and mirroring confirmation of the child's state (through expressions such as pleasure, hilarity, or surprise) in relation to and in proximity with specific objects, events, and behaviors which undergo simultaneously a process of definition, differentiation, and demarcation. In this way, an internal order of events becomes associated lawfully with an external order of events which, through repetition and redundancy, becomes finally recognizable, predictable, and known. Over time, the therapist's designations, descriptions, and identifications will become also a part of the experiential mix and a meaningful aspect of the child's total subjective awareness.

The reader might well ask at this point whether the process described is simply a variant of an associational learning paradigm. Technically, it may be. Operationally, however, it makes sense to think in these terms only if we are willing to account systematically for each of the infinitesimal combinations of association, counterassociation, and interaction (within all related cognitive and affective domains) that go into the negotiation of even a single learned response. Such a process would not be practical, nor would it have any particular relevance to the child's immediate experience. Moreover, were it necessary from a clinical standpoint to disassemble each complex interaction in terms of stimulus-response mechanisms, it would in all likelihood be impossible to move much beyond the opening exchanges of the treatment hour.

Transferential Aspects of Experience

Let us return at this point to an observation made in passing above. I proposed that the preindividuated, preconceptual level child is a creature of moments whose awareness is defined by contrasting and fluctuating states and whose responsiveness is relatively unencumbered by reflection on what has come long before or what will follow long after. We imagine (and this is confirmed empathically) that the world through the child's eye has a freshness and freedom long-forgotten by those who carry meticulous representational images with them. Even preadapted capacities for recognition and anticipation carry an element of surprise and excitement that is lost in the translation of experience into vivid mental imagery. I am not saying, of course, that the child remains totally unaffected by what has come before, only that the impact and influence of things past is preserved in psychophysiological patternings and organizations which do not involve an evocative memory function. In a Piagetian sense (Piaget 1981) such experiences are "cognitively unconscious"; a baby knows not of his own growth, let alone of its formative sources.

Based on the work of Denenberg (1977, 1982) and other investigators relating the effects of early experience to brain function, I believe that factors affecting development have an effect that is both prospective and retrospective. With or without awareness, each succeeding moment is shaped and revised by each preceding moment. With the advent of evocative memory and recollection, the converse is true as well: the meaning of the past is continuously shaped and revised by the meaning of the present. Clinically, the implications of retrospective-prospective processes are most familiar to us in the study of transference phenomena in the psychotherapeutic setting.

As Freud originally conceived, the clinical phenomenon of transference represented "a special class of mental structures" appearing most conspicuously in the therapeutic regression of the analytic treatment situation as facsimiles or new editions of impulses and fantasies replacing as their object "some earlier person by the person of the physician" (Freud 1905, p. 16). These were bits of history repeated, unknown to the subject and particularly well suited to perpetuating the obfuscation of meaning. While definitions vary, most contemporary analytic investigators agree that transference in the broadest possible sense involves experiencing in the context of a present situation attitudes, drives, feelings, fantasies, and defenses derived from an earlier situation, typically infancy or early childhood (Greenson 1967, Menninger 1958, Racher 1968). By definition, transference involves repetition, inappropriate or partially inappropriate, which occurs quite naturally as an aspect of almost every interpersonal interaction but which appears most conspicuously against the relatively neutral background of the analytic situation. With time, the analyst as transference object may come to occupy the center stage in the patient's emotional life, at which point we refer to a transference neurosis. In a therapeutic medium of interpretation and reconstruction, conflicts first repeated are remembered and, finally, resolved and reintegrated into the patient's conscious mental life.

In the psychodynamic treatment of children, the situation is not really so different, though, as Anna Freud noted (Sandler et al. 1980), the transferred past for the child may include current and ongoing developmental situations involving actual rather than internalized object relations. This is consistent with the principle developed earlier that, in general, processes which are mediated intrapsychically by the older child or adult are handled intersystematically by the infant or otherwise preindividuated, preconceptual-level child. Such reactions are not transferential in the sense of a symbolic recapitulation of the distant past, but have the quality of displacement or extension in a context of current and ongoing caregiver-child interactions: the therapist as transference object is "used" by the child to subserve a need or fulfill a specialized function much as the parent is used in the family or primary caregiving situation.

In addition to the transference of current modes of relatedness, past modes of relatedness, and transference neuroses proper, Anna Freud discerned in child analytic patients the transference of habitual modes of relating, akin to the character transference of adult patients. Here again, the element of displacement involves not so much the repetition of an earlier libidinal relationship as the repetition of an attitude, approach, or mannerism which has generalized from a prototypical situation to include entire categories of object relations. As habitual responses, these are relatively autonomous and do not necessarily subserve the purpose of belated conflictual mastery through repetition. I believe that, as a general rule, transference phenomena (beginning with those reactions which relate to a displacement from current and ongoing interaction and culminating with reactions relating to displacements from a representational past of earlier object relations) are a function of the child's developmental stage and may be viewed as an actual line of development within the overall context of psychological development.

How, then, do we account for the preponderance of transference variations among child analytic patients? In the first instance, the displacement of current and ongoing object relations, the problem is relatively straightforward. Most often, children live and grow within the context of a nuclear family. When conflicts occur in the actual object relations, these, too, may be subject to attempts at belated mastery through repetition. Internalization of conflict is not a prerequisite for transference, though in an everyday sense we talk about displacements of this second variety in terms such as "taking it out on someone" and do not customarily think of it as transference.

Where habitual modes of relating are concerned, we see fixed patterns of behavior, attitude, posture, or perceptual organization which may have acquired a relative autonomy from their origins. A child's avoidant attitude, originally adopted as a means of momentarily distancing a seductive or overstimulating parent of the opposite sex, for example, may evolve into a characteristic reticence coloring all interactions with adults of the opposite sex. Where this attitude has outlived its usefulness but has acquired a life of its own, we observe a form of behavior that is reflexive and may or may not be motivated or intentional. In the extreme, habitual responses may become totally automatic modes of physical, social, cognitive, and affective patterning. Here again, we are talking about a process which involves a relatively limited degree of mental organization and differentiation. Habitual patterns require neither the capacity for complex differentiation of means and ends (that is, intentionality) nor the capacity for mental representation and may persist independent of conscious or unconscious ideation. Transference of current relationships may involve some degree of representation but may also function in extension of ongoing family interactions without having undergone actual internal representation and subsequent displacement—a "spillover," as Anna Freud has described it.

The point that needs to be made, I believe, is that transference phenomena, in the broadest possible sense, are not limited to either adults or children of advanced developmental status. They are ubiquitous phenomena with manifestations throughout the life cycle and constitute a distinct line of cognitive and affective development. In their most rudimentary form, transference phenomena may be detected in the first year and perhaps even the first days of life. The cognitive and affective underpinnings are apparent from birth and are seen to undergo continuous organization and reorganization in keeping with the succession of developmental phases and stages. The transferability and displaceability of bio-psycho-social patterning, as a characteristic mode of adaptation, has implications for both the ontogenesis of human development and the phylogenetic development of the species. Like empathy, transference appears to be a capacity of basic human endowment.

Infantile Transference or the Transference of Infants?

As her therapist waited in the office doorway, Ms. S. marched angrily down the clinic corridor, carrying her 14-month-old infant by an ever-tightening grip around the girl's waist. The child did not make a sound. With the exception of an occasional whimper or blink, she seemed in a state of suspended animation. Once she had deposited her baby in the therapist's office, Ms. S. left the room quickly with the put-upon air of someone who has traveled a great distance to deliver a parcel of little importance.

Mara seemed scarcely to have noticed that her mother had left. She remained where Ms. S. had put her, in a needlessly awkward position, and paid little attention to the toys around her. The therapist might just as well have been in the next room. Almost anyone sympathetic to small children, and certainly one whose business it is to entreat and engage, would have responded as the therapist did. Rising from his seat and kneeling down to be at eye level, he softly courted Mara's attention while commenting sadly on the child's troubled mien. In response to Mara's icy indifference, the therapist moved a few inches closer. As though he had crossed some magic line, the infant flew into a paroxysm of wild flailing and striking out which looked and certainly felt like unrequited rage. The salvo seemed oddly directionless, triggered by the therapist's proximity, but aimed at no one and nothing in particular. Surprised and somewhat shaken, the therapist withdrew (certainly the empathic thing to do), but his withdrawal also had little effect on the child's behavior. Once triggered, Mara's tantrum seemed to run its course with little direct orientation to the therapist until, drained and exhausted, Mara resumed her listless repose. Clinically, the child's behavior was reminiscent of the fight-flight/conservation-withdrawal response described by Engel et al. (1956).

Ms. S. listened to the therapist's account of the tantrum with little surprise and even a vague satisfaction that for once someone else had had to handle her child's unexpected blows. Mother had found Mara's "indifference" maddening; her anger in turn was frightening to Mara, who seemed to fight back in her own way in order to keep a safe distance. Not surprisingly, mother and child seldom got very close anymore. To the therapist, however, the child's behavior was perplexing and incongruous with the tone of warmth and invitation he had intended to create. Something had been brought into the treatment hour which in some sense did not belong.

Strictly speaking, the displacement of Mara's evasive behavior from the parent–child interaction (where it served the purpose of modulating, in an all-or-none fashion, her mother's angry, intrusive, overstimulating contact) to the therapeutic situation (where it was unnecessary, given the therapist's benign intentions and modulated approach) is something quite different from what is commonly associated with transference phenomena. It would be inaccurate to attribute to Mara's behavior the transference of unconscious conflict, attitude, or defense, insofar as each of these patterns of cognitive-affective activity implies a level of mental representation which the preindividuated, preconceptual-level child has yet to achieve. In a somewhat broader sense, however (and assuming the full definitional latitude afforded by Anna Freud's more recent formulations), the fundamental aspects of transference still apply. The behavior observed by the therapist in this vignette represents the development of a specific orientation, action pattern, and defense derived from an early object relationship (albeit one that is actual and ongoing) and transferred to another interpersonal situation with quite different interactional characteristics. As is the case with all transference reactions, this displacement involved both an inappropriate generalization and an ineffective discrimination: through her behavior, Mara seemed to be saying that all engagements involving close physical proximity with mother are dangerous and that the therapist is no different.

Given what we know of early mental organization, child development, and parent–child interaction, how do we interpret the extremely precocious transference phenomena observed in cases of early onset psychopathology? What are their clinical implications? Once again, if our model of treatment of the very young and very disturbed is to remain a talk therapy, we need to account for this type of phenomenon in order to arrive at a meaningful understanding of the therapeutic action of our words.

The Constitutional Readiness for Transference

Almost all contemporary investigators of child development agree on one point: human infants begin life in an organized state (Sander 1975, 1983, Lichtenberg 1981, 1982, 1983, Stern 1983). Preprogrammed to seek patterns involving any and all sensory modalities in complex interaction, the child rapidly acquires preferences, hierarchically ordered among pleasurable stimuli, and avoidance, similarly organized to encompass stimuli that are noxious or otherwise disturbing. In the context of early object relations, inborn preferences and avoidances predispose to the development of a specific attachment relationship to the caregiver or caregivers with whom early developmental tasks of state-regulation, biorhythmicity, synchronization, and entrainment are gradually negotiated. The process of negotiation as well as its resolution are quite specific and characteristic of each individual dyad. Based on the repetitions and redundancies of interactional exchange, both parent and child begin to anticipate the quality and quantity of responsiveness they can expect, developing complementary patterns of behavioral orientation. While it is true, perhaps, that the infant does not remember in an evocative sense what may have gone on in a specific exchange with his caregiver, he is nonetheless capable of experiencing moments of tension, loss, love, and grief, each of which yields a specific orientation towards the object. Given constancy over time (or even consistent inconsistency, for that matter), the child will organize gradually patterns of expectancy based on the behavioral cues of the interacting caregiver. As the recognition of and response to such behavioral cues undergo progressive differentiation and discrimination, the child's own response to the caregiver will tend to become increasingly specific and differentiated. Conversely, if the child's recognition and response is based on relatively few cues, cues that are ambiguous or poorly articulated, or cues of an intensity which defies the child's limited organizational and sensory capabilities, the likelihood of generalization to other interactional exchanges increases. As is the case with older children and adults, we can expect that the preconceptual child's capacity to organize and differentiate experiences is optimal in situations where disruptive affect is kept within tolerable limits and the actual content of the interaction is kept within the limits of the child's integrative capabilities. In other words, we must avoid exchanges which err in the direction of too much, too soon, or too new.

Thus, in interactional situations involving extremes of affective intensity, cognitive complexity, or experiential novelty, the child's capacity to organize and discriminate is mininized. This, in turn, is the background against which the relatively indiscriminate generalizations and displacements associated with transference phenomena are most likely to occur. As is the case with all transference reactions, the situations or conditions which predispose to displacement are ones which could not be mastered because of the child's limited adaptive organizational capabilities. In Mara's case, the mother's angry response to the child's rather halfhearted overtures led to Mara's defensive orientation of withdrawal. By shutting out and to some extent shutting down, the child avoided a potential affective overload. So pervasive and automatic was the response, that it followed upon almost any perceived approach behavior initiated by the caregiver. Any response on the mother's part occurring after the mobilization of Mara's shutdown was also obviated. There was no modulation or fine tuning; the baby responded in an all-or-none fashion.

To the extent to which Mara's defensive orientation precluded a potentially affective overload in her interaction with Ms. S., it must be considered an adaptive or at least self-preservative mechanism. But the behavior had other consequences as well. By shutting down in response to any perceived approach cue, the child forfeited the possibility of discrimination based on outcomes other than the dangerous one experienced in interaction with her mother. Mara had come to expect that any approach made by any caregiver would result in distress. That is to say, a defensive orientation mobilized in response to a primary caregiver's repeated and destructive rage had generalized to include all other interactional exchanges involving a particular kind of approach behavior. The therapist's approach, like the mother's, was regarded with mounting fear and apprehension followed by outburst and withdrawal. That which occurred subsequently in the interaction made little difference; for the moment, the child was lost to the world or, at the very least, to the therapist.

Transference Mechanisms

Subject to the scrutiny of analytic investigation—interpretation, reconstruction, reintegration—the transference reactions of adult psychoanalytic patients yield memories of early object relations, remnants of unresolved or insufficiently resolved conflict, reactivated needs for self-confirmation and empathic responsiveness, and the gamut of fantasies and feelings that accompany and accrue to these early experiences. To the extent that the transference is successful, repetitions of conflicted object relations or nonresponsive self- and self-object interactions orchestrated by the patient in the analytic situation replace the memory of these painful sequences as they actually unfolded or unfolded in fantasy within the recesses of the distant biographical past. Conversely, insofar as the analytic work is reparative, with elements of conflict subjected to the integrative capacities of the mature ego and structural deficiencies bolstered by the transmuting internalization of the therapist's confirming and regulatory responsiveness (Kohut, 1971, 1977, 1984), the compulsion to repeat is replaced by the capacity to remember. In either case, the recovery of a complex mental state or representation towards which the person characteristically acts in such a way as to obviate memory, meaning, and awareness is at stake.

As Lichtenberg (1983) has summarized, differentiated, cognitively organized representations in contexts that correspond to actual intrapsychic and extrapsychic experiences do not in all likelihood exist in the 1st year of life. (I believe that this statement extends by degree to those children who, at any point in the first three to four years, have failed to achieve the requisite cognitive-affective structuralization necessary for complex mental representation, object constancy, and object permanence because of severe developmental psychopathology.) It is therefore unlikely that the preindividuated, preconceptual-level child would be motivated, as the more developmentally advanced child or adult would be, to transfer unconscious aspects of experience from one setting to another for the defensive purpose of avoiding memory. The problem is already taken care of by virtue of the child's developmental immaturity. Furthermore, without some form of representational format paralleling and preserving past experience, is it even reasonable to speak in terms of repetition with the aim of mastery? Why should the preindividuated, preconceptual child engage in transference activity and what, if anything, is in fact transferred?

As long as we limit our discussion of transference phenomena among preindividuated, preconceptual-level children to speculations increasingly difficult to support, concerning intrapsychic functioning and mental representation during the first weeks and months of life, our actual observation of displacements of behavioral orientation and object-relatedness among developmentally immature youngsters will continue to defy understanding. But if, as I have suggested earlier, we expand our perspective to encompass the intersystemic realm, including with the child the context of his caregiving, structure-providing developmental environment, then the transference of experiential patterns of action and interaction is not only comprehensible but, as I hope to demonstrate, nearly inevitable.

From birth, the normal infant is endowed with the capacity for recognition. At this rudimentary stage of development, memory is an autonomous function of the ego (Hartman 1939). It allows the child to identify as something previously experienced objects, persons, and events encountered repeatedly over the course of time. Events of special moment, once recognized, may draw from the child certain anticipatory responses which, depending upon past experience, will tend either to perpetuate, elaborate, or terminate an expected sequence of events. The kinds of qualities of events recognized and anticipated and the kinds of patterned response modes which follow will depend both on the child's current developmental status (the ability to organize and differentiate complex patterns of experience) and on the child's current level of interactional structuralization (the level at which dyadic reciprocity, synchronization, complementarity, repetition, and intentionality persist as enduring patterns of relatedness within the child–family system). This distinction, I believe, is crucial. In order to understand the mental life of the preindividuated, preconceptual-level child, we are drawn again to consider that attitudes, orientations, and patterns of relating, which are preserved intrapsychically in stable mental structures for the individuated, conceptual-level child, are preserved for the preconceptual, preindividuated child interactionally in patterns of action, reaction, and transaction negotiated in the context of actual and ongoing object relations. Mutually regulated patterns of action and interaction involving actual and current caregiving persons are the psychic structure of the preconceptual, preindividuated child. The way in which parent and child together negotiate a synchronous patterning of sequential interactive events will determine to a large extent which cues the child is drawn to recognize and attend, how these cues are interpreted (anticipated), and the kinds of responses that follow.

In a clinical context, much as in the primary caregiving environment, the therapist is likely to be engaged by the child in a complex configuration of complementary interactive sequences. Depending on the child's developmental level with its respective issues and tasks, the caregiver's developmental level with its respective issues and tasks, and the caregiver-child interactional level with its respective issues and tasks, the character of engagement will normally follow certain predictable patterns of exchange. The child's developmentally expectable responsiveness, interpreted correctly by the empathically attuned therapist, will evoke appropriately dosed gratification, regulation, or facilitation after which the interactive dyad, its intended purpose accomplished, moves on to the next order of business. Nothing will have occurred to dissuade the child of his expectations or the therapist of his attunement. The therapist will at times also initiate interactions, based on a reading of the child's signals and on his empathic anticipation of where the child seems to be heading or where the child needs to go developmentally.

Let us pause for a moment to look at two somewhat different conditions. The first involves the child who, because of constitutional vulnerabilities in temperament, self-regulatory capacities, and attachment readiness, is unresponsive to even the optimal caregiver—the child for whom no parent is good enough. The second involves the parent who, by virtue of constitutional vulnerabilities, psychopathology, or misinformation, is unable to provide even a modicum of well tuned caregiver responsiveness—the parent who is not good enough and to whom no child can adapt. In either case, we can observe that both parent and child tend to orchestrate their interactions on the basis of an unusually idiosyncratic set of behavioral, postural, affective, and, in some instances, linguistic cues and will respond to these cues with equally idiosyncratic expectations and anticipatory behavior.

When the normally inviting, outstretched arms of the welcoming caregiver are consistently followed by what the infant experiences as a flurry of overstimulating activity, the infant may recognize this invitation to interact as the first motion in a sequence of events which leads predictably to distress. As a cue, the outstretched arms will signal distress to the child and evoke a withdrawing response. It should not surprise us when the child is equally distressed by the inviting approach of other caregiving persons and responds accordingly. The child has generalized both a fear, which, based on an original caregiver-child interaction, anticipates distress in other interactive encounters and the defensive behavior through which the child customarily averts the associated danger. In doing so, the child has eliminated effectively the possibility of experiencing a different and potentially positive outcome, one that might disconfirm his expectations. Finally, by withdrawing, the child has blocked the input of additional cues through which the outstretched arms of the overstimulating caregiver might otherwise have been discriminated from the outstretched arms of the more modulated and benign caregiver-therapist. Recognition of a familiar behavioral cue is followed by anticipation based on the predictable outcome of past caregiver-child interactions and concludes with a defensive orientation which obviates both the anticipated danger and, along with it, the possibility of improved discrimination, disconfirmation of expectations, and a potential reassessment of the situation in question.

The pathological interaction may begin with the congenitally or constitutionally vulnerable youngster (the child described earlier in this chapter, for example), in which case we may expect to find equally idiosyncratic patterns of object relatedness transferred from the primary caregiver-child interaction to other interpersonal situations, the psychotherapeutic interaction among them. The mechanism is similar, only in this instance the therapist is likely to experience difficulty maintaining empathy and modulating responses as the child's internal state undergoes rapid oscillations of affective tone and intensity, often with little apparent reference to the actual interactive situation. Unlike the constitutionally adaptive child, whose inappropriate transference of response maintains a certain interior logic (it was appropriate or at least adaptive within the context in which it originated), the constitutionally disordered youngster who experiences ordinary "average expectable" responsiveness as inundating or insufficient will produce compensatory patterns of signalling even in the face of normal or optimal caregiving. These are the types of cases described in the last section, in which therapist and child must literally create from the ground up a novel developmental context familiar to both in which the therapist can respond empathically to the child's needs for nurturance, regulation, attachment, differentiation, and organization and in which the child can move ahead to a more phase- and age-appropriate adaptation.

In actual practice, we find typically admixtures of both types of transference displacement; even the well modulated, empathically attuned caregiver, in attempting to adapt to the idiosyncratic rhythms and states of the vulnerable, unusually sensitive child, will of necessity adopt equally idiosyncratic patterns of response in the process of tracking and adapting to the child's needs. These in turn will become the basis for the child's initial cue-recognition and anticipatory reactions. Not infrequently, these find their way into the therapeutic interactions as seemingly incongruous, non sequitur reactions to the therapist's interactive overtures.

Chapter Sixteen

The Origins of Transference

Inborn capacities for recognition, recognitory memory, and behavioral anticipation guarantee that the preindividuated, preconceptual-level child is capable of transferring patterns of object relatedness, orientation, affective responding, and expectation from the primary caregiving situation to interactions within the clinical setting (or almost any other setting, for that matter). It is neither reasonable nor necessary to speculate, as was the bent of early object relations theorists, on complex mental representation and precociously differentiated mental structures in order to account for the clinical observation of this kind of response. If, however, we are to view this phenomenon as lawful and meaningful in terms of our current understanding of what a preconceptual-level child can and cannot do, then we must understand what is being transferred as well as the hypothetical mechanism of transference.

The preindividuated, preconceptual-level child, by virtue of developmental immaturity, deficit, or disorder, is not, as was once believed, a repository of highly structured, internally represented or unconscious conflicts, fantasies, and impressions. I do not dispute that the child is a participant in situations that are conflicted or that at least present equivalent possibilities, and that these situations tend to reflect certain phase-specific tasks and issues. I wish only to emphasize that these kinds of formative situations are important as actual events, rather than as events of highly questionable mental registration. To a greater extent than at any other time in the life cycle, mental events unfold in a context of actual caregivers engaged in actual interactions with an actual child. The metaphoric psychological inner world is not a meaningful construct until such interactions can be said truly to occur on the plane of thought as well as on the plane of action, when, in other words, through processes of imitation, internalization, identification, and incorporation these intersystemic relationships become a part of the child's internal representational landscape. Until this occurs, however, functions of regulation, adaptation, integration, and organization belong to a system of exchange in which the preconceptual child is but one (albeit the central) component.

When the child brings into our office patterns of relatedness that seem as though they don't belong and have been carried in over from somewhere or someone else, we ought to think not so much in terms of plumbing the depths of our small patient's unconscious (again, a construct of dubious value) but of analyzing those actual interactions from which these seemingly inappropriate recognitory cues and anticipatory behaviors derive. This is a fundamental complement to our developmental assessment of the child (across all relevant normative-developmental and clinical-empathic domains) as an individual entity. From this third perspective, we will focus on and evaluate those aspects of the child's shared interactive development that have been brought into the clinical hour from the primary caregiving situation. What the child seems to expect of the therapist and how these expectations are brought to bear upon the therapeutic interaction will help to determine, genetically speaking, the developmental levels of caregiver-child interaction which have undergone stagnation or distortion and which the child is attempting belatedly to master through repetition. As in all dynamic psychotherapy, the therapist will be aware not only of the child's responses, but also of the kinds of reactions these seem to draw from the therapist himself—what the child seems to evoke and draw from his interactive partner—in short, the mesh and stability of interactive cycles over time. Depending on the age and developmental phase of the child, the therapist should expect to observe patterns of "fitting together" (Erikson 1950, 1959) that reflect either current interactional issues or earlier interactional issues in the development of the caregiver-child dyad. In some cases, the child's patterning of engagement, disengagement, and attachment, his contribution to the overall dyadic "regulation of exchange" (Sander 1975, 1983), will reflect the current and ongoing negotiation of interactional issues with a current caregiving figure. In other instances, the child's patterning will reflect earlier configurations of interactional development which may or may not include current interactions with current caregivers.

Taking as our point of departure the recent epigenetic models of dyadic development over the first 36 months of life (Greenspan 1981a, 1981b; Sander 1975, 1983; Sroufe 1979), it is possible to identify sources of early interactional disturbance as these are manifest as transferential deviations in the match and mismatch of regulatory exchange between therapist and child.

Maintaining a balanced state of equilibrium in the face of mounting internal and external stimuli remains a crucial regulation throughout life but reaches special intensity as an interactional issue during the first months of life. Together with his dyadic partner, the child negotiates a complex dialogue in which an unrelenting output of information reflecting moment-to-moment changes in the child's inner state is synchronized with equally persistent soothing, consoling, calming, quieting, and need-satisfying ministrations by the caregiver. Every dyad is different, however, and reaches its own terms and tolerances for the negotiation of these crucial regulations. The same irritable banter and fuss that is of sufficient intensity, duration, rhythm, and timbre to elicit the calming gaze and caress of one caregiver may evoke quite a different response from another caregiver.

Individualized patterns of parent–child regulation are established through interactional repetitions and redundancies within each of the child's states and state transitions. With the consolidation of interactional structures organized around state regulation (formalized patterns of regulation, relatedness and exchange which persist over time), the child will have formulated effectively hypotheses about the kinds of regulatory responsiveness that can be expected of his caregiver during moments of unusual affective intensity, state disruption, or behavioral disorganization. Moreover, until such time as the preconceptual-level child has achieved the capacity to make subtle discriminations among caregiving persons, he is likely to generalize these expectations to include almost any caregiver involved with him in mutual regulatory activity. Again, I must emphasize that states of low or moderate tension are most conducive to learning in general and learned discriminations in particular. Thus, states of high tension either leading to or resulting from interactional dyssynchrony not only disrupt biological, neurophysiological, and behavioral organization but lead to reduced cognitive efficiency. For this reason, I believe interactional structures formed around states of intense affect or physical distress are aspecific and are particularly vulnerable to generalization, displacement, and transference to other poorly differentiated interactional situations. Where, as is nearly inevitable, the child's expectations and anticipatory behavior do not meet with a reciprocal synchronous response (Call 1980), an initial escalation of evocative behavior may lead to behavioral disorganization and, ultimately, to a lapse into pained immobility.

Interactional patternings of attachment and disengagement, "reciprocal exchange" as Sander (1975, 1983) has described the associated stage in interactional development, are apparent from birth but reach developmental salience during the second or third months of life. Gradually, the infant's endogenously mediated affective responsiveness undergoes transformation to exogenous, volitionally mediated and modulated expressive behavior. Emde (1980a, 1980b) has described this process in great detail as it pertains to the evolution of the social smile.

The building of solid interpersonal attachments is, of course, the work of a lifetime and a source of ongoing tension, negotiation, and adjustment. When, however, due to early postnatal deprivations of contact or to constitutional limitations either parent or child are impaired in their capacity to direct and maintain a selective interest in the human world, manifestations of dyssynchronous contact (ranging from nearly complete autistic withdrawal to relentless symbiotic clinging) are prone to structuralization as persisting patterns of social-interpersonal recognition, expectation, coordination, and response. Very often, the child will have developed highly idiosyncratic expressions, mannerisms, cues, and other modes of signalling and engagement which have little efficacy beyond the primary interaction. Frequently, these types of behavior suggests a certain interior logic in the context of the interactions from which they were derived, but defy the empathy and expectation of the outsider unaccustomed to the highly personalized meanings and attributions negotiated by parent and child. Carried over as transference reactions into the psychotherapeutic situation, these types of patterning may ultimately succeed in evoking from the therapist the very kinds of responses—anger, withdrawal, disinterest, frustration—which led to pathological adaptation in the first place. In this way, the child's mode of perception and reaction is actually confirmed and perpetuated in the therapeutic encounter.

Where the child's overtures fail to meet with an expected mode of engagement or disengagement (as they do invariably because of the highly specialized interactional context in which they originated), we can expect to see an intensification of response followed by disorganization and, finally, a massive shutdown resembling the "conservation withdrawal" reaction described by Engel and Reichsman (1956). At this point, the possibility that therapist and child can correctively renegotiate a different outcome from the one the child anticipated has been diminished by the severe disruption and disorganization of cognitive/affective functioning that follows upon the overload condition. Thus, in the transference of pathological modes of interaction, the therapist is likely to experience varying degrees of isolation (at the autistic extreme) and intrusion or violation (at the symbiotic extreme). In either case (and there are typically manifestations of both), the child's responsiveness is notably incongruous with the therapist's sense of the current interaction, its intended direction, and the therapist's own feelings, fantasies, and intentions toward the child.

The developmental transition spanning the period from 3 to 7 months (overlapping to some degree the previous stage) has been described as the stage of somatopsychic differentiation (Greenspan 1981), active participation (Sroufe 1979), and initiative (Sander 1983). Optimally, this stage witnesses the structuralization of interactional patterns reflecting the infant's goal-directed initiatives in social exchange and preferred activities. By accurately interpreting the infant's initiatives and responding contingently to expressions of mastery, compromise, success, failure, pleasure, displeasure, and so on, the parent helps the child establish a sense of efficacy, a sense that the child's behavior has had an impact on the environment that is in harmony with what was intended. When the child's initiatives are ignored or misread, this sense of efficacy may be seriously undermined. Causes are disassociated from effects, intentions from outcomes. Finally, parent and infant may organize their interaction around a wholly idiosyncratic world of attributions and meanings, a separate reality, as it were, in which objects events, actions, and reactions are invested with a significance that defies any kind of consensual validation. A fusion or collapsing of cause-and-effect relationships and the persistence of magical expectations predominates over the intricate association of actions with their equal and opposite reactions.

Carried into the transference relationship of the therapeutic situation, the child's misattribution and misinterpretation of cause-and-effect are likely to produce a sense of frustration and confusion in the therapist and may lead to clash. In fact, these are simply the reflection of erroneous and idiosyncratic assumptions about the relationship of the self to objects and events in the environment and the meanings associated with these. Direct confrontation of these assumptions is likely to lead to further entrenchment as the child's sense of causality (however inaccurate this may be) is threatened.

In the fourth stage of interactional patterning, described by Sander (1983) as focalization and by Greenspan (1981b) as behavioral organization, the child's goal-directed manipulation of objects and events extends to the manipulation of people. The 10 to 13-month-old develops certain hypotheses or predictions regarding the availability of the primary caregiver to expedite his intentions and meet his specific needs. Optimally, the interactive partner will respond with blends of facilitation, limit-setting, and nurturance. Tolerant and available but firm, the caregiver is gradually defined as a separate person whose initiatives may or may not be harmonious with those of the child.

When, in the child's experience, caregiving interactions are intrusive, overcontrolling, fragmented, or manifestly fearful of the child's proclivity for self-direction, the child may adapt by pulling back into a premature separation at the first recognition of caregiver intercession. Where interactional patterns of intercession and rejection become structuralized through repetition, expectations of faulty or invasive responsiveness may generalize to other interpersonal situations, including those involving the therapist. The therapist's overtures to facilitate the child's activity may then meet with obstinate and insistent rejection. In clinically evaluating interactional disturbances at this level of development, the therapist should be attuned to his or her own feelings of slight, belittlement, and anxiety when the child insists on doing something independently or in isolation. Assertions of independent initiative seem fragile and unconvincing.

Between 14 and 20 months, beginning with the developmental stage of organization of internal representations (Greenspan 1981b) and the interactional stage of self-assertion (Sander 1983), the adaptive child acquires the capacity to conceptualize and imagine, to experiment on the plane of thought with increasingly complex representations and variations of objects, events, and relationships. The perceptual-affective-action modes (Lichtenberg 1983) through which preindividuated preconceptual-level children know themselves and their world are reorganized around internally generated mental events which are wholly or partially independent of stimulation or sensory-perceptual impressions. Only at this point in development are we truly justified in thinking about the child as a semiautonomous human being, having the capacity to carry within himself identifications derived from the caregiver and to perpetuate autonomously the psychological functions which the care-giving object formerly provided. For the first time, we observe a shift from a dynamic that is predominantly intersystemic to one that is increasingly intrapsychic. In terms of the present discussion, the elaboration of an increasingly differentiated mental apparatus with organized internal structure and content implies an unprecedented independence not only from the actual but also from the immediate. With the capacity to remember, repeat, replay, and reorganize on the plane of thought events that have already taken place (as well as events that have yet to take place), the child can belatedly master situations long past for which the data have already been received and can master premeditatively situations involving future events which exist solely in terms of potential.

These abilities contrast markedly with those of the child who functions at a predominantly preconceptual level, who is locked into a perspective encompassing actual and immediate events, recognized on the basis of previous experience and anticipated on the basis of previous outcome. Where the preconceptual child must act before the fact to obviate situations that are anticipated to produce displeasure or distress, the conceptual-level child has the option of considering a given situation after the fact, and of confirming or disconfirming preconceptions and expectations based on past experience. At this point in the child's development, with the advent of mental representation, most traditional clinical investigators begin to think in terms of the transference reaction proper as both a clinically useful concept and a clinically useful tool. As the child acquires the capacity for evocative memory and fantasy elaboration, entire experiential complexes may be registered consciously or unconsciously in memory, where they act as templates for the organization of subsequent experiences. In this context, transference is conceived as a means both of repeating experiences which have acquired mental registration and simultaneously of resisting such repetitions as are likely to produce anxiety or pain when reexperienced (Racker 1968, p. 501).

While I would certainly agree that transference phenomena undergo extensive elaboration with the advent of mental representation, I have tried to demonstrate that such representation is not the sine qua non of all transference phenomena. Equipped with the inborn capacities for recognition, anticipation, and perceptual-affective-action patterning, even the preconceptual child is capable of transferring aspects of experience from one interactional setting to another. I believe, however, that there is a fundamental distinction to be drawn between preconceptual and conceptual-level trans-

ference phenomena, not as much in terms of aim (which is in both
instances the avoidance of or mastery over situations which produce anxiety or pain), but in terms of the modes through which they
are accomplished.

The preindividuated, preconceptual-level child *recognizes* (re-
members upon being reminded) a situation that *anticipates* a certain danger. In response, the child acts in such a way as to avoid
what is expected. The child acts precisely because a portentous cue
or stimulus is recognized and remembered on the basis of past
experience. The individuated, conceptual-level child may also respond in this way to actual situations that anticipate painful consequences. In addition, however, the child is faced with situations
which may at one time have been actual (though not necessarily so,
as in the case of fantasy) but are now representational. Any situation which at some point in the child's history unfolded intersystemically between the child and his caregiver may now unfold
intrapsychically as an analogous event in the child's memory or
imagination. In the latter case, the child acts not to avoid an anticipated outcome but to avoid the painful memory of an outcome that
had at one time caused anxiety or pain and would likely do so again
were it restored to consciousness. Where the preindividuated,
preconceptual-level child acts to avoid the anticipated repetition of
an actual interpersonal interaction, the individuated, conceptual-
level child repeats an early pattern of interaction to avoid its conscious recollection, this being the source of distress. The pre-individuated, preconceptual-level child acts because he has recognized
a portentous behavior cue—because, that is, he has already remembered; the individuated, conceptual-level child, engaged in transference behavior involving intrapsychically represented events,
begins with action as a means of avoiding memory. The one acts to
obviate an actual danger involving actual intersystemic objects and
events, the other, to obviate the anxiety associated with an internal
danger involving the representational components of a system
which is increasingly intrapsychic.

Again, the shift from transference phenomena rooted in an
intersystemic dynamic to transference phenomena rooted primarily in an intrapsychic dynamic is a gradual one and never complete.
Even in the treatment of adult psychopathology, we frequently
encounter displaced remnants of preverbal perceptual-affective-
action patterns that may well predate the advent of mental representation. Increasingly, however, interactional structures founded
on the repetitious patterning of caregiver-child engagement and

disengagement are reorganized in the elaboration of intrapsychic structure, relatively independent of actual interaction. At this point, avoiding repetition means avoiding recollection.

Tendencies and Ambitendencies

The preindividuated, preconceptual-level child is a being of tendencies, competing tendencies, and "ambitendencies," as Lichtenberg (1983) called them. While he may be drawn simultaneously by the appealing aspects of multiple objects or events, his resulting vacillations are entirely action oriented and persist only as long as each of the alternatives remains in plain view.

To an observer, the child's dilemma when faced with both a highly desirable toy and the invitingly outstretched arms of the primary caregiver is conflictual; the child appears torn by two attractive choices. It is doubtful, however, that the child's dilemma is experienced as conflictual, nor does it register as such to the empathically receptive observer. While there is clearly a competition for the child's attention, to which he is likely to respond with a mosaic of approach and alternate-approach behaviors, the child does not as yet engage in an internal conceptual weighing of choices, alternatives, and consequences. Nor does he include among the criteria for solving his dilemma characteristics inherent in the object itself or its prerogatives and intentions. The child simply faces the push-pull of two equivalent events. Finally, and most importantly, the affect surrounding ambitendency may involve frustration but is unlikely, at least in the case of equally desirable alternatives, to involve anxiety related to that which is invariably lost or given up in making a choice.

Mental representation changes all of this. To the competing desirability of alternatives is added an internal awareness of intentions and prerogatives, those of the self as well as those of the object. The "draw appeal" (Roth 1984) of immediate and apparent choices becomes but one component in the determination of choice. First, what is wished for must be reconciled with what is possible. Later, what is wished for and what is possible must be reconciled with what is acceptable. The process by which these considerations are structured within a hypothetical mental apparatus is well known and constitutes the cornerstone of Freud's (1923) tripartite structural model.

From the standpoint of the current discussion, intrapsychic conflict proper begins when the child's outward directed awareness of multiple possibilities for gratification involving equally appealing present objects (objects, that is, which function interactively within the complex infant-family system) is joined by an inner directed awareness of possibilities for gratification involving actual and representational objects (that is, objects which function either intersystemically or intrapsychically), some of which are associated with discordant intentions, either within the self or between self and object, or with potentially painful consequences. Conflict becomes a clinically meaningful concept when ambitendency is joined by ambivalence. Once again, following what I believe to be a general developmental trend, that which is intrapsychic for the individuated, conceptual-level child and can be elaborated on the plane of thought, meaning, and feeling, is intersystemic for the preindividuated, preconceptual-level child and can be elaborated upon only on the plane of perception, affect, action, and interaction. To the latter we can attest by direct observation; to the former, however, we can attest only by virtue of our capacity as clinicians for attuned empathic receptivity and our patients' capacities for introspective observation. With increasing cognitive competency and affective differentiation, the preconceptual-level child's perceptual-affective-action patterning of competing tendencies towards external objects expands to include internal, intended, yet incompatible actions towards representational fantasies, images, and recollections as well. Finally, there is the capacity for true intrapsychic conflict as an entirely internal process with little or no apparent reference to external or actual objects whatsoever.

To return now to our developmental sequence of interactional processes, we find the 14 to 20-month-old child, the child who has reached the stage of "self-assertion" with his interactional partner, faced with increasingly differentiated and at times incompatible aims and goals. Once aware of his own intentions as actually being his own and of the caregiver's intentions as not his (at best) or opposed to his (at worst), the infant-toddler "between states" must reconcile not only the uncertainty of choice among equivalent possibilities, but the ambivalence of choice given incompatible intentions. The relatively unencumbered recognition-anticipation-action patterning of previous stages is now complicated by a dawning awareness of the separateness of self and other, the potential for incompatible intentions, and the inevitable compromises inherent in all action. The preconceptual-level child recognizes on the basis of behavioral and contextual cues a familiar caregiver response, anticipates its consequences, pleasurable or painful, then acts in order either to perpetuate the gratifying response or to obviate the frustrating or distressing one. The child in transition to a fully individuated being capable of conceptual-representational thinking inserts some extra steps, and begins to demonstrate the capacity for delay. Recognizing his own intention, the child anticipates the caregiver's response (independent of actual behavioral cues), then acts either to expedite his intention or, where it seems risky to do so, abandons the intention lest he invoke the caregiver's anticipated displeasure. The child can act in reference either to the intention itself by committing it to direct and immediate action, or to the predicted consequences of the intention by anticipating the caregiver's response and either modifying the intention or relinquishing it altogether. How intentions are interpreted within the self and between self and other will depend, of course, on the meanings ascribed to them through what may be likened to a type of interactional consensus regarding the aim or ultimate purpose of the intention and the contextual and behavioral cues through which it is communicated. The outcome of the shared attribution will form the basis for the child's recognition and interpretation of the aims and intentions of other persons—a process which over time will become automatic, as in the unconscious apprehension of intuition and empathy—and the recognition and interpretation of self-generated internal events. This latter process of validation will determine the subjective realism of internal states, their efficacy and meaningfulness to the self. The process by which the child and his caregiver negotiate a shared, mutually familiar, and empathically accessible consensus of cross-validated meanings and intentions lies at the interface of that which is intersystemic, involving the actual coordination and fitting together of interactions within a bio-psycho-social system, and that which is intrapsychic, involving the coordination and fitting together of the internally structured registrations of these interactions.

What bearing do these findings have on psychopathology and the kinds of interactional disturbances which are encountered when working with children whose development around the interactional issue of self-assertion is disturbed or arrested? Where the more primitive transference reactions reflecting interactional disturbances in the caregiver-child dyad are built on the child's recognition of actual actions and anticipation of actual outcomes, the individuated, conceptual-level child's expectations are informed by covert intentions to act as well as overt behaviors. Like other purely mental phenomena, intentions need not be grounded in overt behaviors, cues, or signals and are highly susceptible to generalization and displacement. Obviating conflictual intentions is a different problem altogether, one that can hardly be accomplished through the primitive bio-perceptual adaptations to painful stimuli which we have identified as defensive behaviors in our preconceptual-level child.

For the child who is capable of thinking about what he wants to do and of speculating about how those around him will respond the therapist becomes not only a transferential embodiment of every kind of preconception, fantasy, and displacement, but, at the same time, an important source of experiential confirmation and disconfirmation. More than at any previous stage of interactional development, the child is now able to transfer characteristic modes of action and interaction to the therapeutic relationship and to examine and subject these modes to a process of revalidation in the context of the therapeutic situation. The child's readiness to engage in this kind of validation of internal intrapsychic experiences is guaranteed by the primary interactional structures of this stage, that is, the fitting together of caregiver and child around the inference of intentions and the interpretations of shared meanings within the dyadic interaction. Thus, among the expectations that the child of this stage brings into the therapeutic relationship is that the therapist, like the primary caregiver, will engage in a process of defining inner awareness, of thinking about thoughts so to speak, and of staking out a common ground of subjective experience. Once the child has acquired verbal fluency the therapist will join him in the elaboration of a common language for the shared communication of internal states and perceptions. This is, I believe, the very crossroads between the old order of things—the perceptual-affective-action patterning of experiences structured interactionally within a complex bio-psycho-social system—and the new order of things, the internal representation and conceptualization of experiences structured intrapsychically and maintained through a carefully regulated balance of autonomy and interdependence. The opportunity to intervene effectively during this transitional phase is optimal, unparalleled by any other phase in the early life cycle.

From a clinical standpoint, observations of the shift from preconceptual to conceptual-level organization and from preindividuated to individuated functioning suggest that, as early as 18 months and certainly by 36 months, our patient is capable of engaging in a treatment process that is comprehensible in terms of interpersonal dynamics and intrapsychic processes already familiar to us from our work with older children and adults. Furthermore, even prior to 18 months we can begin to understand modes of action and interaction as these relate to the child's past and present developmental experience, and to intervene with the aim of expanding the child's awareness to include possibilities and outcomes other than those to which he is accustomed and which constitute the foundation for his particular biases in perceiving the world and other people. In doing so, however, we understand that the essence of the preindividuated, preconceptual-level child's experience cannot be unlocked by study of the child alone. We must include in our observations and in our treatment interventions the full gamut of systemic and interactive processes which, taken together, constitute the child's primitive psychic reality. Only with the consolidation of a tripartite personality organization are we justified in treating our patient as one truly self-contained, and even then only relatively so (Rapaport 1951). Prior to this point in development, we must carefully track the shifting balance between autonomy and interdependence through the assessment of those specific lines of development, levels of organization, and contexts of functioning which show signs of compromise. Ultimately, this may lead to the treatment of family systems and the direct manipulation of physical environments; invariably, it will entail the treatment of one or both caregiving parents. At whatever level we intervene, we do so with the aim of altering those elements in the extended personality system of the preindividuated, preconceptual-level child that will one day leave its imprint on the individuated, conceptual-level child's internal personality structure.

There is one further implication that is of critical importance here. The discovery and definition of interactional structures and transference reactions at a preindividuated, preconceptual level of personality organization opens the door to the treatment of infants and toddlers within a dynamic psychotherapy paradigm. At the same time, it provides us with an important theoretical rationale for the treatment of those severe psychopathological conditions of childhood, adolescence, and adulthood which have their origins in the early regulation of exchange between parent and infant, a psychopathology manifest in basic modes of perceptual organization, affective organization, and physical patterning which predates the conceptual representation of experience. The basic parameters within which evaluation and treatment are conducted remain essentially the same; after all, a recapitulation of experiential deficits and distortions from any point in the life cycle is most likely to emerge within an intense interpersonal relationship. Within these broad parameters, however, we emphasize as mean-

ingful psychotherapeutic process those aspects of physical patterning, symbolization, communication, and expectation which have
originated in the earliest parent–child and family–child interactions.

Defenses

Long before the preindividuated, preconceptual-level child is
capable of experiencing and expressing in an organized way the
conflictual pain of irreconcilable longings, impulses, wishes, and
feelings, he is faced with situations of mounting tension and need
which require a special kind of action to ease distress and reduce
the threat of stimulus inundation. Once perceived, actual or anticipated danger is met with behaviors that effectively eliminate or
minimize the threat. Defensive behaviors? Strictly speaking, probably not. Most investigators in this area (Lichtenberg 1982, 1983;
Fraiberg 1982) define defense mechanisms as structured organizations of perception, cognition, affect, and action operative on a
symbolic level in a context of intrapsychic self- and object relations and representations. Fraiberg in particular, however, distinguished between defense mechanisms "which can be assumed to
function only when an ego proper has emerged " (1982, p. 612) and
behavior with a "defensive purpose" which may be operative as
soon as the child is capable of recognizing and rejecting a threat to
his functioning, probably from birth. I believe that we can take this
distinction one step further by adding that, while the preindividuated, preconceptual-level child may not be capable of intrapsychically rejecting, repeating, and reorganizing complex interactions
of self and object at a representational level, the child is nonetheless
subject to experiences of tension, loss, love, grief, and shame, with
respect to actual objects. Each of these emotions yields an anticipation of and a specific orientation to the object which, with consistency and redundancy over time, lead to organized patterning of
interactive behaviors (with a defensive purpose or otherwise) and
generalization across interactional situations. The defensive purposes and behaviors of the preindividuated, preconceptual-level
child can be best understood as complex intrasystemic patternings
of interaction between an actual child and an actual caregiving
object engaged in mutual regulation. What the conceptual-level
child accomplishes autonomously, in a medium of intrapsychic
structures, the preconceptual-level child accomplishes interdepen-
dently in a context of interactional structures (enduring patterns of
interactional relatedness, orientation, and regulation).

The defensive behaviors of the preindividuated, preconceptual-level child have as their purpose the alleviation of distress which, given a reasonably responsive caregiver-child dyad, will normally be alleviated interactionally in conjunction with the caregiver's soothing, consoling ministrations. Thus, even where we do not see defensive behavior per se—behavior organized and initiated by the child on his own behalf in response to threat or danger—we will certainly observe behaviors, attitudes, and orientations born from the caregiver-child interaction and designed to elicit the caregiver's distress-reducing response. In this sense, the result of the interaction is defensive in causing the cessation of a painful or distressing event. What will one day operate intrapsychically, given the successful internalization of the caregiver's soothing, tension-reducing function, is, in this precursory stage, operating inter-systemically. The caregiver's defensive-regulatory structures have become the child's defensive-regulating structures, the child's signalling of distress, the caregiver's call to action. The signal and the response it elicits are not coherent or meaningful events unless they are viewed together in the context of the interactive exchange which taken as a whole may be said to have a defensive purpose.

Clinically speaking, in terms of the preconceptual-level child's transference relationship to the therapist, the child may be expected to initiate defensive regulatory exchanges that are structured interactionally on the basis of previous regulatory exchanges with the primary caregiver. The therapist will be coerced into providing a specific mode or configuration of distress-alleviating responsiveness for the child; the role of the primary caregiver as an external auxiliary structure will, therefore, have been transferred effectively to the therapist. A 15-month-old girl, Ellen, illustrated this phenomenon poignantly. In the face of imminent separation from her mother, she would cling desperately to her father's leg. At most, she would venture away a few tentative steps, always maintaining at least fingertip contact. When her father, too, was asked to leave the room, Ellen was beside herself with fear and sadness. She ran to the therapist, grabbed his legs, and maintained a posture of desperate clinging identical to the one she had held with her father. In both instances, the result of Ellen's action was the alleviation of her anxiety at being momentarily left behind by her mother.

In contrast to the pervasively disordered autistic or symbiotic child, Ellen was a relatively adaptive, constitutionally resourceful youngster, whose developmental experience, while not one of optimal maternal responsiveness, had been rich and well-regulated enough to sustain forward developmental motion. But, in cases of extreme deprivation, where effective interactive structures do not develop to serve defensive purposes, the child is vulnerable to repeated, prolonged periods of helplessness and inundation. Here the child is prone to adapt through the elaboration of what are referred to in the literature as pre-ego modes of defense (Fraiberg 1982; Bergman and Escalona 1944); biopsychological organizations built on the preadapted behaviors available to the normal infant for coping with moderate levels of dystonic stimuli, behaviors such as crying, withdrawal into sleep, pushing away, habituation, and gaze aversion.

In the clinical situation, as in the severely disturbed caregiver-child interaction, the therapist as transference object is likely to become the object of defense (the very aspect of experience which must be excluded) rather than a partner in defense (a collaborator in the shared regulation of potentially damaging internal and external stimuli). In other cases, the therapist may be excluded from the interaction altogether as the child seeks to avoid all potentially inundating aspects of the world. By assessing the nature of the child's interactional orientation, the therapist can generate important diagnostic hypotheses based on the quality and degree of his own responsiveness: what he is made to feel towards the child and towards himself and what he is compelled or coerced into doing for the child in the regulatory exchange. The therapist will be led to question, in the context of his own developmental experience, the source of fantasies, associations, or perceptual-affective-action patterns generated spontaneously during the therapeutic interaction. The therapist may, for example, experience the loneliness, tedium, or boredom of having been shut from the child's awareness or of having been relegated to the status of an inanimate object. His thoughts may seem to wander: the hour drags; he may feel restlessness, irritation, and a loss of empathy. At one extreme, the child's withdrawal is met by the therapist's withdrawal, resulting in a self-perpetuating confirmation to the child of the tenuousness of the caregiver-therapist's availability. In other cases, the therapist may feel himself the object of the child's aggression as interactions seem to combust spontaneously, for no apparent reason. Such interaction is likely to evoke irritation at the very least, outright antagonism, hostility, and provocation at the worst.

What are the transference implications of the preindividuated, preconceptual-level child's defensive orientations and what can we surmise about the child's developmental experience on the basis of his choice of defense? While the possible variations of detrimental experiences are endless, the modes of response available to the preindividuated, preconceptual-level child are not. Basically, most defensive orientations involve some form of fight, flight, clinging, or withdrawal. When avoidant or flight-fight reactions predominate, we are seeing the child's half of an interactive pattern that is characteristically nonempathic, exploitative, destructive, or abusive. Where provocative or fight reactions predominate, we may very well be seeing the child's half of an interaction that is provocative in kind, responsive but cruel, teasing, antagonistic, or sadistically hostile.

Variations on avoidant and provocative defenses have received some attention in the psychoanalytic literature but are generally treated as relatively autonomous behaviors defined without reference to the interactive context in which they assume their significance. Engel and Reichsman (1956) have described the conservation-withdrawal reaction in which avoidant behaviors oscillate with wild discharge activity and, finally, complete psychophysiological shutdown. Fraiberg (1982) has described a number of pathological defenses in infancy, including turning aggression towards the self, transforming painful affects into their opposites, fighting, hyperactivity, and "freezing" (a complete immobilization and massive habituation to stimuli). From the point of view of the observer, each of these defensive orientations involves the child in a characteristic patterning of behavior which either limits or accentuates stimulus values, social or otherwise. From the point of view of the interactive partner, however, such defensive variations are identifiable by the kind of resonance or responsiveness that is evoked or coerced. Freezing, for example, may evoke from the therapist a distinct sense of the odd or uncanny and, with it, anxious discomfort leading to active intervention aimed at bringing the child "back to life," which may, in fact, only fortify the defense by confirming its necessity to the child already hypersensitive to intrusiveness. The transformation of affect, turning pain or displeasure into its opposite, will likely evoke in the therapist a sense of incongruity, bewilderment, or confusion. Empathy is led astray as the manifest feeling tone to which the therapist responds is discordant with the child's actual subjective experience. Such was the case with one little boy in our infant-toddler therapeutic play group, whose face frequently registered a bright and beaming smile after he had been hit or infringed upon by another child in the group.

Whether we choose to regard the emergency regulatory mechanisms of the preindividuated, preconceptual-level child as defensive behavior proper or as the precursors of later defense mechanisms is of theoretical importance, perhaps, insofar as human development tends to be most comprehensible in terms of its continuities but is of somewhat less significance from a purely clinical standpoint. What is clinically meaningful, however, and must be kept in mind at all times, is that each of these patterns of responding bears a special significance to a prototypic caregiver-child interaction and provides the clinical observer with invaluable information about the quality and fit of past and present interactive exchange. Each defensive pattern represents a solution to an interaction problem, a solution that has been transferred (inappropriately, we must hope) from a primary caregiver-child interaction to the therapeutic situation. This is how the preindividuated, preconceptual-level child reveals to us something about his distant or recent past. It is the replay of a struggle to adapt, a replay that in all likelihood will never be retold.

Chapter Seventeen

Some Technical Considerations

By "undoing resistances" and returning to the adaptive resources of the neurotic patient "lost provinces of his mental life" (Freud 1938, p. 173) Freud's psychoanalysis accomplished therapeutic successes which in his own words "were second to none in the field of internal medicine" (1916, p. 256). Nevertheless, Freud made quite clear throughout his writing that psychoanalytic treatment was not a panacea for all human ills, nor even the treatment of choice in every case of emotional illness. At its inception, at least, psychoanalytic treatment was well suited to a relatively limited range of patients. Three factors, Freud believed, each relative to the disposition or predisposition of the patient, were decisive to its efficacy: the relative influence of congenital and "accidental" traumas, the congenital strength of the drives, and certain "unfavorable alterations of the ego" acquired as the result of a "defensive struggle" during the earliest phases of development (1937, p. 220). In order to benefit from a treatment based on broadening self-awareness acquired gradually over time, the prospective analytic patient, despite his indisposition, had to maintain a capacity for reflectiveness, relatedness, abstinence from direct gratification and alliance, and to make do with gratifications, often minuscule, symbolic, inferential, or imagined, and almost always painfully slow in coming. All of this called for a well-controlled flexibility, a readiness to invest as the patient had invested in others in the past (that is to say, a mobility of cathexis) but at an optimal distance from which the actor could with little difficulty assume the role of observer and wonder with the analyst at his own mental productions. From an operational standpoint, pathological alterations of the ego were defined by contrast to the "normal ego" which would guarantee "unshakable loyalty" to the work of analysis.

On each of these three counts Freud was skeptical of the prospects for treating psychotic disturbances psychoanalytically, though the door was certainly left open: "We discover that we must renounce the idea of trying our plan of cure upon psychotics . . . perhaps forever, perhaps only for the time being until we have found some plan better adapted for them" (1940, p. 173).

Freud would probably have extended his clinical pessimism to the treatment of psychotic children as well, though the matter was never fully elaborated. In general, child psychoanalysis, even of relatively intact children, presents numerous and endemic technical problems which in and of themselves push conventional wisdom and accepted practice to the limits of theoretical accountability. In working psychotherapeutically with children, Freud wrote that "it is often embarrassing to decide what one would choose to call conscious and what unconscious" (1918, p. 104)—an unfortunate obstacle indeed in a form of treatment based on the transformation of mental events unknown to mental events known. Accommodating though the analyst of children might be, "lending words and thoughts" to fill in the child's sparse associations, the "deepest strata" of primitive mental life, Freud believed, might in the end turn out to be impenetrable. Even Freud's most recent detractors would seem to agree with this point.

A plan "better adapted." Were it simply a matter of scrapping old theory and replacing it with a new body of thought, there would be little more than academic interests in citing Freud's skepticism here. The point, however, is that the phenomena with which I have been dealing throughout this work—developmental disturbances among preindividuated, preconceptual-level children—are, I believe, comprehensible and can be influenced within the context of classical and contemporary psychoanalytic theory. As I hope to demonstrate, the central operational constructs still apply and, given sufficient accommodation to the developmental and interactional status of our young patients, suggest a model of intervention not altogether different from that which we regularly apply in the treatment of adults.

In the classical psychoanalytic model, the resolution of neurotic symptomatology is accomplished through the patient's recapitulation of the origins of symptoms, renewing the conflictual situation in response to which they arose, and, by capitalizing on developmental resources and motivations that were not available at the time, guiding the conflict to a different and more adaptive outcome. It is the opening up of new possibilities for relatedness and problem-solving in situations where once there were believed to be no alternative that is curative. The agent of change in the therapeutic process is the therapist's interpretive intervention aimed at establishing a relationship or connection between drive and defense and at expanding awareness by creating contrast in place of continuity. The theater in which the "decisive battles" (as Freud called them) between the rational and irrational elements of the mental life are fought is the transference relationship. In the context of the transference, the object of interpretation is to demonstrate to the patient that certain feelings, attitudes, and orientations toward the therapist do not arise from the present situation, are not altogether appropriate to the person of the therapist (though they may in fact coalesce around actual attitudes, behaviors, and so on), and are, in fact, apropos of something that happened (or was imagined to have happened) earlier or elsewhere in the patient's life.

The problems involved in applying a psychodynamically oriented treatment model to the emotional and developmental disturbances of infancy and early childhood are manifest, and I shall attempt to highlight only a few. To begin, we have a child whose capacities for verbal communication, abstract-conceptual thought, and symbolic representation are limited or nonexistent. Thus, it follows that the use of interpretive interventions whose efficacy is usually understood in terms of the communication of meaningful symbolic representational motifs is of limited value at least in terms of content or semantic aspects. If, as I mentioned earlier, we are to have a model of psychotherapy for preindividuated, preconceptual-level children based on the interpretive mode, we must reassess the relative significance of the various components of interpretive content and structure as these apply to both the child's subjective organization or preconceptual experiencing and the therapist's empathic reorganization of the child's experience at a conceptual level of experiencing. But what evidence do we have to support the notion that interpretation (as a tool for therapeutically illuminating the disparity between expectations based on past experiences and actualities based on current realities) is even germane to the treatment of preconceptual-level disturbances of the early years of life, devoid as we believe these to be of well-organized intrapsychic experiencing?

Though limited in the ability to represent experience in thought, the preconceptual-level child is capable of rudimentary patterning of perception-affect-action and recognition-anticipation-response which provide the foundation for what we have come to regard as the earliest manifestations of transference phenomena, and behavioral orientations having a defensive purpose aimed at curtailing, limiting, or obviating psychophysiological pain or distress. We find that, like older children and adults, preindividuated, preconceptual-level infants and toddlers who have suffered trauma or deprivation in interaction with their caregivers develop expectations based primarily on learned associations and patterns which influence their subsequent interactional orientation. Based on the recognition of familiar behavioral, affective, communicational, or contextual cues associated with danger, the child will anticipate a likely outcome, one which has proven to be painful in the past, and will act to avert the predictably dire consequences. As Wachtel (1980) has pointed out, however, the act of avoidance or defense may, in fact, evoke unwittingly the very kind of response that is anticipated with such dread. In the context of parent–child interaction, withdrawal on the part of the child fosters intrusion by the parent, a stepped-up effort to engage or stimulate the child, while the child's defensive clinging may elicit a pushing away by a parent uncomfortable with the child's violation of boundary. We have, in other words, a self-fulfilling prophecy: the child's worst fears are substantiated and the original defensive maneuvers fortified. The parent has successfully matched to pattern with the child's expectation and confirmed the efficacy of the dreaded anticipation. This is really not so different from what we observe among adult neurotic patients, who succeed in eliciting from others the kind of responses which confirm their worst fears and expectations about "the way other people are" but who, as Freud noted, are compelled to seek out the very kinds of situations which will justify maintaining habitual modes of reaction and relatedness (1937, p. 220).

Given our observation of certain cognitive-affective behavioral organizations among pre-individuated, preconceptual-level children which resemble in aim and mode similar mechanisms among conceptual-level children and adults, we construct our treatment interventions based on principles and derived from the treatment of related disturbances in interpersonal patterning observed in cases of adult psychopathology. The medium of change in our treatment model will remain an intensive interpersonal relationship between therapist and child, a relationship in which our patient will try to recapitulate the same kinds of interactional exchanges through which adaptation has occurred in the context of the prototypic caregiver-child relationship. We will become the benefactors of a particular configuration of interactional structuralization reflecting the child's present level of intersystemic functioning. The agent of change in our psychotherapeutic model of treatment similarly parallels the types of interventions that facilitate expanded awareness among adult psychotherapy patients: interpretation, confrontation, support, and, more generally, the facilitation and elaboration of preexisting modes of adaptive-interactive functioning. Clearly, the active ingredient inherent in these processes changes as they are applied to children in the early phases of development; we can see shifts in emphasis from content to process, from concept to experience, and from substance to sentience. Our goals, however, remain the same: the confirmation and disconfirmation of expectations, based on a realistic assessment of possible and potential outcomes across the range of life experience; the refinement of discriminatory capabilities and the reduction of tendencies toward unwarranted generalization; the opening of closed systems of self-perpetuating and self-limiting patterns of behavior through the introduction of new information; and the articulation, punctuation, and organization of internal experience and awareness.

The Confirmation and Disconfirmation of Experience

In working clinically with conceptual-level children or adults in a psychodynamic framework, the therapist is confronted with transference phenomena in a variety of configurations, including the development of an artificial neurosis, transference as resistance, and transference as repetition (Racker 1968). In each case we see a form of behavior aimed at maintaining a specific orientation with respect to something remembered about the self, or the self in relation to others, which would cause anxiety or distress were it allowed direct access to consciousness. Isolated from the adaptive resources and broadening experiential data base of the mature aspects of the personality, such memory constellations and the modes of relating which they inform are in some sense left behind and do not participate in the overall growth and development of the person. Interpretation, the tool with which the therapist works to fill in memory gaps, provides a conduit between current experiences and past experiences as these are preserved in memory. Subjected to confirmatory or disconfirmatory feedback, suppositions, presuppositions, and the behaviors which reflect and are informed by them are altered gradually through accommodation to reality. How, then, within a psychodynamic framework, do we modify systems of expectation and belief when there is as yet little or no capacity for evocative memory, where those aspects of experience which constitute the focus of our therapeutic endeavors are preserved not in well organized and retrievable mental representations but in the nonverbal, perceptual-affective-action patterns of the preindividuated, preconceptual-level child?

Here again, the principles of treatment remain largely the same: we seek to open closed patterns of recognition-expectation-response to new sources of experiential input, leading to either a reconfirmation or a disconfirmation of that which is expected. Rather than work within the context of what is remembered or represented from the past, drawing connections and filling in gaps, we work within the context of what is actual and present by creating an alternate interactional experience, a developmental environment of optimal, "good enough" empathic responsiveness in which new interactional structures and a more flexible and adaptive regulation of exchange are possible. We demonstrate to the child by actual example that cues, attributes, orientations, expressions, and communications which have become associated through previous interactions with painful or distressful outcomes may, under certain conditions, yield outcomes significantly different from what is anticipated. Treatment, however, involves more than helping the child to recognize that characteristic modes of response simply do not apply in all relationships; it involves helping the child to make this kind of discrimination on his own. Transference is an aspect of generalization and pattern matching, treatment, a process leading to refined discrimination.

Before the child can experience outcomes to interactive engagements other than the painful ones he expected, he must first risk giving up those behavioral patterns which, in keeping with their defensive purpose, interfere with the opening of patterned feedback regulatory systems to new information and, therefore, to the accommodation of certain maladaptive behavioral schemata to changes in external reality conditions (Watchel 1980). In other words, before the child is even accessible to the confirmation or disconfirmation of expectations, he must first open himself to possibilities other than those he anticipates. Thus, in the psychodynamic treatment of the infant or preconceptual-level child, as in the psychodynamic treatment of the conceptual-level child or adult, we intervene first at the level of defense, gradually working our way towards that against which the patient is defended (Fennichel 1945).

The first step in overcoming resistances is the remobilization of a need or a wish which is defended against because of the child's fear of renewed traumatic rejection, nonresponsiveness, or over-responsiveness (under or overstimulations, for example). We then wait for an opening, for the child to relinquish momentarily the defensive orientation for purpose of surveillance or exploration (and here we must assume that, despite the unfulfilled longings or the pain of early experience, the child continues to harbor some degree of hope and curiosity, however dim it may be). Herein lies the art. Unlike the caregivers of the child's primary and original developmental environment, we do not respond to the child's defensive posture with complementary or reciprocal responses that will confirm to him that his avoidant response is still necessary. Often, this means restraining the impulses, inclinations, and intentions that seem most appropriate or natural to the situation. When a child pulls away, it is natural to move closer; when a child is fearful, to reach out, to reassure. When a child fights, it is natural to try to contain his disorganized lashing-out. For the child who can tolerate the caregiver's regulatory responsiveness, such interventions are thoroughly appropriate, growth-promoting, and structure-building. However, for the child who cannot tolerate this kind of regulatory exchange, for whom the interactional synchronization and patterning of biorhythmicity, contact, and state regulation have become distorted under the impact of innate constitutional vulnerabilities or parental psychopathology, the normal consummation of these natural interventions may only succeed in aggravating the child's fearfulness and confirming the accuracy of his expectations. This in turn can lead to a fortification of behaviors aimed at diffusing the dangerous interaction and its anticipated consequences. Thus, the predicament: how do we reach the child without triggering a defensive response that will block subsequent informational input?

We find among the more severely disturbed of our very young patients that the elegant physical patterning of engagement and disengagement which normally develops between caregiver and child has grown into something only vaguely reminiscent of the smooth and rhythmic fit of the adaptive, growth-promoting caregiver-child interaction. The caregiver's overtures, cues, and initiatives have become associated with danger; the child, having learned the meanings of these behaviors, averts the dreaded outcomes as best he can. Over time, the resonance, the back and forth of such interactions will crystallize as interactional structure and will be carried over in the form of complex recognition-anticipa-tion-action patterns to other interactions, the therapeutic interac-tion among them. Insofar as the therapist courts the child in a manner resembling that of the child's parents, there is no reason why the therapist, too, should not be repelled at the first display of interest.

Fortunately, there are countless variations of interactional ex-change involving multiple configurations of sensory, motor, affec-tive, and cognitive input through which even the most basic dyadic regulations may be expedited. Insofar as the child's immediate response, recognition and initial expectancy are associated with multiple behavioral cues received and registered across an array of psychological and psychophysiological channels, it is likely that certain types of input will have a more immediate valence or will be more salient to the child's experience of a particular event than others. At different phases in the life cycle and even at different moments during relatively circumscribed developmental stages, there are characteristic biases or sensitivities which influence the selection, rejection, and hierarchical organization of experiential input according to the capabilities, interests, and needs of the person during that particular interval. Because many of our prein-dividuated, preconceptual-level children are, for example, most facile at organizing experiences on a sensorimotor, presymbolic level, sensory and behavioral input formatted in a sensorimotor motif is prone to greater emphasis in the child's experience than the same input would be if formatted in a concrete operational or symbolic motif. The child is simply more sensitive and receptive to information organized in this way than to information organized in any of the possible alternate modes. Thus, we find a greater attune-ment on the child's part to overt actions and behaviors than to implicit or covert actions or to behaviors represented symbolically (such as verbal language). While experiences at a symbolic repre-sentational level are certainly registered and recognized, they tend not to have the same valence or impact and may not carry the same associational significance for the preindividuated, preconceptual-level child as experiences organized in, for example, a visual or tactile-kinesthetic motif. In other words, interactions consum-mated through nondominant modes of experiential organization (for example, symbolic representational interaction with a senso-rimotor-level child) may provide a basis for interactional exchange that is not yet subject to the child's prepatterning of recognition, expectation, and responsiveness; moreover, these interactions may transact at a threshold of stimulation more compatible with the child's limited regulatory capabilities than interactions of comparable aim and intent consummated through more dominant modes of experiential organization. Vulnerable children in particular are more open to overtures that are framed in a manner not already associated with negative or painful outcomes and that are more easily tolerated, given their limited stimulus-regulating capabilities. For these reasons we frame our interventions verbally, following the child wherever possible with words rather than overt actions which are more likely to have become associated with negative expectations and, consequently, with behavior patterns aimed at discontinuing interaction. In this respect, our treatment model, like all psychodynamic treatments, is verbal and interpretive. But our words serve a very different purpose.

We verbally interpret aspects of interaction in our treatment of the preindividuated, preconceptual-level child but not with the aim of undoing repression or restoring to the ego (an ego which has yet to coalesce fully) aspects of experience rendered unconscious. Rather, we interpret with the intention of creating a new kind of developmental experience for the child, a new regulation of exchange which, by virtue of its empathically attuned understanding, sensitivity, receptivity, and responsiveness, will disconfirm expectations built on earlier experiences. Certainly, our interpretations, like all other interpretive statements, will have a substantive component. They will have a meaning or content derived from drawing together disconnected or disassociated aspects of experience. However, this component of the interpretation, one which in the conventional wisdom receives special emphasis in the framing of most interventions, is (depending of course on the verbal and linguistic capabilities of the child) itself relatively incidental as an agent of change in our treatment of the preindividuated preconceptual-level child.

Content or semantic aspects are important insofar as they allow the therapist to organize and conceptualize the therapeutic process in both primary and secondary process motifs, a flexibility of experiencing to which the therapist may have relatively limited access by virtue of his developmentally sophisticated cognitive and affective status. This conceptualization allows the therapist to track the movement of the child's preconceptual experience. The child, by contrast, to the extent to which his cognitive capabilities are limited to sensorimotor and preconceptual-level motifs responds to very different aspects of the same communication: inflection, rhythm, cadence, volume, fluctuation, and, most importantly, the affective tone against which these aspects are set. Each of these expressive elements, though nonsemantic, parallels closely the meaningful aspects of the therapist's communication and forms the basis for the preconceptual-level child's tracking of the therapist's conceptual-level interventions. More importantly, each of these nuances of communication contributes to an articulation of experience which, though not totally undifferentiated (Pine 1981), may be organized by the child in idiosyncratic ways that obviate or negate any meaningful informational value (for anyone other than the primary caregiver with whom the child has consolidated interactional structures based on faulty or nonconsensual organizations of experience). Gradually, a new edition of interactional structures built on the synchronous, bidirectional tracking of therapist by child and child by therapist may develop along with the idiosyncratic patterns of exchange negotiated with the primary caregiver. To the extent to which these newly negotiated interactional structures prevail (to this end we engage simultaneously in a complementary therapeutic process with the primary caregiver), a foundation is laid for the consolidation of internalized (intrapsychic) self-regulatory structures subserving a similar but autonomous organizing function. The child will have been enabled by our efforts to articulate his own internal and external experiencing, much as this had formerly been articulated interactionally with the therapist, and will do so in a manner that is shared and comprehensible to others. The child will, in other words, have acquired the capacity for genuine interpersonal relatedness. When language does develop, it will do so around an awareness and organization of experience that can be represented within the common idiom of human discourse.

Verbal linguistic interpretation, then, is a means of reaching the child who has come to associate predominantly nonverbal sensorimotor patterns of action and interaction with danger or distrust. It functions by creating a contrast between an actual interactional situation and an anticipated interactional situation and by opening up once-impenetrable patterns of recognition-expectation-response to new experiential input. Simply put, the therapist's well modulated, nonintrusive mode of verbal contact creates a basis for discrimination. Unlike the caregiver, who challenges the child's withdrawal by moving into closer proximity and increasing the intensity of stimulation, the therapist follows and articulates some of the child's actions, segregating them from the child's total behavioral output, but does so through a carefully regulated synchronization of affect, action, and articulation that has not become associated with devastating consequences and is therefore more likely to be tolerated.

I would agree with Winnicott (1965) at this point that psychotherapy is the work of expanding awareness by replacing continuity with contrast. It is a texturing process as much as it is an uncovering process, one wherein unchallenged connections between cause and effect or action and reaction are examined with heightened acuity for inconsistency and contradiction. Apropos of the present discussion, it may be useful to think of Winnicott's definition in terms of similarity versus discrepancy (dissimilarity) or, more simply, familiarity versus strangeness. What we are, in essence, initiating in our therapeutic interaction is the building in of optimal discrepancy between what is expected and what is actual and doing so through a form of interactional contact that is not as prone to heighten fearfulness and escalate defensive reactions. However, since the child's developmental experience has not, in all likelihood, been all bad (if it had been, the child might well not have survived), the therapist does not seek to disconfirm all aspects of that experience. In other words, similarity and discrepancy, familiarity and strangeness must coexist within a critical balance.

In moderation, the similarity between expectation and actuality facilitates a working alliance between patient and therapist. It connotes "you are not so different from me that you cannot understand me" and, conversely, "I am not so different from you that I cannot make myself understood." At a preconceptual level, where this kind of reasoning could not take place, optimal sameness is experienced as safety and constancy in a situation which is in many respects familiar and not at such variance with the expected as to demand a complete repatterning of recognition and response. There is enough continuity that the child can, when needed, retreat into nonawareness. Taken to an extreme, of course, similarity confirms the child's expectations and lends reality to the transference situation. At this point, the child can only conclude ("adultomorphically" speaking), "I was right all along—this is just the way it is." In this case, the conceptual-level child will cling the more steadfastly to his convictions, the preconceptual child to his expectations.

Optimal discrepancy challenges the child's beliefs, perceptions, and preconceptions (in the transference) in light of the present reality but does so against a background of constancy and familiarity. It invites the child to rectify distorted expectations with alternate attributions of cause and effect, action and reaction. In moderation, it promotes an awareness of separateness and facilitates the child's assumption of those psychological functions provided by the interactional partner. The child's optimal phase-appropriate encounters with discrepancy in expectation and unfamiliarity fuel the internalization of interactionally mediated processes. Thus, discrepancy is the conduit between the intersystemic and the intrapsychic. At an extreme, however, discrepancy crushes the hope of being understood and undermines trust in sameness and predictability. Faced with the unrecognizable and totally unexpected, the child is left with few alternatives but to fight, cling, or withdraw. These are worst-case scenarios, each of which culminates in drastically reduced awareness.

Within a medium of optimum similarity and discrepancy, the preindividuated, preconceptual-level child begins to reorganize and internalize interactionally mediated patterns of recognition-anticipation-response. Such reorganizations occur not so much as a result of the child's reassessment of preexisting sensorimotor patterns which, in the context of malignant caregiver-child interactions may have become associated inextricably with painful outcomes, but as a result of the therapist's introduction and emphasis of alternate modes of interaction which, while effective in establishing contact, are significantly less evocative of dreadful expectations. A wedge is driven between anticipation and outcome, between the child's undifferentiated fearfulness of all caregiving persons who would seem to extend themselves and a reality in which trustworthy empathic responsiveness is possible, if not inevitable. Having established this basic discrimination, the child may go on to recognize that there are not only differences among caregiving persons but that the same caregivers are capable of various intentions and that even subtle differences in behavior and communication can predict radically different interactional outcomes. Few caregivers are all bad, few therapists all good.

More than 50 years ago, Freud (1933, p. 148) recognized that working psychoanalytically with children invariably brought the analyst into a systems-interactional perspective. The "internal resistances" against which the analyst struggles within adult patients, he wrote, are in the treatment of children replaced for the most part by "external difficulties," that is, the parents. If the parents make themselves vehicles of resistance, the aim of analysis, and even the analysis itself, is often imperiled. The solution? To incorporate into the child's treatment "a certain amount of analytic influencing of the parents." I believe that in formulating these remarks, Freud had in mind the more likely treatment candidates of his day, the neurotic child and the neurotic parent. Developmentally, these were children (and parents) who had attained or were at least on the verge of attaining well differentiated tripartite (ego-id-superego) personality organization and had succeeded reasonably well in negotiating earlier interactional stages. In most cases, the extent of pregenital arrest was not so pervasive as to undermine or forestall the entire developmental process. Freud's neurotic child was conflicted and carried much of his conflict internally, but interactional structuralization had already been superseded by intrapsychic structuralization, intersystemic conflict by intrapsychic conflict.

As we move back in developmental time from the oedipal to the preoedipal disturbances of infancy and early childhood, we find that the relative significance of mental events which are, strictly speaking, intrapsychic, diminishes with a commensurate rise in the significance of events at a systems-interactional level of organization. Those functions of regulation, organization, self-confirmation, and reality testing, which will one day enter the autonomous domain of the individuated self, are relegated to the various caregiving persons and environments which, as a cohesive system of exchange and interchange, function as the child's primitive personality organization. Much more is involved here, however, than the defensive resistance of the parent or parents, as Freud once believed. Indeed, if contemporary developmental research has demonstrated anything, it is the extent to which factors and influences external to the preindividuated, preconceptual-level child's immediate psychophysiological being are involved at almost every level of functional organization, from regulation to attachment, to initiative, and, finally, to internal representation.

A part of the experience which will effect the child's development is not, strictly speaking, the child's experience at all. Rather, it is the developmental experience, past and present, of those persons composing the complex family–child system who provide those functions which the child is unable to provide autonomously for himself. If, for example, a caregiving parent is the source of the child's capacity for tension regulation, then we must concern ourselves with the parent's experience of homeostatic regulation as much as with the child's inborn capacity to maintain a balanced state equilibrium when we evaluate the child's capacities in this area. Similarly, insofar as the caregiving parent is the source of the child's capacity for differentiating events internal to the self from events external we must take into account the parent's current and historical experiences in the area of reality testing in order to understand the genesis and current status of the child's functioning in this area. In short, anything which the child is unable to accomplish without the caregiving parents' supportive or facilitative functioning must be assumed to involve not only the child's adaptive resources but the adaptive resources of the caregiving parents and the family system as a whole. As an interactive event, such collaborative behavior must be defined in terms of the adaptive or preadapted psychic structures of the child with their genetic-historical-biographical antecedents, the adaptive intrapsychic structures of the adult caregivers with their respective antecedents, and the interactive structures of the caregiver-child system with their historical and biographical antecedents. The child's behavior cannot be defined as a fully comprehensible event if it is defined from a single vantage point. Clinically, this in no way reduces the child's centrality in the treatment process; we simply acknowledge that developmentally, autonomy and interdependency are always relative, from the first day of life on. Human beings are never wholly dependent upon nor wholly independent of their social and physical surroundings.

To summarize, for the child who has already internalized the world of objects and made their functions his own, the medium in which the treatment process unfolds is weighted relatively toward the intrapsychic realm, in which the important regulations of exchange between the child and the caregiving environment are preserved representationally. Much of what is needed in order to bring the treatment to a successful conclusion is contained within the child's stored and retrievable representations of experience. For the child who has yet to bridge the gap from interactional structuralization to intrapsychic structuralization, our medium is relatively more complex and extends beyond even the personal biographical history of the immediate child. It may bring into focus a diverse system of actual interactions, their effects, countereffects, and resonances throughout any and all contexts of functioning. While the child is certainly ready to meet us halfway in orchestrating his contribution to the interactional regulation of exchange, we must be aware of the other elements of the system as well, those with which the child has negotiated and continues to negotiate a complex patterning of mutual facilitation and exchange. The developmental experiences of the child's interactive partners as caregiving providers in the present and as caregiving recipients in the past will be no less important to the treatment process than the more immediate developmental experiences of the child himself. For in modifying the intrapsychic structures within which the caregivers' own developmental experiences are preserved, we lay the foundations for a more adaptive and successful consolidation of interactional structures in the current dyadic relationship and, ultimately, for the consolidation of stable, self-regulating intrapsychic structures in the child's increasingly autonomous personality organization.

PART THREE

The Case of Kathy M.

Chapter Eighteen

Background Information and Diagnostic Impressions

A clinical case presentation illustrates the application of corrective developmental principles to the treatment of a pervasive developmentally disordered 3-year-old, Kathy M., and her mother, Ms. L. The actual treatment process, spanning a period of some 15 months, is relatively brief by most standards, particularly in light of the severity of pathology involved. However, the results obtained, while necessarily incomplete, will, I believe, demonstrate the effectiveness with which a psychotherapy informed by our broadened understanding of empathy, transference, and the development of human interaction can alter favorably the course of even the most intractable disturbances of infancy and early childhood and their extension into adulthood and later life.

By its own definition, the corrective developmental paradigm is more encompassing than simply a child therapy. It is, rather, a treatment of systems or, more precisely, of dynamic intersystemic regulations of exchange as these are structured in the interaction of caregiver and child. Thus, our case illustration is really a compendium of three treatments: that of the child, that of the mother, and that of the parent-child dyad as a psychological and psychosocial entity in its own right with its own synergistic characteristics of structure and function. The division and segregation of these three components into separate and isolated process segments is to some extent an artifact of the presentation. In reality, there is considerable overlap among the treatments. However, to appreciate the systems dynamic fully, the reader must keep in mind not only the concurrence of events but also the resonance of effects originating in one treatment context throughout other contexts of treatment and throughout the life system of the family as a whole. The complexity of description involved in documenting this kind of flow-through relationship goes beyond the scope and intention of my text, but it should be kept in mind as a quiet but potent factor in the overall treatment design.

I will consider technical and theoretical issues raised during the course of the therapy at the conclusion of the case presentation.

Case History

Name: Kathy M. (child)
　　　Ms. Barbara L. (mother)

Age: Kathy—2 years, 9 months at initial intake. 4 years, 8 months at termination.
　　　Ms. L.—24 years at intake. 26 years at termination.

Dates of Birth: Kathy: 9 October 1977
　　　　　　　　Ms. L: 29 July 1955

Dates of Clinical Contact: 30 January 1980–19 May 1980 (Initial Dx evaluation)
　　　　　　　　　　　　6 March 1981–30 June 1982 (Reevaluation and treatment)

Identifying Data: Kathy M., a 4-year-old black female, is the second daughter of Ms. Barbara L. by Mr. Walter M. (age 35). Both Kathy and her older sister, Carol (age 8), live with their mother in a housing project on Chicago's south side. Mr. M. and Ms. L. are both single but have lived together on an irregular basis since Ms. L. moved to Chicago in 1977.

Ms. L., a former nurse, is unemployed and supported on ADC. Although she had contemplated resuming her career pending Kathy's school placement in September 1981, no positive steps had been taken in this direction as of treatment termination in June 1982. Mr. M. is also unemployed but works periodically as a musician.

Kathy M. currently attends a hospital-based child development center where she has been enrolled in a therapeutic day school program since September 1981. Carol, Kathy's older sister, is a second grade student at a public elementary school.

This summary represents the family's second and most recent contact with the Child Psychiatry Clinic-Parent–Infant Development Service (PIDS) at the University of Chicago Hospital. At the completion of an initial diagnostic evaluation in May of 1980, Ms. L. chose not to pursue treatment follow-up for either herself or her daughter. When contact was reestablished in February 1981, Kathy's former diagnostician-therapist was preparing to leave the clinic staff and referred the family back to PIDS where arrangements were made for mother and child to be seen by the current therapist. From the outset, Ms. L's compliance with the treatment process was inconsistent. While she generally kept at least one and often two weekly appointments for Kathy, she had been known to fail her own individual sessions for several weeks at a time.

Reasons for Referral

Kathy was originally referred to PIDS by a Chicago Board of Health clinic. At 2 years, 3 months of age, the child presented with a "profound language delay," failure to establish age-appropriate social contact and a variety of repetitive stereotyped behaviors. She was an extremely temperamental child, intolerant of most any frustration, particularly where this involved separation from her mother.

At the completion of her intake evaluation in May of 1980, Kathy was diagnosed reactive attachment disorder of infancy, her mother, borderline personality disorder. A treatment plan including work with both mother and child was proposed, but, as mentioned above, Ms. L. dropped out of the program shortly thereafter.

It was not until 6 March 1981 that Kathy and her mother resumed contact with the Child Psychiatry Clinic. Following the initial evaluation, Ms. L. had felt that by simply pronouncing words more clearly for Kathy and "just being there when she needed me" she could help her daughter to speak without outside help. Little progress was made during the nine-month hiatus, however. On the advice of a concerned relative and an article on childhood autism in the *Readers Digest*, Ms. L. reestablished clinic contact. It was mother's impression that, while much had changed in her parenting of Kathy, there had been little change in Kathy, who, if anything, had become increasingly aggressive, defiant, and tyrannical. Most disturbing, however, was the child's failure to develop speech and language use. The single words that she spoke were mostly imitative and perseverative; comprehension was equally poor. Kathy's nonverbal behaviors had become increasingly rote and repetitive. In fact, her most persistent activities seemed to be rocking and ear twiddling either of which could monopolize her attention for long periods of time.

Developmental History of the Child

Ms. L. was able to provide an account of Kathy's recent difficulties in convincing detail. When documenting events from the first 18 to 24 months of her daughter's life, however, she recalled mainly her own emotions at the time and had few vivid impressions of Kathy's early experiences. In trying to account for these "gaps" in her memory, Ms. L. dismissed large stretches of time by simply stating that things were just "OK" or "average." Occasionally, current difficulties were projected into the past. Ms. L. explained her confused recollection as an artifact of having been away from her baby a great deal during the first 12 months of Kathy's life while Ms. L. trained to become an LPN. Kathy was frequently left with neighbors during the day.

In giving an account of Kathy's development, Ms. L. went back spontaneously to the period before conception. Somewhat perplexedly she spoke of the pregnancy as an entirely unexpected event that "just happened" without special planning. Her relationship with Mr. M. was also described as having been more "accidentally than intentionally" maintained. Although Ms. L. originally moved to Chicago from her family home in Arkansas at Mr. M.'s encouragement, the two saw very little of each other following the first pregnancy.

When Ms. L. realized that she was pregnant for the second time, she recalled "hating the thought" as this would interfere with her plans to "better herself" by returning to school. She was also concerned about her ability to support the child on her own, since Mr. M. was completely uninterested in contributing to the family's welfare. Despite having been tense and anxious throughout the pregnancy and hating the changes in her appearance, Ms. L. never considered abortion. "Once you're pregnant," she believed, "you've got nothing to do. My mother didn't abort me."

Early in her second pregnancy, Ms. L. began to have fantasies that the child would be born damaged in some way or that both she and her baby would die during childbirth. In the second trimester she began spotting and her obstetrician recommended rest. Still, she kept up a frenetic, round-the-clock pace though it was difficult for her to account for her activities. Some of the doctor's orders were followed meticulously, however. Ms. L. gave up smoking and drinking and was exceedingly careful to take vitamins and iron supplements.

During the third trimester, Ms. L. received word that her mother (who had undergone a severe stroke) was terminally ill. Believing this to be her final opportunity to reconcile what had become a rather ambivalent relationship over the years, she wished desperately to return home. Her doctor, however, advised her not to travel and she complied. Still, Ms. L. recalled feeling "very depressed" and wished that her baby would spontaneously abort so that she could consumate this longed-for reunion.

Labor and delivery with Kathy (named after a kindly obstetrical nurse) were relatively uneventful except that mother was bothered by persistent thoughts that her baby would be born brain damaged (as the result of her depression). The use of general anesthesia during the delivery only added to these fears. Ms. L.'s immediate feelings following delivery were a mixture of relief and disappointment—relief that the ordeal was over, disappointment that the child was female. She had hoped for a boy this time believing that "you don't have to worry about them when they're growing up." Excited at first in anticipation of seeing her baby, Ms. L. turned away upon actually being presented with the infant. This, too, seemed to puzzle her: "I don't know why I did that, I don't know if I was resentful or what."

As noted above, details of Kathy's early life history are rather vague. Mother perceived her daughter, then as now, as being of difficult temperament and poor disposition. Somewhat incongruously, however, Ms. L. described Kathy as having been, in most respects, an "average" baby presenting only average difficulties. Still, there was the feeling that Kathy was not connected emotionally with either herself or any other adult caregivers. The baby did not seem to care about being held and was, at best, tolerant of even the most affectionate overtures.

At first it seemed to mother that "one person was about as good as another" in Kathy's eyes. It was a matter of apparent indifference to her who held or cared for her. Mother did not become differentiated as a distinct and special caregiver until sometime around 24 months, at which point Kathy developed an intense separation reaction. Ms. L. attributed Kathy's initial "indifference" to her own emotional unavailability during the aftermath of her mother's death. This, she believed, was her punishment.

Ms. L. recalled few of Kathy's early developmental milestones other than walking, which occurred by 14 months. At 18 months

Kathy spoke her first words, "mama" and "no," but these remained her only intelligible vocabulary throughout the first 2½ years. About this time, mother noted that Kathy had adopted a repetitious rocking behavior with which she would occupy herself for hours at a time. Mother would find her rocking in the morning upon waking, and again, shortly after she was returned to bed in the evening. Similar behaviors were noted during the day when she was frustrated or upset. Other times, when mother refused to accede to her demands, Kathy tantrumed to the point of exhaustion, then withdrew altogether. When restrained or limited in any way, she reverted to rocking once again. It was difficult, however, for Ms. L. to set limits for Kathy or discipline her for those of her behaviors that were unacceptable. Often she simply allowed the child to have her way in order to avoid the outbursts that inevitably followed upon any frustration. Mother also maintained the idea that Kathy might be suffering from some kind of congenital disorder that was causing her visceral pain and on that account found it difficult to deny her what she wanted.

Around 24 months, when Kathy first exhibited a specific, differentiated response to her mother she began desperately clinging to her caregiver and became increasingly intolerant of even brief separations. She also adopted her first transitional objects at this point: a bottle and a blanket. In keeping with her general laissez-faire policy of letting Kathy "have her way," Ms. L. did not begin toilet training until 30 months, and then only with the encouragement of her first therapist, Dr. G. Much to her surprise, Kathy trained in a matter of days. Up until this time Ms. L. had believed that her incorrigibly obstinate daughter could not possibly be influenced by her in this way.

Discussion

Based on what we know about pervasive developmental disorders and on our knowledge of adaptive and maladaptive development, could we have predicted Kathy's pathological outcome given the historical data at hand? While I believe we would be hard pressed to point to a single "damning" piece of evidence, there is clearly a constellation of potentially pathogenic factors which, retrospectively, put Kathy at high risk for psychiatric difficulties.

Throughout her pregnancy with Kathy, Ms. L. experienced a number of significant obstetrical and psychological problems. Some of these, like her depression, anxiety, and self-doubt were apparently stress-related or reactive to longstanding, unresolved developmental issues stemming from her own childhood and re-awakened by the impending childbirth. Spotting during the second trimester, which may have been stress related, has been shown by some (Campbell et al. 1978) to be the most frequently reported prenatal complication associated with early onset psychotic disorders. Although both smoking and alcohol misuse have been correlated to fetal distress syndromes and later clinical and subclinical neurological dysfunction, Ms. L. claimed to have discontinued the use of these substances by her second trimester. Kathy's delivery, full term and obstetrically uneventful, also provides few useful clues.

Developmentally, we know that Kathy was an irritable, temperamentally difficult infant. Though mother's reporting was inconsistent at times, one has the overall impression of a child who was not easily consoled when distressed, for whatever reason, and whose ability to maintain a balanced, relatively well-regulated inner state was extremely limited, even with the provision of adequate maternal intervention. At a time when most infants develop their first specific attachments, Kathy seemed unconnected to her mother and indifferent to her availability or unavailability. Until 24 months, Kathy did not differentiate her various caregivers— "one seemed as good as another"—then developed an inflexible attachment to her mother. Where earlier she had been unable to establish any affective bond with her caregiver, she was now unable to relinquish mother's attention for even a moment. Although there are indications that Kathy adopted several transitional objects, it would appear that these failed to provide the intermediate bridge between mother's actual presence and the internalization of the comforting maternal image.

Kathy's physical and maturational growth progressed more rapidly than her cognitive development. All early psychomotor milestones appear to have occurred within the normal range. Although she toilet-trained somewhat later than most, this apparently had more to do with mother's belief that she was incorrigible and could not be influenced by her efforts than with a specific maturational delay. In contrast, Kathy's language development faltered almost from the start; she acquired one or two words but made little progress beyond this.

Genetically, we know very little about Kathy's background. While there were suggestions of familial psychopathology in both the paternal and maternal lines, most of this was only hearsay and could not be solidly documented. We do know, however, that Kathy's older sister, Carol, exhibited certain learning problems in school and had undergone speech therapy. This is consistent with current research which suggests that learning and speech difficulties occur in around 25 percent of the families of psychotic children (Bartak et al. 1975, DeMyer 1979) representing a nonspecific hereditary factor which may, in some instances, given other constitutional and experiential deficiencies, manifest in a full pervasive developmental syndrome.

The best evidence we have for factors predisposing to early onset psychosis comes from Ms. L.'s recollection of the early mother–child interaction. Though it is unlikely that any of these "psychogenic" factors taken in isolation would account for a pervasive developmental disorder, when taken together with a probable "constitutional anlage" they are very likely to have had significant influence on both the course of the illness and its specific manifestations. We know from the history that Kathy was a temperamentally difficult infant. She did not respond easily to mother's efforts to console and in general seemed more occupied than most infants with inner tensions and distresses which exceeded her capacity for balanced regulation. We can speculate that at the point in development during which outward-directed attention normally undergoes its first differentiation in the establishment of a specific attachment relationship, Kathy remained absorbed in poorly modulated, internal somatic states and was invested only marginally in the world around her. The optimally responsive caregiver might have met Kathy's difficulties in maintaining internal regulation with a special sensitivity to potential sources of overstimulation, creating an environment of limited sensory input to which Kathy could have more easily adapted. A concerted investment in wooing this child's interest and attention may have been necessary in order to build a solid attachment.

At the time of Kathy's birth it is unlikely that Ms. L. had the capacity to mobilize fully her emotional resources around a constitutionally vulnerable infant. The developmental history tells us that she experienced an immediate animosity toward her daughter whose birth interferred with her plans to "better herself" and whose unusual demandingness depreciated her sense of maternal competence and esteem. Furthermore, this was the child who had taken her away from her own mother, the one human being who "understood," whose empathy made her feel vital and alive. Even the physical changes of pregnancy made Ms. L. feel unattractive and still more resentful. She harbored a wish to be purged of the child, but feared that the fetus, as through magically attuned to her malevolent thoughts, would destroy her from within and both would die in childbirth.

Ms. L. first responded to her infant by "turning away," denying, in effect, what she had created. In place of the wished-for son, about whom she would "not have to worry," whom she imagined would take care of his own needs (and perhaps hers as well), she delivered a little girl whose demands for gratification seemed limitless. Mother adapted to what had become a nearly prophetic situation by continuing in some sense to "turn away" from her infant throughout much of the first year. Kathy was cared for by a number of different caretakers and is not known to have established a specific attachment relationship with any one person in particular. If mother had made herself unavailable to Kathy she did so believing that it was her dauther's disaffection that had undermined the bond. The baby, she reasoned was punishing her.

As Kathy grew, so did her mother's mixed feelings of guilt and resentment. Ms. L. found herself unable to set limits for her daughter or help her structure her needs and impulses. By acceding to Kathy's tyrannical demands she would make up to her for the damage that she believed herself to have inflicted. In the end, mother could trust neither her own ability to influence Kathy nor Kathy's capacity to be influenced by her. She perceived both her daughter and herself as damaged and defective.

Maternal History

Ms. L. was the fourth of seven children in a poor, intact working class family. She was born and raised in Arkansas where the remainder of her family still resides. As discussed above in the developmental history, Ms. L.'s mother died in 1977 from the sequelae of a stroke. Her father and siblings are still alive and well.

Despite Ms. L.'s earlier emphasis on the impact of her mother's death, when asked about her own growing-up she talked spontaneously about her father with whom she had been in continuous conflict for as long as she could remember. Ms. L. recalled having wanted desperately to gain her father's approval, admiration, and attention but felt that she could never do anything right in his eyes. He criticized her endlessly yet gave her little opportunity to demonstrate her worthiness. Although she could not recall ever having been punished by her father, his incessant ridicule reverberated in her memory. Father was not as intolerant or overbearing with all his children, however. According to Ms. L., he preferred his sons and took little care to hide his favoritism. As if to accommodate this preference, Ms. L. recalled that for many years she adopted the habits and interests of her older brothers, always preferring to work in the fields, "doing the men's work," to working around the house with her mother and sisters.

Gender, however, was not the only issue. None of the other children, male or female, were depreciated and overlooked in quite the same way that Ms. L. perceived that she had been. The younger children were regarded as "cuter and brighter," the older children "were always ahead of me." Ms. L. was somehow lost in the middle. In one particularly poignant incident, Ms. L. and her younger sister switched sewing to see how father would respond to their work. As she had predicted, father praised her sister's work (which was really her own) but ridiculed the work he believed that she had done.

Ms. L.'s recollections of her mother were vague and idealized. Mother was portrayed as a hard working, if somewhat overbearing woman who "never spent much time with [her]." Nevertheless, Ms. L. always had the feeling that her mother understood her in a special way: "I don't know why, but I just felt she knew my mind. She was the only person I ever felt really understood me." At 17, Ms. L. met Mr. M. (Kathy and Carol's father) who was visiting relatives in Arkansas at the time. He was ten years older than Ms. L. who recalled having been very impressed by his worldly acumen and by the fact that he was from Chicago. Although Ms. L. did not have a good recollection of this period in her life, she did recall having dated Mr. M. only a few times before becoming pregnant. This was the first dating she had ever done. Again, there seemed to be some confusion surrounding conception, as though the connection between intercourse and pregnancy had come as a surprise to her.

By the time Ms. L. had discovered that she was pregnant, Mr. M. had returned to Chicago. Ms. L. made plans at this time with a friendly acquaintance (she had no close friends) to move out on her own and the two decided to travel to Chicago where the acquaintance had relatives with whom the two could stay. Ms. L. indicated that it was in the back of [her] mind to look up Mr. M. upon arriving in Chicago, though, as things turned out, it was more than two years before she "ran into him" once again. Initially, Ms. L. stayed with the older sister of her acquaintance, but found her own apartment and began working at a variety of different jobs after Carol was born.

Ms. L. spoke regretfully of her decision to leave home believing that if she had stayed with her mother, "everything would have worked out somehow." At this time, however, she was determined to leave Arkansas for good, vowing never to return "unless something happened." Ms. L. was not exactly sure what she meant by this but felt that her mother's stroke was just such an event. Her thinking here bordered on the magical, as though her secret wish that something "big" might happen, something that would allow her to return home, had in fact precipitated her mother's illness.

Ms. L. gave up working in 1975 so that she could spend more time taking care of Carol but managed in the meanwhile to finish high school through correspondence courses. Beyond this she stayed at home with her two children. At the point of initial evaluation, Ms. L. rarely went out without taking one or both of the children with her. She maintained no close friendships.

Dynamic Speculations

Pregnancy, childbirth, and parenting assumed a special significance for Ms. L. in the context of her own family background. From early childhood, she found herself in the unfortunate situation of being at home with a father who didn't admire her, for whom she had no worth, and a mother whose support only diminished her own sense of competence and esteem. At 17, she fell in love with a man ten years her senior; this renewed her sense of personal worth. In order to redeem herself fully, however, she needed to feel competent as a mother. Shortly after leaving home, Ms. L. became pregnant. With the help of her mother she raised a healthy child. As long as she had her mother to refuel her sense of competence she was capable and resourceful.

Three years later, Ms. L. became pregnant again. This time, her mother fell seriously ill and died. Ms. L. experienced this loss as a death within herself, or, more specifically, the death of a part of herself. With Kathy she would have shown her mother that she could raise a child on her own and then it was too late. Mother's death represented both the loss of a valued object and the loss of that part of herself that could have been maternally resourceful. In her mother's absence she felt damaged and incomplete; a "gap" had been created within her.

It is known from the history that the first 18 to 24 months of Kathy's life were remembered by Ms. L. as simply a "blank." Mother's investment in the child was marginal while Kathy, for her part, seemed poorly connected and unresponsive. From the beginning, we see a complimentarity between mother's emotional distance and a child who came into the world difficult to console and highly temperamental.

Kathy was perceived by mother as a representation of that part of herself that was deficient (i.e., her "gap") but the one responsible for this deficiency in the first place. "Were it not for Kathy," she seemed to be saying "I could have saved my mother. Without my mother I have nothing to give. My child is responsible for my mother's death, my mother's death is responsible for my child's illness. Because of my mother's not being here I am empty. I cannot raise my child without her."

The 'gap' Ms. L. experienced during Kathy's infancy was a gap that she transmitted to her daughter. For Kathy this transmission represented a missed opportunity to experience mother's consistent emotional presence and to utilize this as a base from which to begin the process of self-other differentiation. In the place of normal bonding and attachment, mother fused with Kathy. Where the two connected there was not true empathy but total identification and merger, a complete loss of distance and boundary.

Behavioral Observations: Pre-Treatment Diagnostic Interview with Kathy M.

Kathy first impressed me as a delightfully pretty little girl, physically robust and surprisingly poised for a child who had been described as totally unmanageable by her mother. Neither did she seem "woefully, pathetically sad" as Dr. G. has described her during her first clinic visit a year earlier. From her chair in the reception area she gazed blithely about the room singing quietly to herself in a stream of cheerful babble, legs swinging rhythmically beneath her. It was not until her mother rose to speak with me that Kathy showed signs of alarm. Bolting from her chair she lodged herself between mother and myself and whined in speechless protest until we all left together for the office.

Once securely within the office, Kathy occupied herself with a toy phone and had no apparent difficulty relinquishing mother's full attention. She used the toy appropriately for the most part (as a toy phone) but mother insisted that she "say hello . . . can I talk to Carol" which was clearly beyond her ability. Feeling that Kathy was ignoring or defying her by refusing to speak, mother attempted to take the phone away. At first, Kathy pulled back furiously, but every so often her anger turned abruptly into pleasure. Mother too seemed to vacillate between rage and the most solicitous affection. One moment she was scolding Kathy, hugging and kissing her the next. To an outside observer, it was nearly impossible to gauge the tenor of the interaction, so confused were these communications.

While Kathy seemed content to play by herself with mother and I looking on or following, she was intolerant of any activity that pointed up her relative weaknesses or incompetence. Mother and Kathy spent, for example, a part of the session drawing pictures together. Mother produced a flower, Kathy a page full of scribbles. Upon seeing her mother's rendering, Kathy became furious and insisted on coloring over the image until it was entirely unrecognizable.

Midway through the interview, I asked Ms. L. to leave the room so that Kathy and I could play alone for a few minutes. Kathy showed some slight distress but allowed mother to leave without her. (This was the first and last time Kathy would allow this kind of abrupt separation to occur for the next six months.) Again, Kathy busied herself with the phone though in mother's absence her use of this item was markedly less proficient. After babbling for a few moments she began chewing on the receiver and absently spinning the wheels on the toy's base.

Being in a room with Kathy was often like being with no one at all or being no one at all. She had a way of shutting one out that was nearly impenetrable. When she did make contact, it was usually to use me as a tool or convenience, something useful for opening doors or reaching toys that had fallen behind the desk. In either case, only my hand, (chosen for its remarkable grasping characteristics) was of interest to her, the rest of my person was ignored. Kathy's gaze often fixed on me but seemed to focus at a point somewhere in the distance. Unless I intervened in such a way as to limit or contain her behavior, she seemed unaffected by my physical proximity or contact. When taken into my lap, for example, she continued to play obliviously and without interruption, quite as if nothing had happened. When her activity was restrained in any way, she protested, often violently, but in the end usually acceded to the imposed limitation. On several occasions she responded to frustration by withdrawing herself from the interaction entirely, rocking listlessly or twiddling her ear.

Kathy's withdrawal seldom took her far, however, and sometimes seemed to make her even more uneasy than had the frustrating interaction that led to the flight in the first place. Every so often, as the rocking or twiddling intensified it was necessary for her to stop for a moment as if to reorient herself. With an odd stereotyped motion she lifted a hand to within a few inches of her face and stared fixedly at it for several moments. It was not entirely clear, however, whether she was using this behavior to reaffirm to herself that she was in fact "still there" despite her momentary lapse or as a shield to further limit the influx of stimulation.

When mother returned to the office (she had stationed herself just outside the door) Kathy acknowledged her presence with a glance but seemed otherwise unaffected by the reunion. If anything, mother appeared the more shaken of the two.

As Ms. L. and Kathy rose to leave, Kathy looked back and forth from mother to me as if noting, for the first time, that there was a distinct difference between us. Ms. L. instructed her to say "bye bye" which she dutifully repeated (this was the first intelligible word she had spoken that day). Then mother and daughter moved toward the door. Suddenly, Kathy turned around, extended her hand to me and took my fingers as if expecting me to follow.

Pre-Treatment Diagnostic Interview with Ms. L.

Ms. L. is a tall, attractive 26-year-old woman. Her manner of dress showed considerable attention to fashion and added to an impression of poise and sophistication. If Ms. L.'s outward appearance was confident and self-assured, however, her personal manner reflected painful self-doubt, awkwardness and trepidation. One might, at first, have considered Ms. L. a shy individual, though once she began to speak freely, her thoughts seemed to race ahead of her as if she were opening up to another person for the first time in a long while. Occasionally, she seemed to lose track of herself or to move off in several different directions without completing a single thought. When describing situations that were painful or affect-laden it was particularly difficult for her to compose herself; her thinking became disconnected and moderately disorganized. When making a point that in any way implied hostility, assertiveness or disagreement Ms. L. punctuated her statements with anxious laughter as if to diminish the impact of her words. The net effect, however, was strikingly incongruous; a woman obviously angry or upset, forcing a smile or giggling joylessly over experiences or impressions that were anything but humorous for her. One got little sense of genuine pleasure from these expressions which, if anything, only added to the impression of an extremely beleaguered and unhappy woman.

Ms. L. used words accurately and was reasonably fluent in getting across her ideas even when this involved a fair degree of abstraction. Despite a tendency toward disorganization around emotionally evocative subjects, she rarely seemed disoriented or completely confused. If she was difficult to understand at times, this had more to do with poor articulation than with conceptual difficulties. She had the habit of speaking with a heavy nasal inflection and imprecise enunciation and her voice often trailed off before she had completed a sentence, as if it were not important for her to be heard. This effect may have been partially under her control, however, as my obvious straining to understand seemed to induce her to sharpen her diction.

Throughout this first interview, Ms. L. appeared tense and somewhat frightened. She kept her coat on for the duration of the hour and sat at the edge of her chair as if poised to bolt from the office in the event that the interchange suddenly became unbearable. Arms crossed rigidly, each hand grasping the opposite side of her chest, she gave the impression of a woman literally trying to hold herself together in face of what must have been an extremely unsettling experience for her.

Ms. L. freely admitted that her return with Kathy to the child psychiatric clinic was born out of discouragement with a deteriorating situation. The child was becoming increasingly unmanageable at home. Most frustrating, however, was her belief that despite Kathy's apparent incognizance, she really understood much of what was said to her and that her defiance and misbehavior were willfully and pointedly malevolent. She had become mother's persecutor.

At several points during the interview it seemed as if Ms. L.'s attribution of meaning and motivation to her daughter's behaviors became confused with some of her own intentions. This was most apparent in her perception of Kathy's defiance but was suggested by certain incongruous or unsubstantiated impressions of other persons as well. In each of the interpersonal relationships described by Ms. L. there was a certain fluidity of boundary and identity. Characterizations were often confused or organized according to "split" or overly simplistic characteristics: a mother who seemed magically and omnisciently to "know [her] mind," whose death was experienced as "a part of myself dying." A father who showed her no understanding whatsoever and who seemed insensitive to her needs for admiration and affection. One daughter who, "like a little sister," looked after her and helped her make decisions, another daughter whose relentless provocations punished her for secret wishes and resentments. Even Ms. L.'s concerns for Kathy might have applied equally to herself: "She'll grow up and no one will understand her . . . If I send her to school the teacher's won't know what she means the way I do . . . I'm afraid that if I leave her maybe she'll pee on herself and lose control and won't be able to talk at all anymore." At times it seemed that Kathy had become a metaphor for her mother. Perhaps, as she worried over her daughter's well being, Ms. L. was also "asking" me whether I would understand her (Ms. L.) or allow her to lose control.

In summary, Ms. L. impressed me as a woman who, though of average intelligence, was experiencing a number of difficulties communicating her thoughts and feelings and making herself understood. Particularly in situations where her emotions were stirred (an occurrence which she seemed to go to great lengths to avoid), she had a tendency to become disorganized, though this rarely went as far as to compromise her basic orientation and reality sense. She seemed quite capable of evaluating situations that did not touch her personally, but had a tendency in interpersonal situations to confuse identities and misattribute (project) certain of her own motives and intentions to other persons. This had no doubt limited her capacity to respond empathically in the parenting situation and was likely to have made it difficult for her to manage other mature emotional relationships as well. By her own admission, Ms. L. was an extremely lonely and isolated young woman.

Discussion

It has been said by some that the course of an entire psychotherapy is contained within the first hour of contact; a recapitulation of the whole in the part. Unfortunately, from an operational standpoint, we as psychotherapists generally do much better accounting for our patients' first communications retrospectively with the work of an entire psychotherapy behind us than we do in predicting, prospectively, the unfolding of an entire treatment from the first brief encounter. While I cannot, in good faith, claim to have distilled the essence of a fully developed psychotherapy from the single pretreatment interviews with Kathy and Ms. L., a number of important themes, issues, and impressions, some of which would appear repeatedly during the course of the treatment, were revealed for the first time during these initial meetings.

Kathy began her first session by "demonstrating" what was perhaps the defining characteristic of her illness: the inability to separate from the symbiotic, maternal object. As mother rose to leave the reception room, Kathy, who had been sitting complacently at her side, rose in furious protest, throwing herself between mother and I. No one would leave without her, Kathy seemed to be telling us, unless of course she went first. Once in the office, Kathy began by playing with the telephone. I told her that this was not acceptable and offered a substitute, a toy phone, in which she took an immediate interest. Kathy had responded flexibily to an imposed limitation by substituting a pretend object for a real one. This was no small accomplishment for a little girl with serious deficits in her capacity for impulse control, symbolization and delay of gratification.

With mother it was a different story, however; Kathy would make no concessions. A struggle over the toy phone ensued, a very puzzling struggle. Furiously, Kathy tore at mother's face and clothes. At first, mother attempted to contain the child's aggression but after a few moments the anger disappeared from her face. Pulling Kathy close to her body she appeared almost to envelope her. The two lay embracing each other on the floor, Kathy pulling so tightly that it seemed as though she were trying to meld herself into mother who by this time was again showing signs of discomfort. Giggling rapturously, the child tore with renewed force at mother's face. Mother smiled and caressed as she pushed her angry daughter away. The interaction had become an indecipherable amalgam of irreconcilable feelings and incongruous expressions. To watch mother and child interact, the tyranny of Kathy's control, mother's submission and ultimately, the physical union of the dyad, one felt a sense of participation in something oddly erotic, but only vaguely maternal.

Whatever activity mother and child engaged in, Kathy carefully maintained the illusion of parity. Any independent initiative on mother's part was intolerable unless it could be construed as an extension of her (Kathy's) own willfulness. When mother and daughter drew pictures together, there was at first an unusual tranquility between them until mother's scribbling took on the recognizable form of a flower. This was something Kathy could not do and it reminded her of her weakness and incompetence. In a fury she scribbled over mother's drawing until no trace of the image remained.

Kathy's sense of causality was based on the illusion (or delusion) of omnipotence, of complete control over the events going on around her, and of a limitless capacity for effecting desired outcomes. Maintaining this illusion, however, required a willing accomplice. Mother was obviously capable of doing things that her daughter was not, yet she allowed Kathy to obliterate any evidence of this. When Kathy defaced mother's drawing, the illusion of parity was restored. Mother had helped Kathy to deny that the two of them were separate human beings with separate and independent abilities.

Ironically, Kathy's "allowing" mother to leave the room during this session was the only time the two would accomplish temporary separation for many months to come. It was as though Kathy was letting everyone know what might be possible, where she was able, if not yet willing, to go developmentally. Once mother had left, Kathy resumed babbling playfully into the toy phone quite as if nothing had happened (although the quality of her play seemed to deteriorate somewhat in mother's absence) and no one were with her. That a child whose play demonstrated so poignantly the struggle to establish contact was so completely isolated from the person still in her midst, was, again, oddly incongruous. I was made to feel virtually quarantined or at best, like a convenient tool. Kathy was not as much indifferent as oblivious to my presence. This, too, was instructive, however. Isolated and alone, the I was given the opportunity to experience something of what my young patient must have herself experienced much of the time.

Kathy's confused behavior, though troubling for mother, gave some indication of what might be possible psychotherapeutically. She could stand on her own or she could cling tyrannically. She could tolerate other's independent initiatives or she could destroy every evidence of individual difference. She could unhesitatingly violate personal boundaries or she could make one feel isolated and alone. That Kathy had a will of her own and could operate as an independent entity seemed clear. However arbitrary its expression, her willfulness indicated that at least the foundations for autonomous functioning had been established, that she was indeed a primitive, but potentially viable self.

Not unlike Kathy, Ms. L. impressed me as a person struggling to establish contact and make herself understood. A relatively articulate woman (when she focused on communicating clearly and was not anxious or emotionally stressed), she had the capacity to express herself in ways that Kathy could not. Developmentally, mother and child stood worlds apart. It seemed at times, however, that Ms. L. worked at cross-purposes with herself, that certain of her personal and interpersonal resources were pitted against each other in such a way as to diminish the impact of her presence and obscure the meaning of her communications.

Like Kathy, Ms. L. conveyed a sense of the incongruous. Though she struggled to make herself understood, everything about her seemed to obfuscate meaning. For example, Ms. L. obviously took great pains to make herself physically and cosmetically attractive if not provocative, yet her manner of relating was painfully awkward and reticent. She seemed to draw one in and push one away at the same time (recall her interaction with Kathy). If it was important for Ms. L. to make herself heard and felt, this was not apparent from her style of communication either. As she spoke, her words seemed to race ahead of her and run into each another. Sentences dropped off before completion as if it were not important for her to finish her thought. Perhaps she felt that no one would hear her out in any event. As we know from the history, this had been her experience in the past.

Finally, I had the distinct impression in talking with Ms. L. and watching her play with her daughter that she was not perceiving clearly the persons with whom she was interacting. Toward Kathy, she pitched herself at a level, developmentally, to which her daughter could not possibly have responded. Although she believed that she understood Kathy in a way that no one else could, her

---

Kathy M.

Axis I: 299.90 Childhood Onset Pervasive Developmental Disorder.
Axis II: V79.09 No. Diagnosis on Axis II.
Axis III: Physical Disorders: None.
Axis IV: Severity of Psychosocial Stressors: (5) Severe.
Axis V: Highest Level of Adaptive Functioning Past Year: (7) Grossly Impaired.

Ms. Barbara L.

Axis I: 300.40 Dysthymic Disorder
Axis II: 301.22 Schizotypal Personality Disorder
Axis III: Physical Disorders: None.
Axis IV: Severity of Psychosocial Stressors: (5) Severe.
Axis V: Highest Level of Adaptive Functioning Past Year: (5) Poor.

Figure 1. Diagnostic Impressions (*DSM III*) of Kathy M. and her mother, Barbara L.

impressions and interpretations often seemed more reflective of her own intentions than the child's. Thus, her responding was inappropriate and oddly dyssynchronous. Despite my efforts to understand, I was also misperceived by Ms. L. as someone who could never really know what she was experiencing and who was unlikely to be interested in her, independent of her child, in any event. Once again, her expectations seemed inconsistent with what had, in fact, been offered.

If this first interview was any indication of what lay ahead, psychotherapy with Ms. L. was likely to focus upon a style of communicating, coping, and relating that seemed to insure the inevitability of isolation and aloneness. If she was to make herself understood, she would first need to examine the ways in which her own confused interpersonal perceptions and self-experience made her difficult to reach, where these impressions came from, and what was to be gained by maintaining them. Therapeutic exploration would help Ms. L. to see herself as an active agent in orchestrating the kinds of relationships in which it was difficult for her to create an impact on others. Genetic reconstructions would connect current patterns of relating to developmental precedents. However, only the experience of empathic understanding would bring to life for Ms. L. the possibility of being "known" and the experience of connectedness that comes with feeling oneself understood by other persons. The "fact" of the treatment relationship, the alliance between patient and therapist, would, in all likelihood, be every bit as important as the "process" of treatment itself.

Chapter Nineteen

Treatment Plan and
Initial Treatment Phases

For both Kathy and Ms. L., psychological growth must begin with separation. Before either can move ahead, both must begin to look at who they are and what they carry within themselves as separate human beings. For Kathy, this process will begin with a loss of self experienced as limitlessly powerful and a loss of other experienced as a part of the self. She must begin to see that she is a little girl with limited powers who can use and rely upon those around her without commanding complete control. First, however, she must trust. This will develop over time with the building in of permanence, sameness and predictability.

For Ms. L. the problem is twofold: she must see that she is neither as powerful nor as weak as she believes, that her wishes can neither kill nor bring back to life, and finally, that she need not be limited and incompetent in order to keep a fantasy alive. She will mourn the death of her mother. Perhaps most importantly, Ms. L. must realize that she is not as different from other people as she thinks and that she need not isolate herself in order to preserve a sense of separateness and identity.

Specific treatment goals for Kathy and Ms. L. are the same at many points. For Kathy the treatment process will provide corrective therapeutic relationships (interactive as well as individual) in which she can work out of her symbiotic fusion with mother. She must develop the capacities for self regulation with less reliance on perseverative, ritualized activities and excessive self-stimulation and for a more adaptive channeling, focusing and containing of impulses. Finally, together with her mother she must negotiate a sustained empathic, mutually responsive and gratifying parent-child interaction.

It is anticipated that through play and well tuned therapeutic interaction Kathy will derive an enhanced understanding of who she is as a person apart from her mother and what she can do on her own. Over time, she will acquire fantasies and ideas that are her own and that she needn't share with mother. She will develop her own internalized structures, her own conflicts, and her own distortions. She will learn that she is truly her own entity.

Treatment will move at a pace of which Kathy is capable. She will demonstrate what she can do; I will follow her empathically and help her to elaborate where appropriate. As Kathy experiences herself as accessible and understood, she will feel more substantial, that she is a self with real coherence and continuity across time and place. With the awareness of being separate she will begin to look at who she is in terms of her potentials and limitations.

Again, for Ms. L., specific treatment goals will be similar and at many points symmetrical to those set forth for her daughter. By exploring her own inner resources within the therapeutic process, she will derive an enhanced understanding of personal identity and greater assurance of her competence and capability as an autonomous human being. By engaging in a relationship in which fantasy and reality are differentiated clearly for her, she will develop a heightened capacity for reality testing and will no longer need to isolate herself as a means of maintaining a sense of boundary and separateness. Finally, and most importantly, as Ms. L. experiences herself as accessible and "knowable" from the point of view of another person, she, too, will feel more substantial and coherent, that she is not really so different from other people, and that she need not be alone.

Treatment Summary: The Parent–Child Interaction

Kathy was seen in treatment by me from 3 March 1981 through 10 June 1982. During this 15-month period she attended a total of 74 sessions: 21 in interaction work with her mother and 53 by herself; once she was able to separate from mother. Until June 1981, Kathy and her mother were seen together on a once-per-week basis. From that point on, Kathy was seen twice-a-week, individually. Throughout the treatment process, Ms. L. also had her own weekly, individual therapy sessions. Of 56 scheduled appointments, she kept 34.

The initial phase of Kathy's treatment, comprised of 21 sessions, was, by necessity, carried out conjointly (interactively) with mother and child. The primary goal here was separation. This was reflected in both the quality of interaction among mother, child, and therapist, and thematically in the content of Kathy's play. We will begin with a session in the early weeks of treatment.

After hurriedly pushing the door shut behind her, Kathy dumped an array of Tinkertoys and blocks on the floor around her—before settling in, she needed to be sure that all commerce in and out of the room had ended. She built while mother and I watched. Kathy allowed slavish imitation of her play but was intolerant of variations or independent activity. She was equally insistent upon working by herself. As she returned each individual piece to the container meticulously, mother teasingly tossed a stick into the can. Kathy spilled out the contents furiously and began once again. I followed the interchange, empathized with mother's hurt at exclusion and Kathy's anger at having been intruded upon but continued at that point to comply with the "rules" which Kathy had established. Kathy was "violated" by mother in this way two or three times more, in each instance becoming progressively angrier. Finally, she was out of control, slashing and biting at mother who deflected her blows, blandly ordered her to stop, but smiled incongruously all the while. Kathy stepped up on mother's leg and pulled herself tightly against her then alternately tore at her blouse, pulled at her hair, and clutched at her breast for comfort. One moment she was screaming through a flood of tears, the next moment laughing rapturously. Mother scolded, giggled nervously, and protected herself.

The interchange between Kathy and Ms. L. was garbled, dissynchronous, and poorly differentiated. I intervened by attempting to differentiate the various strains of contradictory affect and behavior while acting as a buffer between the two. In the end, Kathy calmed, backed away and reconstituted around a simple, repetitious activity that captured beautifully the source of both her terror and her rapture. Removing a pen from my pocket, she alternately turned the cap, pulled the pen apart, then reassembled it once again. I followed: "things that come apart go back together again." This was Kathy's earliest demonstration of symbolic play and a good sign that she had at least a rudimentary capacity for mental representation, a capacity that might ultimately form the basis for organized thought and language.

In the weeks that followed, themes of separation and reunion were gradually elaborated in both the mother–child interaction and in Kathy's isolated play. Mother continued, however, to taunt

Kathy by imposing upon her inflexible regimens with subtle variations that seemed almost calculated to send the child flying into a rage. With a knowing smile, she moved this piece or that ever so slightly until Kathy finally took notice. Suddenly, as if an explosion had been triggered, toys and people alike flew across the room.

Kathy's intolerance of mother's impositions was born, we believed, out of the fear of reengulfment in a symbiotic entanglement and the loss of whatever fragmentary vestiges of self had been maintained through the illusion of complete omnipotent control. Once enraged, her ability to organize and regulate her feelings and behavior deteriorated still further. What control and articulation she had been able to sustain through an unyielding insistence on sameness were lost. The same child who one moment played carelessly, constructively and was almost oblivious of the other persons in the room, clung frantically the next moment to her mother's breast, in an odd mosaic of pulling closer and pushing away. Both mother and child rolled around on the floor fighting, biting, crying, kissing and smiling. While there was tremendous force in these interactions, there was very rarely any real differentiation of feelings, just rapid oscillations of unbridled aggression and passive erotic hanging on.

Intervention began with my interposing myself between mother and child, setting limits and sifting through the morass of contradictory feelings expressed in the confused interaction. This was a first step toward differentiation. What each seemed to be experiencing was followed, reflected, and interpreted for each patient. What was explained or interpreted to mother was then reexplained and reinterpreted for Kathy. Every intervention was framed in terms of the "double alliance" in order to emphasize the separateness of mother and child and the developmental differences between the two.

Gradually, Kathy's play became more flexible, creative and well-differentiated. From time to time she even allowed mother and me to play independently, off to the side, without demanding that we mimic or imitate her activity. It was also about this time (after the fifth session) that Kathy began to elaborate on her first rudimentary symbolizations of separation and reunion. For example, taking a small blue block and a larger red one, she would rub the two together, slowly at first, then more rapidly. Stopping suddenly she would begin a careful inspection of each. Did the one block rub off on the other? Could the little blue block rub the big red block without the big one coming off on the little one? Could the big one be close to the little one without the little one becoming the big one and vice versa? The theme was worked over and over again.

With each reflecting back, the therapist brought the symbol closer to its referent: can a little girl remain herself yet be close to her mother who is so big and can do so many things?

From week to week a sense of continuity developed, and over time, familiarity and permanence. Games were repeated, toys remembered, special objects hidden and retrieved. By the third month of treatment, however, we began to think about splitting up the hour into two individual sessions: Kathy's followed by her mother's. While the work of self-other differentiation had gotten off to a good start in the interaction sessions, it was felt that now both Kathy and Ms. L. must pull out of the fused relationship. Some progress had been made; Kathy was now willing, for example, to relinquish some of her control over mother and did not cling quite so insistently. In stressful moments however, all boundaries seemed to dissolve. Mother and child reverted to the odd, poorly differentiated entanglements of anger and seductiveness that had characterized their earlier interactions.

Over the course of the next ten sessions (May 1981–August 1981) a variety of strategies, each incorporating a different transitional phase from joint to independent sessions, were tried without success. Kathy was walked to the office by her mother, by me, by her mother and me, and so on in every possible combination. Later, mother attempted to leave the room after a 15 minute preliminary interaction session. Kathy stuck all the more tenaciously to her side, however, and each became increasingly infuriated with the other.

Despite Kathy's overt resistance to separation there were other indications suggesting a gradual movement away from mother. For instance, before her sessions began, she would often run out of the waiting room alone to play with her sister or watch the elevator mechanism. During sessions, she seemed to gravitate more than in the past towards me, standing on my foot or sitting in my lap while she played. What remained of her clinging behavior seemed largely oppositional in nature, the residue of a prolonged domination over mother which she was only gradually willing to relinquish. A harrowing struggle was anticipated in getting Kathy to enter my office without mother at her side, but it was felt that she could now tolerate this brief separation and recover on her own from any momentary setbacks. A foundation of trust built on sameness, predictability, and permanence had been built. Now mother had to go.

On 10 July 1981, both Kathy and her mother were prepared for Kathy's first individual session. I led Kathy into the office, first by the hand, then kicking and screaming in both arms. Once in the office, she trampled wrathfully around the room, cried pitiously, and occasionally struck out at me, but she did so with clear, unambiguous anger. Her signals were assertive and unmistakably forthright and she was not as hopelessly disorganized as in the past when the rigid order of things had been interrupted. Though she cried, she was reachable, and her anger was not paralyzing. I intervened by helping Kathy to calm herself so that she could think about what she was feeling and by identifying and differentiating subtle changes in her tenor and temperament: "Kathy you're angry (sad-mad-lonely) right now. You're angry because you can't be without your mommy and she's left you." Finally something caught her attention and a memory seemed to flicker. Kathy looked across the room, saw the Tinkertoys she had thrown in her anger, and began to pick them up one at a time. Then my help was accepted without protest.

The second phase of treatment, comprised of 23 sessions, began with Kathy's first individual session. Now that she had separated, we wondered what she could do on her own and more specifically when she would begin to talk. Arrangements were under way at this time for her to begin school at a hospital-based child development center. This was a behaviorally oriented program in which she would work on, among other things, the cognitive component of language development. In her individual treatment we had tried to help her to explore her own inclinations and to structure and organize her experiences in a way that reflected things going on within her, "working from the inside out." The day school program in which Kathy was enrolled approached the problem somewhat from the opposite direction. Here, she would be provided with a carefully regulated structure (a highly prescriptive classroom situation) within which she would have to adapt and around which she would have to organize herself. Her behavior in this setting would be evaluated according to certain predetermined performance criteria. This was "working from the outside in." It was our belief that in order for Kathy to adapt herself to the widest possible range of situations she would need the flexibility to adjust to both types of situations: those in which structure was created from "within" on the basis of her own inner resources and directives and those in which structure was imposed prescriptively from "without."

Kathy adjusted to her newly instituted individual sessions more quickly than any of us who had worked with her had anticipated. Before the second session there were a few moments of sorrowful protest at mother's leavetaking, a brief skirmish in the hall, but then of her own volition she moved into the office and began to play contentedly. Despite mother's absence the process during the hour (how Kathy played and what Kathy played, themes and patterns of interaction) remained remarkably unchanged. She played much as she had with her mother, but now mother's role was transferred to the therapist. When she built with blocks or Tinkertoys, for example, she did so from my lap. When she drew, she stood with both feet anchored on my foot. In each instance she seemed almost to meld herself with me much as she had with her mother.

Kathy adapted nicely to the modified therapeutic situation. In contrast, I experienced my own role as "mother substitute" with a vague sense of discomfort and apprehension. Kathy had moved in too quickly and too closely. Without a trace of hesitation she moved back and forth across that elusive perimeter of personal space that one seldom notices except when it is violated. My first inclination was to pull away, but then I considered that this might indicate to her my anxiety or, worse yet, my disaffection. Thus instead of distancing myself, I pulled in closer. Suddenly, I realized what was happening. Not only was I being cast in mother's role, but I was playing the part as well—pulling away, pushing closer, no less ambivalently than the original. Having made this connection for myself, I tried to interpret it for Kathy as well: "You like to be close to me. . . . You like to be close to your mother, too. It felt good when you were little. It made you feel like you could do anything you wanted to. . . . You were a baby then but now you are bigger. . . . If you stay in my lap you won't be able to play like a little girl." When I felt that Kathy was ready to progress, more developmentally appropriate forms of play and self-expression were introduced though in each instance she was encouraged to explore the various possibilities for herself.

Eventually Kathy was able to "give up the lap" as she discovered other means of remaining connected to me without actually maintaining physical contact. A simple game of catch in which a ball was rolled back and forth between us captured this new possibility poignantly. Genuine exchange as a mode of interaction allowed both of us to maintain contact while respecting each other's separateness and boundaries. Gradually we could begin to communicate with one another in terms of "you and I" or "yours and mine" (symbolically that is; pronoun use was still considerably beyond Kathy's limited linguistic capabilities) instead of a hopelessly confused "we" and "ours." This subtle but important distinction was stressed in every interaction. Kathy was no longer allowed, for example, to grab at my clothing or belongings as if these were just another part or extension of her own personal domain. Instead, she was given objects that were her own and which she could use as she pleased: "Kathy, that is mine. It belongs to me but here, I'll give you one that will be yours. . . . It belongs to you."

The first seven months of treatment had shown considerable progress. Kathy was now an individual patient in the fullest sense with all that this implied in terms of developmental progress. Still, things did not always go forward smoothly. Kathy continued to have difficulty containing, modifying and modulating her feelings, particularly where anger was concerned. When she became upset, for example, and began to throw objects around the room, it was still necessary for me to hold her hands, usually while talking to her about feelings that "you just couldn't keep inside."

During one session (19 October 1981) Kathy walked into the office, went for her toybox, and dumped the Tinkertoys on the floor. She then sat down in the pile and began to stir up the pieces. I said, "Kathy you are mixing everything up today . . . everything is mixed up." After a few moments, she stopped and began to rock herself. For a while she was quiet but obviously agitated about something. I continued, "Kathy, there's something going on inside of you today. I don't know what it is but rocking seems to help you to get it out." Perhaps it did, but not sufficiently; once again she began to throw Tinkertoys across the room. I responded, "Kathy, you're very excited and now you have to throw to get it out." On the second throw I stopped her, adding: "I think you can do better than that with your excitement. . . . I'm not going to let you throw." This was to let Kathy know that she had it within herself to hold back and contain her feelings and that there were other more effective and developmentally appropriate ways of letting me know what she was experiencing.

Most workers in the field seem to agree that helping the psychotic child establish capacities for delay and detour of impulses is a fundamental treatment goal. Conceptually, this makes a great deal of sense; indeed, one could argue that "delay of discharge" is the "motor" of psychological development and a peculiarly human capability. What, however, does the development of "ego control" look like from a practical, clinical standpoint? From what does it develop? In Kathy's case, the capacity for regulating impulses first began to appear as a brief moment of hesitation before she abandoned herself to diffuse, often explosive outbursts of anger or excitement. During one session, for example, she began the hour by walking into the office and immediately dumping an ashtray on the floor. Again, I had to restrain her before she smeared the cigarette butts and wads of chewing gum into the carpeting. Undaunted, however, she grabbed a can of crayons and deposited its contents on the floor, then raised a handful into the air and readied herself to throw once again. Normally, in one fluid motion the entire fistful would have been strewn across the room. This time, however, Kathy paused at the peak of her backswing. Poised to throw, she hesitated for a moment and looked over at me, as if she were considering whether to complete the motion. Finally, she let go, but her release was restrained and without force as if something were holding her back. I responded by trying to organize and identify for her what had happened: "You tried to hold back. You were thinking about it. Then you threw, but just a little. There's still a lot of excitement in you today."

Gradually, the affect behind Kathy's diffuse outbursts was channeled into her play where it could be focused and articulated symbolically. Following one episode of wild, angry throwing, she procurred a favorite doll which she alternately kissed and bit. What had begun as an unintelligible tantrum could now be followed and interpreted: "Sometimes Kathy, you kiss the doll and sometimes you bite it. Sometimes you love the doll, sometimes you hate it."

Mid-Treatment Summary (November 1981, Rx Review)

Kathy is beginning at last to move ahead on her own. Interpersonally her interactions are less driven, tyrannical and stereotyped. She can afford to lose herself or those around her momentarily as she becomes absorbed in her own activity. Her play is now better-organized and shows the beginnings of coherent theme and symbolization. This indicates that Kathy can use play as a means of attaining active mastery over conflict or trauma, for practicing new skills, or simply for the pleasure that comes with exercising newly discovered abilities and potentials. Most importantly, it represents the beginning of a capacity for delay and, ultimately, the ability to think in symbolic terms.

Still, there are setbacks; the old is never far from the new. As if to remind both of us of just where she is coming from, Kathy now begins her sessions by heaving the contents of a Tinkertoy can across the room. With this accomplished, she picks up each piece carefully, puts it aways, seals up the contents of the can, and settles in with a favorite doll. Meticulously, she brushes, braids, and feeds the doll, having assumed the apparent identity of the mother. Depending on her mood, she can play quietly by herself while I look on or engage in a lively interactional game of patticake. New words appear here and there.

At times, growth is painful for Kathy. There are those moments when she stops whatever it is she's doing, looks around her as if seeing for the first time where she is and with whom, then begins to cry softly. This is not the diffuse banshee-like wailing of a year ago, however. It is the despair of a four-year-old girl coming to the awareness that she is a self, that she can only be herself and that there are limits to what she can do by herself.

Chapter Twenty

The Third and Fourth Phases of Treatment

By her eighth month in treatment, Kathy had completed the transition from shared interaction sessions with her mother and me to individual hours of her own. This created an unprecedented situation different in many ways from anything in her experience and involving altogether different modes of adaptation and adjustment. How did Kathy respond? In one sense, she responded as she had always responded in the only other dyadic relationship she had ever known, that shared with her mother. Finding herself amid the unfamilar and unexpected, she created a situation that was knowable and coherent in terms of her past experiences. This was the transference relationship, the revitalization of the past in the present. Symbolically in her play and interactionally in the therapeutic process, Kathy reenacted with me aspects of the early, ongoing developmental environment that continued to influence her perception and organization of current experiences. Having shown me during the first phase of treatment what had happened as a result of these early experiences, Kathy would now show me how it had happened.

For many weeks following her separation from mother in the treatment hour, Kathy began her sessions very deeply absorbed in play with a doll (a little black girl) that I gave to her for her birthday. The content of this play was nearly always the same. Kathy began by combing or brushing the doll's hair thoroughly, then braiding it (like her own hair) or setting it with a rubber band. Both her concentration at the task and the care that she took were exceptional for a child who in most instances showed only the most fleeting investment and attention. Intermittently, however, she would pause, put down the brush and begin shooting the doll with a toy gun. On other occasions the play took a slightly different form though with a similar theme and a comparable intensity of interest. To begin, Kathy gently fed the doll from a bottle, but after a few moments began forcing the bottle into its mouth until its face collapsed under the pressure. In either case, the game usually ended with Kathy abandoning the doll, throwing it away, then standing up at the door and signalling me to let her out of the room.

At first, I simply followed Kathy's behavior: "Kathy you're playing very hard. You're taking very good care of the baby. . . . You're making her very pretty. . . . You're feeding her." Occasionally, a connection was drawn between mothers taking good care of their children and Kathy's mother taking good care of her: "Kathy, you're combing the doll's hair like mommy combs your hair" or "You're feeding the doll like mommy fed you when you were a baby." The oscillations between tender nurturance and destructive-sadistic assaultiveness were somewhat more baffling. Again, to begin with, I simply followed the behavior: "Kathy, you were taking such good care of the baby, now you are hurting her"; or identified what seemed to be the two opposite extremes of affect: "Kathy, sometimes you love the baby, sometimes you hate her."

The first real clue to the meaning of this play came not from direct observation of the child but from feelings stirred up within me as a participant in the dramatization. As Kathy became increasingly absorbed in her play, I found myself gradually withdrawing from her. Often, after ten or fifteen minutes into the hour, it took a real effort just to stay awake. Upon returning my attention to her play I would once again experience a tendency to daydream or drift off distractedly. For some reason, either I had shut Kathy out or Kathy had shut me out. In fact, both were true. Kathy entered the office almost oblivious to my presence, then preoccupied herself with the doll, as if no one were with her in the room. My response seemed to say that if she didn't need me, I would forget about her. Withdrawal on my part was a defense against the narcissistic injury of not being needed and not being responded to. Ms. L., too, must have felt this way quite often. The next time this happened, I stayed with the process rather than the manifest behavior: "Sometimes Kathy, you play so hard that you don't even know I'm here." But to what end, I wondered, was it necessary for her to do so?

Kathy began her play by isolating herself in total preoccupation with "her baby." This is when I began to feel shut out. Next, she alternately nursed and injured the child. Finally, she abandoned the doll and ran away. Isolation, preoccupation, nurturance, injury, abandonment—the pieces began to fall into place. Perhaps Kathy was reenacting something from her early, nurturant experience, but this time she was active; the doll, passive and dependent.

Finding herself alone in a room with me, a therapist towards whom she had strong affectionate feelings, awakened in Kathy the fear of reengulfment (loss of self) in the symbiosis. To need or depend on the loved object, to seduce closeness and contact meant total reabsorption by or merger with the object and a terrifying disintegration of whatever autonomous functioning had been achieved. Thus, isolation from me was Kathy's defense against fusion and the dissolution of her primitive self. The anticipated consequences of 'getting too close' were revealed in the interaction between the child and her doll: oscillating affection and destructiveness and the condensation of sadistic-aggressive and nurturant impulses. The doll, fed until its face collapsed, was literally killed by its caregiver's kindness.

In the end, the doll was abandoned and Kathy anxiously attempted to flee from the room. Like the dreamer who can neither hide nor escape some formless horror, whose every evasion seems to bring closer the ubiquitous assailant, Kathy's initial defense against the dreaded fusion with me only delivered her into fusion at a different, symbolic level. The doll had been cast as a self-representation, Kathy as the alternatingly nurturant-sadistic maternal figure. As a piece of fantasy, this play might have helped her to work through the original traumatic situation, turning a passive-victimized role into one of active mastery. The actual "production," however, was too transparent and Kathy became anxious. The representation of the traumatic situation incited the same intensity of terror as had the actual trauma. Finally, in a panic, all was abandoned as Kathy attempted to flee the situation altogether.

The real symbiosis between mother and child was gradually being released. Kathy had separated from her mother and was now reenacting with me that which had occurred. At this point it became possible to intervene in such a way as to make the experience a new and different one. Gradually, in pieces small enough for Kathy to assimilate, elements of conflict between the wish for nurturant gratification and the fear of symbiotic re-engulfment were interpreted. Interpretations were also used to draw connections between the past and present situations ("The baby likes to drink from her bottle. When you were a baby you liked when your mommy let you drink from your bottle, too"), to identify conflicts and defenses ("When you let me play with you it makes you feel like you're not Kathy anymore . . . so you pretend that I'm not here"), and to identify aspects of the transference relationship ("Sometimes you feel that way when you play with your mommy").

What did Kathy understand about these interventions? This is difficult to assess as immediate signs of confirmation were rarely forthcoming. It may, one could argue, have simply been the "auto-therapeutic" aspects of play (Erikson, 1940) that allowed Kathy to relive, resolve, and reintegrate this developmental conflict, but I believe that, in many instances, my words helped to fill in gaps so that she could remember things long forgotten or never fully represented in consciousness in the first place.

At the same time that Kathy relived with me the troubling interactions that had made it so difficult for her to grow psychologically, parts of the script were reworked and rewritten as well. I offered a new kind of relationship, one in which there could be closeness without engulfment and collaboration without merger and one in which she could expand in terms of language, symbolic play, and physical self-expression. Obviously, this was not something that happened overnight. In order for Kathy to become satisfied with herself and accept me as a person who could help her to see what she was capable of doing on her own, she first had to confront her feelings about not being a normal 4-year-old and acknowledge that there were things with which she needed help.

Kathy defended herself against the painful awareness of being able to do so little on her own by creating an illusion of being able to do everything and anything on her own. This was the omnipotent fantasy. When playing with Kathy, no one was permitted to engage in independent activities that might point out the frailty or inadequacy of her performance. Only slavish imitation or silent observation were tolerated. When we were engaged in activities together, Kathy orchestrated her play in such a way as would allow her to believe that I was simply an extension of herself, that my relatively greater abilities were, in fact, her own. When a toy fell behind the desk Kathy used my hand as a tool for retrieval as if it were an appendage of her own body. When she was unable to braid her doll's hair, she briefly allowed me to do this for her, then, tearing the doll from my hands, furiously undid the braids and redid them herself as if she had been able to do this all along. On many occasions, Kathy took great pleasure in climbing up on my chair and free-falling into my arms, closing her eyes on the descent as if to sustain the illusion of invulnerability, of having miraculously caught herself.

Paring the omnipotent fantasy down to size and building in its place an awareness of actual abilities and realistic possibilities laid the groundwork for a more accurate awareness and defintion of self and a more realistic recognition of the essential dependency and interdependency of the self in relation to other persons. Rather than collude with Kathy's illusion of complete control I responded by gently but insistently directing her attention to those aspects of the interaction that were a direct consequence of her own initiative and those that were only made possible because I intervened. The illusion of omnipotence was challenged. In its place Kathy was given something with which she could grow:

> Kathy, you are using my hand to get your toy but that hand is a part of me. Tell me what you want and then I will help you. . . . You wanted to see how I tied the braid in the doll's hair but then you wanted to think that you did it without me. It makes you mad that there are things that I can do that you can't do by yourself yet. I'm bigger than you, though. Someday you'll be big too. . . . Kathy, you don't want to see me when you're falling. You're pretending that you can catch yourself.

Gradually, a wedge was driven between the fantasy of limitless power and the reality of painfully limited abilities. More often than not, however, Kathy continued to react furiously to my challenge that she see what she could either do on her own or with full awareness of my participation. The illusion that it was she who had reached the inaccessible toy or that it was her own invulnerability that protected her from injury when she jumped off the chair, eyes closed into my arms, was shattered. Left to struggle with her own resources and abilities, she found herself small, wanting and unsatisfactory. With my collusion she could be all that she wanted to be. Without me she felt she was nothing at all.

Much as I had "known," based on my knowledge of child development and my empathic receptivity, that Kathy was ready to separate from her mother even before this was evident in her own inclinations, it was now equally apparent that Kathy was ready to engage in the struggle to differentiate that for which she wished (omnipotent ability and control) from that which was actual (limited but rapidly developing abilities), a struggle that would ultimately result in an enhanced awareness of self-definition and personal identity. It was time that Kathy realize there were two people in the room and that she had feelings about not being able to do everything she would have liked to do on her own. Again, my decision to facilitate Kathy's movement in this direction was based on both a developmental timetable which suggested the high probability of her readiness to take this step forward and an empathic receptivity to certain nascent strivings apparent during the treatment hour which suggested her capacity to expand in the direction of greater autonomy and independence. What I knew, however, was one step beyond what Kathy was prepared to know about herself—that she could tolerate the pain and loneliness of autonomous functioning precisely because she was not bereft of resources. She was something on her own and did not need me to support her omnipotent fantasy in order to feel satisfied with herself.

Toward the end of the first year of treatment I began to notice a subtle change in the direction of Kathy's spontaneous activity during the therapy hours. For example, there was a broadening of interest. Kathy was not absorbed so rigidly in the kinds of isolated, ritualized play that had occupied much of her attention during the first half of the year. She was becoming aware of new objects in the room and was more openly receptive when I joined her exploration and experimentation. From one session to the next there was greater consistency and continuity; possibilities hinted at during one treatment hour were elaborated and expanded upon during the next. Kathy was taking something home with her and bringing it back. She was beginning to organize and represent her experiences mentally. She was filling up with images and ideas.

One item, a wind-up music box with a colorful dancing clown inside, was of special interest to Kathy. Often, for 15 or 20 minutes at a time she would watch the gyrating figure with rapt attention and could hardly wait to wind it up for another performance when it ran down. She even began asking for the clown by name and seemed quite concerned when, on occasion, it was not occupying its customary position on the bookshelf when she first entered the office. Sometimes, after Kathy had finished playing with the toy, she danced around the office imitating the doll's movements. Again, something had been taken inside, thought about, and remembered.

Kathy began her 18 March 1982 session by demanding that I take the beloved music box down from the shelf so that she could play with it. Before giving her the toy, however, I insisted that she first tell me what she wanted rather than assume that I just understood her wish. Together we practiced saying "clown" and Kathy observed her face in the mirror as she struggled to articulate the correct sounds. Once accomplished, she was given that for which she had successfully asked. Kathy played with the music box for some time and finally seemed to grow weary of it though her insistence that I continue to wind it up was undiminished. Finally, I returned the toy to the shelf telling her that I thought she had had enough. When she began to whine irritably, however, I suggested another possibility rather than simply accede to her half-hearted demand: "Kathy, maybe you and I can draw a clown just like the one in the box." For a few moments she watched me draw and then, as if suddenly remembering what she had allowed to take place, insisted that I stop. This time however, I did not permit her to tear up the "evidence." Instead, I gave her a crayon and a piece of paper and told her to see what she could do. After a few disappointing starts she took my hand, placed it on top of her own, then held a piece of crayon over the paper:

Kathy: Clown! Clown!

Therapist: You want to draw a clown, too.

Kathy: (beginning to cry) Clown!

Therapist: But you want me to help you. You're not sure you can do it yourself.

Together, my hand on top of hers, we drew a clown's face, stopping periodically to point out a particular detail and compare it to the corresponding detail on Kathy's own face. Kathy was elated by the finished product—a clown's face that looked remarkably similar to the one I had drawn myself (Figure 2). When Kathy again took my "helping hand," I told her that this time she would have to see what she could do for herself. This was the moment of real triumph. Kathy drew a shaky but clearly recognizable face! (Figure 3).

The importance of this accomplishment cannot be overestimated. However inauspicious a beginning, the rendering, unassisted and from memory, of a human image indicated the capacity to represent objects, events, and most importantly, other persons, on the plane of thought. This was the basis for processes of internalization and identification and a foundation for the building of a stable, structured internal world. Even more, perhaps, than Kathy's physical separation from mother, this first precarious image laid the groundwork for a truly autonomous psychological organization. With the capacity for mental representation and coherent object relations, Kathy could begin to free herself from a

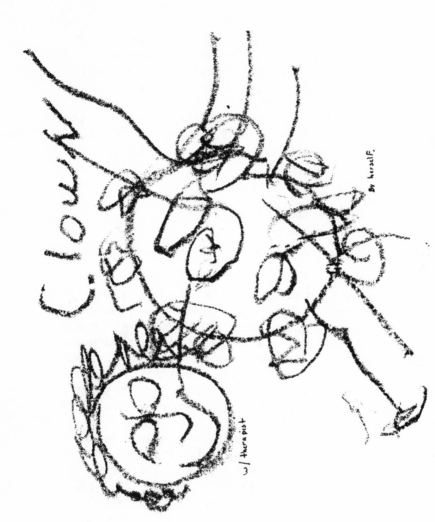

Figure 2. The first attempt by Kathy M. to draw a clown.

Figure 3. The second attempt by Kathy M. to draw a clown.

slavish dependence on actual objects and actual object relations. Now, perhaps, she could begin to perform many of the soothing, regulating, and comforting functions formerly provided by her symbiotically attached partner.

A single image transposed from thought to paper is still far from the complex mental representation and internalization of experience that ultimately leads to personality growth and structuralization. Even at this primitive level of psychological organization, however, Kathy was beginning to think about things that interested her and worry about things that troubled her. Conflicts enacted very literally with dolls or in interaction with the therapist during the earlier phases of treatment were now undergoing simple but nonetheless cogent symbolization. Kathy was gaining a psychological distance from events in the actual past. Rather than repeat these in action, she could now represent them symbolically in thought.

In the weeks that followed Kathy's newfound ability to draw things from memory, she continued to struggle with the wish to merge with the therapist as a person who made her feel that she could do things that were otherwise impossible; she experienced his relatively greater competence as her own. Before trying to draw, she almost always attempted to do whatever she could to coerce me into guiding her as I had during the earlier session.

> Kathy, you want me to help you because it makes you feel like you're doing it yourself. . . . When I don't help, you don't feel good about you[rself].

Sometimes, after a few disappointing starts, Kathy would sink back sadly into her chair and begin tearing up her paper or unraveling the wrapper from her crayon.

> Kathy you're making a mess like a baby because you don't think you can play like a little girl. . . . You feel mad when you can't do something you'd like to do. . . . You don't think you can do it without me. . . . It's hard to draw, I know. It's easier to make a mess. . . . If you're going to grow up you have to do things that are hard.

For several weeks, Kathy seemed a child obsessed with regaining the image that had so charmed both the therapist and herself. Before her sessions she could be found fitfully drawing small circles, one after another, on the waiting room blackboard, erasing each after a brief dissatisfied inspection. Slowly, she was coming to terms with what she could do on her own—more than she had expected, but less than she could do with the therapist's unacknowledged help. One month before her treatment with me was to end, Kathy began her session by insisting that she be allowed to sit in my lap as she drew. Well-acquainted by that time with the meaning this had for her, I was equally insistent that she sit beside rather than on top and in front of me: "Kathy, you like being close to me and I like being close to you. But you're not a baby now. Why don't you sit here so I can play with you." Kathy acquiesced and began to draw a big circle intersecting a little circle (Figure 4). Once completed, the rendering was carefully folded and stapled shut enclosing the two figures inside. I followed closely then attempted to draw a connection, first to what had just happened in the therapeutic process and finally to the transference aspects of the interaction:

> Kathy, there's a big one and a little one. The big one and the little one are very close. The little one is almost inside the big one. Sometimes you like to sit in my lap. I'm bigger than you and it makes you feel like you can do anything. But it's scary to be that big when you're really so little. Like it's not really you. Sometimes you feel that way with mommy too.

Kathy began the hour by indicating to me her desire to sit in my lap and play, again, as if I were a part of her. But this was thwarted. This time, however, rather than becoming enraged, she represented the conflict in a primitive but eloquently simple symbolization. It was not necessary for her to insist on my repeating the entire elaborate and literal sequence of events. With two intersect-

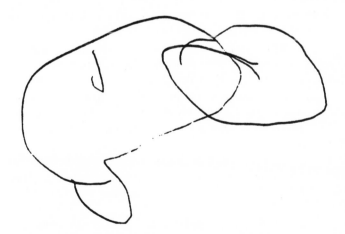

Figure 4. The two circles drawn by Kathy M.

ing circles, one large and one small, she had captured the essence successfully. Reduced to its most elemental proportions, Kathy had rendered her struggle in a form that was accessible and comprehensible to both of us.

Two weeks later, Kathy once again began her treatment hour with figure drawing. This time she sat down next to me but insisted neither that I take her into my lap nor that I guide her hand through the drawing. Again she drew first a big circle then a little one beside it. This time however, the circles were clearly defined from one another; they were separate (Figure 5).

Of the four phases in Kathy's psychotherapy, only the final phase of treatment, "termination," was planned well in advance and did not reflect a significant transition in the actual therapeutic process. Optimally, Kathy might have continued to work with the same therapist on an ongoing basis until each of the treatment goals mentioned already had been achieved or until a more viable alternative to psychotherapy seemed appropriate. Compromising our "best case" treatment plan was unfortunate but unavoidable.

Although premature, termination was nonetheless an important experience for Kathy and one which had a direct bearing on the kinds of issues she had struggled to resolve throughout the course of her psychotherapy. During normal development, the "promise" that sustains the child undergoing separation-individuation assures that the loved caregiver, if not always available, will be regularly available to provide for the gratification of those periodic needs that the child, by virtue of his psychological and physiological immaturity cannot gratify directly for himself. It is the primary caregiver's optimal presence, rather than omnipresence, that creates the "outer predictability" upon which a sense of "inner certainty" is built (Erikson 1950). Reality dictates, however, that while most separations are followed by reunion, some are not. "Things that come apart" usually, but not always, "go back together again." Invariably, some leavetakings are permanent. Treatment termination was one such leavetaking for Kathy. As of 19 April 1982, she would meet with me a dozen more times and then, very possibly, never see me again.

In some sense, I began to leave Kathy long before our final farewell. Increasingly, she was encouraged to "see what [she] could do on her own" without my help and as time went on, I both said less and did less during the treatment hours. Comment and interpretation were offered sparingly in order to create a vacuum that Kathy would have to fill for herself. What I did say, however, would be remembered.

Figure 5. Kathy M.'s two separate circles.

The interventions offered during this phase of the treatment aimed at further enhancing Kathy's awareness of her essential separateness and separate functioning. This meant not only separate abilities, however, but also separate feelings. It was not enough for her to acknowledge what she could and could not do on her own. In order to define herself as an autonomous entity, she needed to understand that there were feelings that belonged to her alone and that others did not always share these feelings with her. Kathy needed to become empathic with other persons and with herself.

Throughout the final weeks of treatment Kathy continued to exercise and experiment with her own growing resources. She was gratified that she could accomplish things of which she had not believed herself capable, but was angered at not being able to perform as well as she would have liked, or, more specifically, as well as her therapist. On one occasion, Kathy began to draw a picture of the now-familiar clown but became increasingly upset when she could not remember all of its features. As her frustration mounted, she began to scribble recklessly on her drawing and then over the entire desk. Finally, she threw the crayons across the room and began lashing out at me, pinching and scratching. While restraining her, I interpreted: "You don't like what you're doing and that makes you angry, so you're hurting me. But it's not me you're mad at. You're mad at you!" Kathy was dissatisfied with herself, but, in my refusal to capitulate to her delusion of fused symbiotic competency, I had become both a persecutor and a reminder of that part of herself which she experienced as weak and powerless.

The source of Kathy's aggressive behavior was not always this clear. Sometimes, for no apparent reason, she would grab at my face or scratch at my arms with her nails, giggling with delight all the while. My anger and efforts at restraining her only seemed to heighten her pleasure. The scratching, I explained, only hurt me; although she could not feel it, her lashing out in this way was a source of pain. Other times, the situation was reversed. Later in the treatment, Kathy began to use self-injurious behaviors such as biting herself in order to regain her mother's attention when she felt herself excluded or ignored (This occurred typically during the aftermath of her treatment hours when I often conferred briefly with Ms. L.). Standing directly in front of mother, Kathy would put her wrist in her mouth and bite down until the pain was unbearable, as if to say "Look at what I'm doing to myself because you won't give me your full attention. I will hurt myself to cause you pain." Here, again, I tried to empathize with Kathy's anger while at the same time differentiating for her exactly who was feeling what: "I don't like when you hurt yourself Kathy, but you are not hurting me when you bite yourself, you are hurting you."

Empathy is a difficult if not impossible process to instill in another person other than by example. The most I was able to provide for Kathy was a foundation for empathy through the careful differentiation of our respective internal experiences: what's mine, what's yours; what I am feeling, what you are feeling. It is difficult to know whether Kathy was able to take the leap from self-other differentiation to momentary empathic identification. Yet there were any number of situations in which she did seem to use her own memory and subjective "referents" to gauge the therapist's internal state. Perhaps the most striking example of this occurred following a minor bicycle accident in which Kathy had scraped her knee. The hour began with Kathy quietly showing me her wound and my empathizing with both the pain and the surprise that all children feel upon first coming to terms with their own frailty and vulnerability: "You hurt yourself Kathy. Sometimes that happens. But you'll get better because the hurt's not a big one . . . Sometimes even when people take good care of you you get hurt." At first, Kathy responded by playing out her traumatic injury with a handful of small plastic dolls which she alternately dropped or threw, then examined for injury. Satisfied that none had suffered irreparable damage, she seemed to forget the matter and moved off to another activity. Later in the hour, however, frustrated by the difficulty she was having blowing bubbles, Kathy suddenly turned to me and began to scratch at my arm. Before I could restrain her she had drawn a small amount of blood. Typically, she would not have noticed this or would have continued undaunted with her tirade. This time, however, she stopped of her own volition and looked very closely at the torn skin on my wrist. From my wound she looked down at her own wound, then back again. For the rest of the hour she seemed unusually subdued, even sad.

Kathy had lashed out at me many times before, seemingly unaware of or at least unconcerned with the consequences of her behavior. This time, however, due to the coincidence of her own misfortune she was able to put herself in my place for a moment and share something of what I might have been feeling. The experience of her own painful wound was the referent in relationship to which she gauged my subjective experience of the injury she had inflicted. In this sense, she had been empathically receptive. However, having made the connection between my experience and her own, she was responsive empathically as well. Her uncharacteristically subdued behavior seemed to reflect both remorse at having caused her therapist, someone towards whom she felt very close, to experience pain, and, in response, a certain amount of restraint. I had the distinct impression that Kathy had "gone easy on me" for the remainder of the hour.

Beginning with the thirteenth month of treatment (14 April 1982) and continuing until our last session (10 June 1982), each therapy hour ended in my counting off with Kathy the number of treatment sessions remaining until termination: "I'm going to say goodbye to you today and then I will see you 12 (11, 10, 9, 8, 7, . . . 1) more time(s). After that, I won't see you any more and you won't be seeing me anymore either." Everything was offered in terms of complementary pairs, as in "my experience, your experience." By the time we had reached the last three or four weeks, Kathy was quite familiar with this ritual and followed my counting by tallying the remaining sessions on her fingers. Did she really understand what would occur at the end of our countdown? Perhaps not, but I do believe that there had been enough subtle variations, both concrete and symbolic, during the course of the termination process to signal, at the very least, the imminence of an important transition. Kathy would have perceived, for example, that prior to termination, I spoke to her with an unusual economy of words and was increasingly insistent that she do things on her own which we had formerly worked at collaboratively. She might have also noticed that towards the end of each session, and with each passing hour, something once numerous (numbers, fingers, sessions) was steadily diminishing, that a lot was becoming a little and that soon there would be no more. Again, I believe, these subtle variations created the cumulative impression of a gradual separation prior to actual termination.

I began Kathy's last treatment hour by reminding her that there were no subsequent sessions remaining and that the two of us would no longer meet with each other. Beyond this, the hour, as any other, was hers to use as she pleased. Befittingly, Kathy's "choice" seemed to capture the essence of what we had worked so hard to achieve and of the struggle that lay ahead for her. Sitting down next to me, (but no longer demanding my active participation) she drew two faces, one large, one small, a short distance apart from one another. The finished work was examined appraisingly, then quickly scribbled over. I noted her dissatisfaction, empathizing with how hard it was sometimes to "do things as well as you'd like" but emphasized how nice it was that even though the "big one" and the "little one" were very close to one another, there were still two of them nonetheless.

The hour ended unceremoniously. Kathy was given the doll she had received from me for her birthday to take home with her— "This is something you used to play with when you came here to see me"—then I assured her that even though she would not be coming back to play and we would probably not see each other again, we would certainly remember each other often.

Kathy met her mother and sister in the reception area, then boarded the waiting elevator. She waved goodbye through the glass doors until I disappeared from view. This time, however, out of sight was not out of mind. Kathy was going home with more than a doll.

Chapter Twenty-One

The Treatment of Ms. L.

"Why am I coming here? Kathy is starting to learn some new words. Me? I feel . . . OK . . . No problems . . . Really. I don't think I need this. I'm only coming here for Kathy."

Like many parents who had initially sought help from the Parent-Infant Development Service due to their children's psychological difficulties, Ms. L. was surprised and more than a little concerned to learn that she herself would have an important role to play in the treatment process. It had taken her a long time to accept that Kathy would require the kind of help that she could not provide on her own; now she was being told that her own treatment would also be an essential aspect of a growth process aimed at facilitating not only Kathy's development but her own development as well. As Kathy's parent and primary caregiver, she would be an active participant in her daughter's therapy; as a woman struggling to meet personal goals and expectations, she would be a patient in her own right. Even as Ms. L. questioned her role in the treatment process, however, she seemed to allude to the answer: "I didn't think I'd be coming here to talk about myself . . . It feels kind ~~ny~~ even being here without Kathy. I never go anywhere ~~~~ days. It's like I'm missing something."

~~ed~~ on the discomfort this seemed to cause her, ~~l~~gate of doubts and concerns. Ms. L. never left ~~a~~r that if she did, something terrible would ~~~~she would lose control and relinquish what little ~~g~~ up she had made: "She'll go back and pee on herself and stop talking completely. No one else will understand her." Once before, during her delivery, she had turned her back on Kathy. Now she could not be sure that the doctors hadn't damaged her child during childbirth, or worse yet, that she herself had not done so unwittingly. Thus, Kathy could no longer be left alone. "Abandoning" the child for even a short while, she believed, courted tragic consequences for both herself and her daughter. Thus, at least one reason for Ms. L.'s participation in the treatment process was evident from the start:

> *Therapist:* It seems like Kathy relies on you a great deal, Ms. L., but you don't feel quite the same without her either.

Kathy's difficulties in achieving psychological separation were mother's difficulties as well. Ms. L. had brought to the parenting situation a history of problematic attachments and a propensity for relationships built on domination, submission and inflexible bondage-like dependency. Her tendency to sustain states of fused psychological unity was as pronounced as her daughter's. Thus, the first therapeutic task was to define the symmetry of the symbiotic relationship between Kathy and Ms. L.

By definition, the symbiotic attachment involves a blurring of boundaries and a peculiarly confused representation of self and object. Aspects of the self are experienced as aspects of the other, and aspects of the other as aspects of the self. As a defense, as a means of disclaiming reprehensible, frightening or shameful aspects of the self, it offers a means of altering the image one carries of oneself at the "expense" of the other. It is the use of the other as a metaphor for the self.

By placing Kathy in treatment, Ms. L. had in some sense already put forth a part of herself, a part which she experienced only indirectly, perhaps even vicariously! If she had not expected to be an actual participant in the treatment process, this had to do with a belief (of which she was initially unaware) that she was already represented "by proxy," as it were, in the person of her daughter. Throughout the treatment, Kathy was used by Ms. L. as a representation or embodiment of those aspects of herself that were vulnerable, unacceptable, or painful to see. She had become mother's "metaphor."

At first, it was a mystery to me that a woman who wanted something of her own so desperately found it so difficult to accept a weekly treatment hour which she could use as she pleased, ostensibly to explore possibilities for a richer, more gratifying life for herself. Nearly every hour began, however, with a discussi

point that on her first day of school, she had literally been dragged to the bus kicking and screaming.) The reality of a child who was not overly frightened and who did not lose control contrasted markedly with her fantasy of a little girl who would surely "break" under the strain of independent functioning. Now, having already explored the possibility of sharing with Kathy certain fears and vulnerabilities associated with autonomy and separation, Ms. L. was able to take the next step of differentiating those feelings which, though actually her own, had been experienced as if they belonged only to her daughter. This is illustrated in a process segment from the 11 September 1981 treatment hour. Again, Ms. L. began the hour by "putting Kathy first" before allowing herself to focus on issues that she could identify as her own:

> *Therapist:* I wonder if you noticed . . .
>
> *Ms. L.:* Yeah (smiles knowingly), here I am talking about Kathy again. It seems like even when I start talking about myself there's Kathy again. . . . It's just that I'm so used to spending all my time with her. . . . I'm just not used to talking about myself. Maybe I've used Kathy as a way of escaping something. I've thought of that before. I sometimes think I use her as an excuse not to go out and do new things. Whenever I do something for the first time I freeze. I get frightened.
>
> *Therapist:* What do you think about that?
>
> *Ms. L.:* Well, I guess I feel that I'll fail. That I won't be able to do it.
>
> *Therapist:* Do you very often fail at things?
>
> *Ms. L.:* No. . . . In fact, when I put my mind to it I usually do a pretty good job.
>
> *Therapist:* Then I wonder where this idea comes from that you'll fail?

Ms. L. pondered this question for a few moments, recalled her father's bitter criticism of her as a child, then sidetracked once again to Kathy's difficulties in growing up:

> *Ms. L.:* You know, Kathy does a lot of things just like a little girl her age but she still drinks milk out of a bottle. When she sees me eating, she'll drop it to get what I've got, so I know she can eat regularly.
>
> *Therapist:* But in some ways Kathy still needs to act like a baby.
>
> *Ms. L.:* I think it's for security. In fact, she used to carry around a blanket.
>
> *Therapist:* What do you think Kathy's insecure about?

Ms. L.: Well, I think she's afraid that she just won't be able to do things very well.

Therapist: That she'll fail?

Ms. L.: Yeah, that she'll try something new and just won't be able to do it.

Therapist: That sounds a lot like what you were saying about yourself a while ago.

Ms. L.: It does . . . except that I'm afraid that I'll fail other people. Kathy's afraid that she'll fail herself. You know she can't let me know exactly what it is she's feeling so she's afraid to go ahead by herself.

Therapist: I see. She's afraid she won't be heard by anyone if something goes wrong so she won't risk taking a chance.

For many months Ms. L. moved in and out of the metaphor, each time bringing something back with her that she had been able to reclaim as her own. Freed from some of her misperceptions of Kathy, she became less hesitant about encouraging her daughter's independent initiatives and began to see herself as an active agent in a process that might ultimately lead to her child's growth and recovery. Other aspects of the metaphor remained intact, however, and may, to some extent, have actually facilitated the establishment of a treatment alliance. As Kathy became more trusting of the therapist, Ms. L. also seemed to become more trusting. As she perceived that her child was becoming increasingly accessible to the therapist, she began to perceive the therapist as someone who seemed intent upon understanding her as well.

Reclaiming the various aspects of the symbiotic metaphor came more easily to Ms. L. than did resolving these aspects and reconciling them with the person she had come to see herself as. Suddenly, with Kathy's enrollment in school, the opportunity to take a portion of each day for herself, to have something of her own, became a reality. She no longer had a practical reason not to be independent. But the hours during which Kathy was away seemed to pass unaccounted for: "I listen to the radio, then I think, then I look at the time and it's two o'clock. Kathy will be coming home soon." Once important ambitions of pursuing a career or reentering the social mainstream seemed to have been relinquished. Old obstacles had been replaced by new. Now, Ms. L. feared not for her daughter, but for herself. It was as if Kathy had abandoned her: "I'm afraid that Kathy is going to grow up and see that she can depend on herself and that she won't want to be around me anymore. If she gets healthy, she'll have expectations of me and see what a failure I've become."

Just what could Ms. L. do? Why, in the face of substantial evidence to the contrary, did she believe that failure was inevitable? Psychological testing, offered at this point in the treatment (October 1981), was administered, in part, to demonstrate to Ms. L. exactly what she could do, what she was capable of feeling and how certain preconceptions based on earlier life experiences prevented her from pursuing a more fully actualized life for herself. Testing proved to be a valuable diagnostic-therapeutic tool but certainly not for the reasons I had anticipated. What Ms. L. could do was not the point. This was not a woman looking for concrete evidence of intelligence or ability. She had a reason not to succeed and a reason to blame herself for every misfortune that had befallen herself and her family. More to the point, she was fearful of succeeding and believed that to have shown herself competent would have been tantamount to depriving, even destroying, something very important to her—an image of herself and a very special relationship from her past. Thus, the last thing she wanted was the therapist to demonstrate her resourcefulness and undermine the rationale for her low estimation of herself.

Had I stayed attuned to the metaphor, I might have heard Ms. L.'s trepidation and protest. A short time after the testing (6 November 1981), she began her treatment hour talking about Kathy's "total disregard" for her feelings:

Ms. L.: Kathy's been throwing a lot lately. She doesn't listen to me and she laughs at me when I tell her to stop. I think she knows what she's doing 'cause she can control it when she wants.

Therapist: Why does she laugh at you?

Ms. L.: Because she doesn't really care about how I feel. I try to be a good mother but I guess I'm not. . . . She needs to be pushed. She doesn't really want to move ahead.

This interesting excerpt contains a subtle but important shift in process. At first, Kathy is perceived as a malevolent persecutor, one who knows mother's feelings but persists in deliberately forcing her to confront her failings. One can immediately draw a connection here to the father who belittled Ms. L. and the mother whose competence reminded her of her own inadequacy. Was this not also a reference, however, to the therapist who dared her to look at herself and what she was capable of? Later in the sequence, Ms. L.'s frame of reference seems to change, as Kathy becomes a manifestation of her (Ms. L.'s) own beleaguered self—passive, resistant, and recalcitrant.

The Transference Relationship

The 11 November 1982 therapy hour began with a long, somewhat awkward silence:

Therapist: What would you like to talk about today?

Ms. L.: Well, there's something ... I don't know if I can talk about it. I just don't know if I can tell you. I was thinking about it before I came in. Can I tell him or not?

Therapist: What do you think would happen if you told me?

Ms. L.: Well, I really don't know. You're a man and well, I know you're a doctor but you're also a man and I don't know ... you're supposed to under ... well this is child psychiatry and ...

Therapist: Maybe I only understand children ... and I won't be able to understand you?

Ms. L.: Well, it's just that I'm so used to coming in here and talking about Kathy.

Therapist: So you'd be taking a risk talking about yourself. But you know, already you're handling things a little bit differently today. . . . You're telling me there's something going on inside of you, a struggle of some kind, and you don't know if you can talk about it.

Ms. L.: Well, it's just that you're a man and I'd feel ... I know you're a doctor ...

Therapist: What do you think I'd feel as a man?

Ms. L.: Well, men feel that they're powerful, that they can overpower women, that women can't do things that they can. I don't believe that but ...

Therapist: So maybe if you told me what you've been thinking about, it would give me some power over you that you'd rather I not have.

Ms. L.: I'd be embarrassed. What would you think of me? I used to be able to tell people about things but not lately. I've thought about it a lot though. Things are going pretty good with Kathy now and I'm starting to think about this more and more.

Therapist: Well, you may not be ready to talk about it today but you've let me know there's something that you're struggling with. If and when you feel like talking about it ... that'll be up to you.

Ms. L.: (long silent pause) Well, it's about Kathy's father. I don't want to tell you what it is but I just can't get him out of my life. Sometimes I feel like I want to take a gun and kill him. He tells me that if I call the police, someday he'll come back and find me, wherever I go. He says he wants to help, but he's hurting me and the kids. I can talk about what he's doing to the kids but I can't really talk about what he's doing to me. It's like when my mother died. For a long time I couldn't talk about it to anyone.

Therapist: I wonder if sometimes you feel that, while I am trying to help, maybe I am hurting you also. . . . I know that last time, when you didn't come in for your session, I called you at home. Maybe you feel that you can't get away from me either?

Ms. L.: Sometimes I feel you're too demanding. I only want Kathy to come in once a week and you tell me she should come in twice. But it's not really like that with Kathy's father. They say that you marry a man who is like your father and it was really my father who was the same way . . . the things he did to me as a teenager. I could never tell him how I felt. I mean, he never abused me or anything, but I was so angry with him I couldn't tell him. . . . He never tried to understand what was going on.

Therapist: So maybe if you tell me what happened [the secret] I won't understand you either. You'd be taking a chance.

Ms. L.: (Seems to ignore therapist's remarks) I just don't know what to do. He'll find me wherever I go. He's just like my father. He doesn't understand. I don't need him. I can get along better without him. I don't need someone to tell me how to do things then just leave me to do it by myself!

The therapist, like the paternal figure of early childhood (and more recently, Mr. M.) had been construed by Ms. L., within the transference, as a person unwilling or unable to understand, relentlessly critical, yet towards whom she was unable to express her rage directly. In most respects, Ms. L. was closely in touch with these feelings even if they had been difficult for her to communicate at the time. What she seemed unaware of, however, were certain strong negative feelings toward the maternal figure. Mother was invariably remembered as having been the complete antithesis of father, one who always understood, who was always there for her and for whom she felt only love and admiration. A somewhat different impression emerged from within the transference relationship, however. Ms. L.'s reference to Kathy's father (and by association the therapist) as a person who seemed omnisciently ever-present, who studied her and found her out wherever she went, were later revived as early impressions of her mother.

Mother's understanding was perhaps too complete, for it undermined autonomy and a sense of solid personal boundary. In a very real sense, she had become Ms. L.'s "better half" without whom she (Ms. L.) felt empty, incomplete, and incompetent.

Years ago, Ms. L. ran away from home to show her mother that she could "do it on her own" and raise her own child. Then mother died. There was a profound sense of loss, but there was anger as well. It was as though Ms. L.'s striving to be independent, competent, and successful had destroyed her mother, a mother who would continue to be there for her only so long as she remained weak, dependent and inept.

Now there was another person with the help of whom her daughter seemed to be thriving. The therapist, in the eyes of Ms. L., was able to accomplish things with Kathy that she herself could not. While it was gratifying to see her child grow, the fact that this occurred apparently for the therapist, undermined her sense of esteem, of being able to do it on her own. The therapist also appeared to be interested in her, but his efforts to understand made her uncomfortable, even frightened, at times. Here was a person who seemed to mean well but who had an uncanny knack for illuminating things about her that she would rather not have seen. Once again, Ms. L. responded by "running away." This time, however, rather than simply repeat a painful childhood scene, she would, with the therapist's help, begin to remember, reconstruct, and reintegrate a segment of her personal history, and in doing so, return it to its rightful place in the distant past.

For the next month (17 November 1981–18 December 1981) Ms. L. missed all of her scheduled appointments. At first, she explained her absence as the result of having felt "blamed" by Dr. R. (the psychologist who had tested Kathy) for Kathy's disability. This stemmed from a testing feedback session during which a question had been raised concerning Kathy's illness and its probable causes. Responding to Ms. L.'s concern that she herself had been the source of the problem, Dr. R. explained that undoubtedly she had asserted an influence over her daughter's development, psychological as well as physiological, but that this meant she also had the capacity to produce a positive, growth-enhancing effect as well. In all of this, however, Ms. L. heard only that her impact on Kathy had been a destructive one and that she was to blame for her daughter's illness (from 18 December 1980 session):

> *Ms. L.:* You know, Dr. R. telling me I was to blame for Kathy . . . just when I was beginning to feel better. I don't believe that I could have had that effect on her.

Therapist: What's important though is the effect you can have in helping her to get better.

Ms. L.: It wasn't that way with Carol.

Therapist: That's right, but things were different when you were raising Carol.

Ms. L.: That's true. With Kathy I was tense and upset and depressed.

Therapist: You'd just lost your mother.

Ms. L.: I had to raise Kathy alone. With Carol there was someone to help me. My mother was there to help me.

Therapist: And then she left you.

It was more than Dr. R.'s perceived criticism, however, that kept Ms. L. from returning to treatment. On a number of occasions she insisted, rather bitterly, that she "understood herself perfectly" and didn't need help from anyone else. As for the therapist: "You may say you do, but you don't really understand me." I asked her whether she really believed that she was so different from me to prevent my getting to know her, but she insisted that she could find out all she wanted to know about herself by herself. Besides, Kathy would probably need her exclusive attention for at least the next two or three years. What would she do in the meanwhile? Or, more to the point, what could she do? I reminded her that what she did with her life was up to her. I could, however, help her to evaluate what was possible. We agreed that the next treatment hour would be devoted to a feedback of her psychological testing results.

Ms. L. returned to the clinic following the 4-week hiatus complaining that Kathy's father had caused her to miss her individual appointments. He had been keeping close surveillance on her, she maintained, and had even threatened her life. At first, Ms. L. also claimed that Mr. M. believed treatment would do no good for either Kathy or herself, but was later able to see that these reservations were really her own and had more to do with her fear of what treatment might do rather than what it could not do. Even if he were able to offer her insight or advice, however, the therapist, like "everyone else," was perceived as someone who told her what to do but in the end left her to handle a very difficult life situation on her own. This was not at all unlike what had happened when her mother died three years earlier (from 29 December 1981 session):

Ms. L.: [Kathy's father] thinks Kathy will just get better on her own and that there isn't any reason to be coming here. He doesn't think you'd be able to understand her problems anyways. You won't know what's wrong with her.

Therapist: The last time we met, you had some real doubts about whether I would be able to understand you either.

Ms. L.: Well yes . . . I feel that way sometimes. You know, what good is this going to do. I know it's helping Kathy and all but . . . Nobody has any answers.

Therapist: Maybe you've felt that I've been telling you what to do a lot also. I know you didn't exactly look forward to those 12:45 P.M. phone calls on Friday afternoons when you didn't come in for your sessions.

Ms. L.: (Sighs) It's just that I'm always doing these things for other people. My father, Kathy's father. What can I do? How am I going to get out?

Therapist: You'd like it if I could give you the answers.

Ms. L.: I know you can't do that. It's got to come from me. I've got to do that for myself.

Therapist. I can't tell you what to do. . . . I can only tell you what I think you're doing and what I think you can do.

Chapter Twenty-Two

The Confirmation and Disconfirmation of Expectations

Experience had taught Ms. L. that doing things for herself and functioning as an independent human being entailed a variety of grave risks. As a child she recalled that demonstrating new abilities to her father met invariably with the expectation that henceforth, she would have to rely exclusively on her own resources and not expect to "fall back" on others for support. When people did things for her she was suspicious, for it always seemed that in the end the intention was motivated by self-interest.

Within the context of Ms. L.'s psychotherapy (through the testing and test feedback) I had, in effect, shown her what she could do on her own, that she had many untapped intellectual and emotional resources and could, if she chose, engage herself in any number of rewarding social and career situations. In terms of the transference, however, this set up the expectation that I, like the father, would now pull away and deny her my support. It meant that she could no longer expect to rely on me as someone to fall back on. Whatever I might offer her, she seemed to anticipate, would in the end prove to be self-aggrandizing and at her expense. This suspicion is illustrated (though in the "voice" of Mr. M.) during an interchange during Ms. L.'s 22 January 1982 treatment hour:

> *Ms. L.:* At first I wasn't going to come in today then I decided to. Kathy's father keeps asking me, "Why do you keep going in? What's all this doing for Kathy? And why do you have to go in every week anyways? How's it going to help? You'd be going in every day if it was up to the doctor."

Therapist: I see, so maybe he feels that really you're coming in for me, that I want you to come in for something I'm getting out of it.

Ms. L.: He thinks all doctors are that way. Now Kathy's starting to talk and all, he would just stick his hand down her throat and pull the words out of her.

Therapist: I wonder if it sometimes feels to you like I'm having you come here for something I need.

Ms. L.: Well sometimes. I don't always know how this is going to help me.

Therapist: But you finally decided to come in today.

Ms. L.: Yeah (laughs nervously). Well, I was already in the neighborhood visiting someone else so I just decided I would come in.

The past cannot be rewritten though it is subject to the editing of time—forgetfulness and distortion. Expectations built on past experiences, however, are subject to confirmation or disconfirmation in the present. Psychotherapy is one such instance in which the expected is pitted against the unexpected, in which "unlikely" outcomes throw into question the foundations of belief. Where one expects betrayal, one is supported; where one expects to be shamed, one is accepted without judgment; where one expects to be ignored or misinterpreted, one is listened to and understood. It is the therapist's interpretation of the patient's material that brings coherence to the patient's experience by helping him to differentiate things past from things present and things real from things imagined. It is, however, the kind of experience offered in the process of this exploration that confirms for the patient the reality of these distinctions and the possibilities for new and unexpected outcomes.

Ms. L. anticipated that, having shown the therapist her potential for resourcefulness, she would be left alone and with only herself on which to depend. Beyond this point, anything the therapist might offer would be suspect for the offering would prove certainly to have been self-serving. In actuality, however, the kind and quality of interaction between myself and Ms. L. was much different than what she had expected. For example, during the same session excerpted above, the process moved from Ms. L.'s complaining about "Mr. M.'s distrust" of the therapist's intentions to a discussion of Kathy's increasing respect for her mother's authority. Having myself witnessed an extremely impressive scene in the hallway before the hour began in which Ms. L. demanded, forcefully and without yielding, that Kathy sit quietly in her chair, I was able to admire the strength, clarity and insistence of her communication, in contrast to earlier mother–child interactions.

Again, this was not what Ms. L. had anticipated. The actual father could not or would not have admired her growing competence and would have used any demonstration of new strength or ability to pull back still further. The "therapist–father," in contrast, was able to admire her accomplishment and mirror the pride that she felt in exercising greater authority and control over her child. This had been a shared triumph, one that strengthened rather than weakened the bond between therapist and patient. I, unlike father, had not been driven away by her success.

The process of therapeutic change, however, is not always as straightforward as facilitating an awareness of new possibilities. Preconceptions may not be easily abandoned even in the face of disconfirming evidence. Old patterns of relating and perceiving, however painful, are often sustained for a reason. What is consciously wished-for is often unconsciously abhorrent.

On the Monday following the 22 January 1982 session cited above, Ms. L. brought Kathy to the clinic for her scheduled treatment hour. As I walked into the reception area I found the child standing at the blackboard, scribbling quietly. Usually, upon seeing me she would erase her drawing and run out of the room ahead of me towards the office. This time, however, she refused to leave. Laughing tauntingly, she held her ground at the board and could not be persuaded to move under her own power. When I put my hand out to her, she dropped in a heap on the floor. When I went to pick her up she resisted, screaming, giggling, and flailing wildly in my arms. It so happened, that on this particular occasion, the waiting room was packed and all eyes were turned to my heavy-handed struggle with the wildly resistant Kathy. One face in particular caught my attention. It was Ms. L., beaming radiantly, knowingly. She appeared to be thoroughly enjoying herself, delighted by my awkward mishandling of the situation. When her own session arrived the following Friday, she was again in unusually high spirits. "How did you feel," she asked, "fighting with Kathy in the waiting room last Monday?" I replied that the experience had evoked a number of unpleasant sensations, anger, embarrassment and helplessness not the least among them. Ms. L. seemed elated: "Now you know what it's like for me every single day of my life."

On the face of it, this seemed to be one of those powerful therapeutic moments in which new realizations are reached and old indefensible positions are relinquished. The pleasure that Ms. L. took in viewing my struggle with Kathy was neither malevolent nor sadistic. Rather, it was the pleasure of sharing with another person the anger, humiliation, and helplessness of being outwitted and outmaneuvered by a child's teasing caprice. None of my attempts at reasoning with Ms. L. that I could understand her because we were not really so different in certain respects carried the weight and conviction of this one wholly spontaneous interaction with Kathy. For a few moments, we had traded places. Quite unexpectedly for Ms. L., I reacted much as she had countless times in the past and with many of the same feelings. This realization was a gratifying one for her and seemed to carry a number of important implications for the kinds of contact and communcation that were possible between two human beings. For a moment Ms. L. felt vital, connected, and understood. This, in turn, contributed to a gradually developing sense of intiative, authority, and control.

The immediate effect of Ms. L.'s growing autonomy could be detected in subtle shifts within the therapeutic process. A new metaphor, previously unheard, was beginning to emerge:

> *Ms. L.:* You know, Carol is more in control now over Kathy than she used to be. Kathy used to push her around a lot and scratch her, but she doesn't do that anymore. Now she's afraid of Carol.
>
> *Therapist:* Tell me how Carol handles Kathy.
>
> *Ms. L.:* Well, she used to act like Kathy wasn't even her sister.
>
> *Therapist:* Maybe she felt ashamed.
>
> *Ms. L.:* I think so. And she just felt helpless with Kathy, didn't understand what was going on with her. Carol was having a bad time in school too, I guess. I think it had something to do with my not paying attention to her. I was giving all my attention to Kathy.
>
> *Therapist:* Carol must have felt like she didn't have anything that was her own.
>
> *Ms. L.:* You're right (smiles knowingly).
>
> *Therapist:* You were always putting Kathy first.
>
> *Ms. L.:* I don't do that anymore. Well, sometimes I do but I give more to Carol now. They're both my children.

Much as Kathy had been incorporated by Ms. L. as a metaphor for that part of herself that was damaged, fiercely angry and out of control, Carol had gradually come to represent those aspects that were bright and attractive but painfully neglected. The gradual development of this metaphor in the treatment process was accompanied by a range of fairly dramatic changes in Ms. L.'s personal conduct and in her handling of the parenting situation. Like Carol, she had become increasingly assertive, consistent, and coherent in her demands and expectations. There was little doubt now that

Kathy. The alternative to a fused symbiotic attachment with the therapist was a wholly erotic relationship in which she could remain close but separate. If the relationship was sexualized then the therapist would remain an object and she could remain a self; otherwise, she would be swallowed up in the symbiosis. From this point of view, Ms. L.'s retreat from treatment appeared to be connected with her anger at the therapist for not giving her what she needed in order to remain in contact yet separate and autonomous, a sexual relationship.

Kathy's father, Ms. L. maintained, would not allow her to come back to the clinic because he believed she was becoming "too involved" with me and was, in her estimation, quite jealous. I associated this immediately with a similar feeling that I had experienced when Ms. L. described intimate situations involving Kathy's father. There had been, in addition, sessions when Ms. L.'s manner of dress seemed deliberately yet incongruously provocative. Perhaps, it occurred to me, Ms. L. was pitting Mr. M. and me against each other. What would it have meant to her to have had two male rivals fighting for her attention?

Beyond acknowledging that there were times during which she thought about her therapist, Ms. L. had few associations to this interpretation. If her behavior was provocative, she believed, this had more to do with a wish for attention or admiration in the broader sense than with sexual attractiveness. Sexualizing the treatment relationship, it appeared, had as its primary aim the gratification of a pregenital, narcissistic need for mirroring self-confirmation, and more specifically, for the firming, strengthening responsiveness (Tolpin and Kohut, 1980) of the paternal self-object in whose eyes she had experienced herself as "nothing at all." As a sexual object she was "an item," one sought after and esteemed. As a person, however, and someone to be valued as a total human being, she seemed to share father's opinion of herself.

Ms. L. returned to the clinic on 12 March 1982. Again, she shifted the blame for her absence to Mr. M. who, she insisted, had made it difficult for her to attend her therapy sessions and continued to be suspicious of the therapist. This time, however, a bridge between those sentiments attributed to Mr. M. and feelings, doubts and fears that were in fact her own was established more easily. With little preliminary exploration, Ms. L. began to elaborate on the connection between her failed treatment hours and other times in the past when she had run from painful situations. As she spoke, her voice filled with anger. This time she was not acquiescing passively to the therapist's interpretations. Her own associations and reconstructions were active, animated, and emotionally charged.

In the following excerpt, the therapist's interpretation of Ms. L.'s defensive avoidance of the treatment situation in terms of feelings towards the maternal figure met with a storm of protest:

> *Ms. L.:* No! It was my father [not my mother] who was no good! Now, I've got Kathy's father. He wants to tell me what to do but doesn't want to take any responsibility for the family. I can't leave, though; I don't know whether I feel scared or guilty.
>
> *Therapist:* Maybe you're not sure whether you can make it on your own.
>
> *Ms. L.:* (Pause) No, I guess I'm not. He's always studying me, watching what I do, telling me where I should go. Who I should talk to!

Had the therapist also engendered a dependent relationship that was hateful to Ms. L.? She had run from therapy because the accessibility she felt in the therapist's presence had awakened a fear of fusion analagous to that experienced earlier in her life with her now-deceased mother. The therapist (like the maternal figure) listened to her and tried to understand, but perhaps, she considered, he was really doing this (like the paternal figure) exploitively for some personal gain. If, however, the therapist could be seduced sexually, then his admiration and esteem would be assured, but this possibility, too, had been frustrated as something to be understood rather than acted upon.

The momentum that carried Ms. L. beyond this therapeutic deadlock came not from the therapist's interpretations but from a series of subtle but extremely important interactions in which areas of responsibility and decision making were turned over to her by the therapist. Toward the end of the session excerpted above, for example, Ms. L. complained that the weekly family therapy sessions that had begun a few weeks earlier were, in her opinion, of little value as Kathy's father refused to participate: "It just defeats the purpose," she reasoned, "he won't get involved so it's really not a family." I acknowledged that her sense of the situation seemed well-founded and that, pending her decision, we would discontinue the weekly family meetings. Ms. L. had ventured an opinion, the therapist had deferred to her judgment. A seemingly minor negotiation, but one interpreted by Ms. L. as an indication that I could allow her to think for herself, that I trusted her judgment, and that

I respected her decision. Metaphorically, in the transference, I had become like the mother who could facilitate and augment her initiatives while encouraging her autonomy, and the father who could offer advice but listen to reason, who could admire her for the kind of person she was. Unlike the mother of early childhood, I could never be "enough" for her in that I refused to support a fused symbiotic relationship of "perfect" empathic responding. Nor would I gratify her sexually. I had, however, helped her to understand how these wishes were related to her needs for esteem, admiration, and self-confirmation. In the end, I could only help her to decide what she wanted to do for herself and respect her for her decisions.

As an interesting footnote to the process material described above, Ms. L. reported, several weeks later (2 April 1982) during her therapy hour, that she was romantically involved with someone new, "someone who I think I'm in love with. A man who cares about the kids and who seems to understand me. He wants to marry me. It's just that he's worried that I'm not going to do anything to get out of my current situation." While the possible transference implications of Ms. L.'s new relationship were not fully explored, it did appear as though the experience in treatment of "a new kind of relationship," one in which nonexploitive help, understanding, and interest had been forthcoming, had opened up the possibility of seeking out new, genuinely intimate relationships outside of the treatment hour. Ms. L. was now ready, it seemed, to take the risk.

Termination

Ms. L. was told of the therapist's plans to leave the clinic approximately eight weeks before the actual termination would occur (16 April 1982). Her response was immediate and unequivocal. The following day she appeared for her scheduled treatment hour and announced that she, too, had decided to move away, "back south" to live with her sister. This would be an opportune time to do so, she believed, because if she were to stay "it would be so hard to get started with someone new." More than just the loss of a person who had become very important in her life, the therapist's impending departure reminded Ms. L. of her isolation. It was not so much the therapist's departure that disturbed her, however, as the awareness of being left behind (passively) or, more to the point perhaps, of leaving something behind:

Ms. L.: I feel like everyone is moving ahead but me. You're going on with your career . . . you're going to do what you want. And Carol is growing up. Kathy is in school right now. For me it just feels like I've left something behind.

Ms. L. had begun to look around her, to see what other people were doing with their lives. Having experienced herself as accessible, and not as different as she had once believed, it was no longer inconceivable to her that she might have the kinds of things that her contemporaries had. Gradually, "their values" were becoming "her values" and a standard against which she measured herself. Not having what other people had gotten for themselves and their families made her feel inadequate, blundering and inept, as though there was something missing. What had been left behind?

Ms. L. could not answer this question at first. Talking about it only seemed to make her anxious. Yet somehow the feeling was a familiar one; she had experienced this kind of uneasiness before, when Kathy was born and her mother died:

Ms. L.: I mean she really knew me and cared about me. She listened to me . . . sort of like you do. . . .

Therapist: Maybe you feel then that when I go away I'll be taking some part of you with me. . . . When you had Kathy you were going to show your mother that you could raise her by yourself. Then she died and you felt you just couldn't do it on your own. Kathy has grown while she's been here at the clinic. Now I'm leaving and maybe you're wondering if you'll be able to do it on your own."

Ms. L. had been left behind. The mother within Ms. L. had been left behind as well. To have taken over, to have become a mother for her children would have meant acknowledging her own mother's death and this was a loss she had yet to mourn. By remaining a child herself, helpless, needy, and incompetent she would keep her mother alive:

Therapist: I've noticed that Kathy and Carol both call you Barbie instead of mommy.

Ms. L.: Yeah they do. I don't mind it though. I guess I just don't feel like a mother to them. Occasionally I do but mostly just like a big sister. . . . It's hard for me to think of myself as a mother sometimes.

Therapist: Three sisters . . . like three orphans without a mother.

Ms. L.: That's what I feel like sometimes.

Before Ms. L. could invest herself fully in mothering her two children, she would first have to mourn the death of her own mother. This, in turn, would entail a radical shift in defenses. Rather than denying the loss by preserving those conditions of helplessness and inadequacy through which mother's presence had been assured in the past, she would keep her mother alive by identification, by providing for Kathy something of the maternal resourcefulness that had once been provided for her. She would no longer need to blame herself for Kathy's illness.

The mourning process, as it unfolded in the final weeks of treatment, began in the past, with recollections of mother's sudden, unexpected death and the anger, guilt and disorientation that followed (from 30 April 1982 session):

Ms. L.: When I was pregnant with Kathy I was in a bad way and I might have transmitted it to Kathy.

Therapist: What do you think you transmitted?

Ms. L.: Well, my emotional disturbance. During the pregnancy I moved eight times and I was going to school and I just had to be a hundred places at once. I just couldn't be a good mother.

Therapist: It was different than with Carol. You had enormous responsibilities to take care of and no one to take care of you.

Ms. L.: With Carol I still lived with my mother. She could baby-sit for her, and I had my brothers.

Therapist: With Kathy you were alone.

Ms. L.: In the last weeks of the pregnancy I always wondered whether there was something I could have done, if I could have saved her if I had been there. She had a stroke and I didn't even know about it. I still blame my father for that. My mother just told me she was worried and that was all. I didn't know she was near death.

Therapist: How did you feel?

Ms. L.: Like I lost something . . . a big loss . . . like maybe I could have done more for her. But Kathy . . .

Therapist: I wonder if you were angry at Kathy for making it impossible for you to help?

Ms. L.: I was. But that was only after she was really finished, at the end [of the pregnancy]. It didn't make any difference.

Kathy had been the child who had kept Ms. L. away from her mother. Were it not for Kathy, Ms. L. believed, she might have saved her mother's life. With her mother to fall back on, she might have raised a healthy child (later in the same hour):

> *Ms. L.:* With most people I'm afraid that if I ask for something I'll owe something in return. It was that way with my father. So I always did everything for myself. With my mother, I didn't owe her anything. She didn't owe me anything. I just wish I'd been able to tell her how much I loved her before she died.
>
> *Therapist:* It was hard for you to tell your mother how you felt towards her.
>
> *Ms. L.:* I think it was hard for both of us. I knew she cared about me, though. I used to ask her how to do things sometimes and she would tell me to do what I thought was right.
>
> *Therapist:* She helped you to grow.
>
> *Ms. L.:* Now I usually do the same thing. I ask people what they think but I end up doing what I think even if it's not always right.

This was precisely what had occurred in the therapeutic process. Ms. L. began the hour by asking me what I wanted to talk about and what I was going to do with her family when I left the clinic. When, however, I asked her what she thought would be most appropriate, what she wanted to do, she produced a sensible and well-thought-out plan for ongoing treatment. "Usually," she explained, "I can make up my own mind so long as I have someone to fall back on. It's when I'm alone that I get panicky and don't know if I can do it." This seemed to get to the heart of the matter. In Ms. L.'s experience, demonstrating competence meant being left alone and not having anyone to "fall back on." The message seemed to be: if you can do it, then do it by yourself! This was exactly what Ms. L. had done throughout most of her life.

Ms. L. had demonstrated during the course of her treatment that she could grow as both a parent and a mature adult pursuing her own goals. Now I, too, was leaving her. As had been the case with her mother, the leavetaking was experienced as a kind of death. The one person who seemed to know and understand her and who supported her growth would no longer be there. Like her father, I was leaving just when she had something to show for herself that she could be proud of.

The final weeks of treatment, I believe, consolidated many of the gains that had been made during the previous year by once again offering new possibilities in place of anticipated outcomes. It was true, for example, that the loss of the therapist as a supportive, growth-facilitating object would be irretrievable, but this time there was much Ms. L. would hold onto and take with her. She would "keep" the therapist not by "keeping a place open for him" through her impotence and incompetence, but by identifying with him as a caregiving individual who had listened with interest and objectivity to what she had to say, who tried to understand what she was feeling without imposing, and who showed her new possibilities while respecting her ability to make decisions for herself. Those psychological functions that the therapist had provided for Ms. L.—impulse control, reality testing, internal tension regulation—had undergone a steady internalization and consolidation. Ms. L. was now doing for herself many of the things that the therapist had once done for her.

Functions that I might have performed earlier in the treatment were turned over to Ms. L. When it came time, for example, to propose a follow-up treatment plan, she was consulted much as a staff person would have been to determine the disposition of "the case," in order to assure her of the primacy of her own prerogatives, intentions, and opinions in any course of action that would affect her life and the lives of her children. My interest in what she wanted to do and how she wanted to do it, and my willingness to stand by her while she tested out her decisions, seemed to reassure her that, although her abilities were trustworthy and reliable, I (like her mother) would (for the duration of our work together) still be there for her to fall back on if she needed my help. More importantly, I (unlike her father) would share her pride when she succeeded without me. Ms. L. was left more in control of her own remaining treatment hours as well. I no longer called her on the phone, for example, following every missed appointment. The decision when and how to reestablish contact was hers. "If you don't come in one week," I confided, "I know you'll come back at some point, when you're ready." Other people, too, Ms. L. believed, seemed to be allowing her more control over her own affairs.

Gradually, Ms. L. was beginning to experience herself as a more accessible, substantial, and coherent human being. She recognized in herself more of "the same person" from one situation to the next and felt a greater sense of inner compatibility and resolve. Her actions and expressions, once confused and incongruous, now seemed to reflect more accurately her feelings and intentions. More often than in the past, she experienced a sense of singlemindedness and direction, being certain about the things she wanted to do. As the scope of Ms. L.'s ongoing developmental experience was broadened and enriched in the therapeutic context, a similar expansion was also observed in the quality and diversity of growth-promoting experiences generated within the developmental context which

Ms. L. created together with her daughter. For the first time, she was beginning to perceive herself as an active agent in Kathy's development, that it was she for whom and with whom Kathy was beginning to grow. Simply put, Ms. L. was becoming a competent and confident parent. At last, the third "orphan" was stepping forward as a mother and everyone in the family seemed to know it. Kathy rarely summoned her "Barbie" any more. Now, she wanted her "mommie."

Chapter Twenty-Three

A Termination Summary

What had 15 months of treatment accomplished? What had changed for Kathy and Ms. L. as the result of our endeavors? These, perhaps the most obvious and natural questions to be asked, deserve both a general estimation of progress and some in-depth explanation of the relationship between the results obtained and the model of treatment applied. Any treatment purporting to have produced significant therapeutic effects in so short a time, whatever its point of intervention (biological, psychological, or sociological), must be viewed with skepticism and a certain amount of doubt. Disturbances like those we have considered do not remediate overnight, or, for that matter, over one and one-half years. What we can claim realistically, however, if not global improvement, is a change of course in the direction of adaptive function and age- and stage-appropriate development. We are looking for signs of readiness rather than breakthroughs, the psychophysiological potential for forward-moving development. We saw these signs in both Kathy and Ms. L. by the end of our initial course of treatment.

In Kathy, we saw a readiness to experience both herself and other people as separate, self-directing human beings having feelings, thoughts, fantasies, and intentions that are essentially private, to be shared or kept private according to individual choice. Once she recognized this distinct inner dimension of personal, self-contained experiencing, Kathy could move on to the tasks of representation—the symbolic elaboration of internal events—and the building-in of intentionality. Knowing what she wanted and where she wanted to go, knowing her preferences, began with a process of affective differentiation, with her discovering a continuum of distinct feeling states ranging from pleasure to displeasure. The capacity to determine for herself what she could in fact have or obtain on her own, given a reality of limited abilities and resources, remained a different kind of problem, one which began with the gradual replacement of a highly tenuous self-image based on an illusion of omnicompetence with a revised and eminently more durable and flexible sense of self based on a realistic awareness of what she could possibly accomplish on her own, what she could do with the help of others, and what remained altogether impossible and out of reach. Accepting her own smallness and the dependency on others which this implied demanded of Kathy a new mode of relatedness to replace the symbiotic mode she had gradually abandoned. She had to recognize her own feelings, wishes, and prerogatives as well as the feelings of the other persons in her life and to understand that sometimes she would have to postpone or forego altogether something she would have liked for herself. She had to develop empathy, the capacity to put herself in the place of the other momentarily and without sustained fusion, merger, or loss of boundary. In short, during the course of treatment Kathy had become more of a person with an organized, increasingly well structured inner life and a readiness to interact with people around her in a manner truly interpersonal. Domination had been replaced by communication. Literally and figuratively, Kathy was learning to speak.

Like Kathy, Ms. L. was, by treatment's end, beginning to move out on her own and to think about what she wanted to do with the rest of her life. For the first time since Kathy's birth, she was able to draw a distinction between her role as a mother and her life outside of parenting and to formulate realistic and attainable goals and ambitions for herself. She had developed insight into her fears: fears about intimacy, fears of engulfment and of losing her sense of self and identity in relation to others; fears of exploitation and entrapment; and, most importantly, the fear of being unknowable, of being so different from and out of step with the mainstream of humanity, as to preclude understanding and empathy. Finally, Ms. L. had begun to examine conflicts around competence and competitiveness: what it meant to act assertively and independently, to follow up on her own initiatives. Like Kathy, she was developing her own voice and making herself heard.

For both Kathy and Ms. L., interactions, once garbled amalgams of love, hate, anger, and fear, had become less amorphous and more readily decipherable. Kathy's sending power had improved and her mother had become increasingly receptive to her signals. In fact, Ms. L. had become quite expert at identifying her daughter's feelings and at following the movement and sentient flow of Kathy's internal state and her more overt expressions and behaviors. More generally, the clarity and quality of dyadic communication from both sides of the interaction had improved greatly. Mother and child had become increasingly articulate with and understanding of one another. Genuine empathy had largely replaced the forced empathy of projective identification.

Despite a truly gratifying margin of therapeutic success, we must face the fact that the treatment of Kathy and Ms. L. remained incomplete at termination. Both had, I believe, reached natural junctures in the treatment process—fundamental changes in interactional and individual functioning had created a base from which continued growth and development were now possible—but neither had completely relinquished earlier developmental or interactional positions or attained all of the goals set forth at the outset. How far might they have gone if they had received further treatment? Had a sufficient reorganization at levels of intrapsychic and interactional functioning set in motion a revised developmental sequence, one which would continue forward of its own momentum? And, finally, what of the inherent limits to individual and interactional growth? Upon how much plasticity could we have relied realistically in the modification of preexisting structures? Such questions will remain unanswered in the present case because there is no reliable follow-up information on either Kathy or her mother. We know only that Kathy continued on in a therapeutic day-school program and that Ms. L. decided following termination to remain in the Midwest rather than return to her family's home in the South as she had originally planned.

To speculate, I believe that a good case could be made for a favorable longterm prognosis with continued treatment and, perhaps, even without it. A simple but fundamental characteristic of the systems perspective incorporated in our treatment model favors continued improvement for both mother and child: we returned a now-rapidly developing child to a family system which had itself undergone radical change and only vaguely resembled the severely pathological system in which the core developmental disturbance had first evolved. In the same way, we returned a rapidly developing adult and parent to a parenting situation over which she had gained control and in which she was no longer subjugated to the tyranny of a wildly angry and demanding child.

Mother had changed, Kathy had changed, and the structure of interactive patterning had changed so much that the likelihood of either mother or child returning to earlier patterns of engagement seems quite remote. Even if we were to assume that Kathy and her mother were essentially the same persons before and after treatment, there can be no question that the interaction between them had been altered radically. While we could not possibly have inoculated our patients against all of the countless and unforeseeable obstacles to ongoing development, we had, I believe, at least insured against a recurrence of those same difficulties and a reliance upon those same solutions as had first brought them to our attention. For better or worse, their future would not unfold in the same way as had their past.

Case Discussion

At 2½, Kathy was a fearful, clinging, and angrily demanding child. She was intolerant of even momentary lapses in her caregiver's attention, becoming panicky, raging, and disorganized in its absence. Even the close proximity to her mother that she demanded was problematic for this required that mother respond in a way that would not challenge the appearance of two persons functioning as one. At all costs Kathy avoided the realization of her own weakness, helplessness, and vulnerability, and to this end she could accommodate neither distance nor closeness. She occupied a very narrow, carefully measured margin midway between separation and symbiotic fusion.

The 3½ year old Kathy who returned for treatment after a yearlong hiatus was little changed, though she had grown physically and, in certain respects, psychologically. Her growth made sustaining a convincing illusion of shared, undifferentiated functioning with her mother a great deal more difficult. Holding on to the appearance of shared functioning demanded a lockstep synchronization of need and gratification, wish and wish-fulfillment, in which empathy gave way to wild and consuming oscillations of over-identification and projection. In order to ensure her mother's absolute understanding, she had first to impose on her an experience of rage and domination which approximated the conditions of her own helpless dependency. She found in her mother a willing accomplice. Ms. L. acceded to the child's wishes in order to ensure that she herself would never have to become a competent, fully functioning adult, something which she did not believe possible in the absence of her own mother. She identified herself fully with her child, creating the kind of "perfect union" that makes the consolidation of autonomy-enhancing psychological structure virtually impossible.

To have begun the diagnostic and treatment process by intervening at the level of individual child or individual parent, or even at the level of individual child and individual parent, would have overlooked what was manifest in this parent–child relationship: a child who, by the very nature of her illness, had failed to consolidate autonomous intrapsychic structure and the kind of independence which this normally facilitates, and a parent who, though capable of relatively independent functioning, sustained this precarious autonomy by preserving in the person of her daughter that part of herself that was weak, angry, and dependent. Clearly, the relationship possessed a certain enduring and characteristic patterning of exchange; it had, in other words, attained a level of structuralization. The salient context of this structuralization from a clinical standpoint, however, was not intrapsychic but interactional, involving the child in actual patterns of mutual regulatory exchange with an actual (as opposed to internally represented) caregiving figure. By its design, the interaction excluded virtually any input which might disconfirm the symbiotic illusion or open up to normal phase-appropriate reevaluation those highly idiosyncratic patterns of recognition-expectation-response which maintained it. The interaction was almost impenetrable; to have treated it as something permeable and readily divisible would, I believe, have led nowhere. We might only have lost our patients a second time.

As therapist, I interposed myself verbally, rather than imposing myself physically, following, reflecting, and interpreting elements of the confused interaction, introducing periodically those modes of exchange which had not yet become suffused with expectations of painful or injurious consequences. This occurred in a therapeutic medium which respected the interaction as a coherent, structuralized entity with its own laws of coherence and organization. The introduction of symbolic motifs paralleling interactional motifs around the problems of separation and reunion (such as "things that come apart go back together again") produced an interface between the interactional and the intrapsychic; it reformulated the garbled, physical intertwining of two psychologically fused human beings in a medium in which thought rather than impulse dominated action, while preserving the sentience of the original interaction. Symbolism functioned both interactionally (as a mode of communication) and intrapsychically (as a medium for internalization) where confused patterns of physical-motor interchange only functioned in the most primitive interactional sense and provided little or no basis for coherent structuralization at either level of organization.

Beginning with Kathy's third month in intensive interaction therapy, we began to notice better-organized and better-differentiated interchange between mother and daughter. In addition, Kathy was beginning (first in the context of the interaction itself) to play alone in her mother's presence without demanding unyielding attention and participation. Furthermore, the character of her independent play, its themes and development, borrowed much from the interlocking exchange of the formerly joint dyadic interaction; she had combined her mother's play function with her own. Something had been taken inside. Deep within the interactive orbit we observed the emergence of embryonic precursors to intrapsychic structuralization, gradually expanding and differentiating from the still dominant interactive structures. If Kathy was now in fact capable of carrying with her aspects of experience in replicable, representational form, then she could, we reasoned, begin to carry with her the essence of the interaction itself: its soothing, regulating functions. The interaction was becoming portable, so to speak; Kathy was no longer bound to the actual engagement of her actual dyadic partner. She could orchestrate with a person other than her mother patterns of engagment which anticipated mother's response but which were independent of mother's actual physical presence. She could generalize and therefore she could transfer from one situation to another those modes of relatedness that were most salient in her experience.

Following several weeks of furiously willful struggle, Kathy accepted her mother's leavetaking during therapy hours and, in her absence, engaged me as her interactive partner. To say that Kathy reconciled herself to my solitary presence with her is not, however, quite accurate. It is true, perhaps, that she accommodated to the situation given her expectation that I, like her mother, would respond to her in such a way as to sustain the delusion of symbiotic unity; in fact, until I began to understand the meaning of her behavior and its sources in the ongoing parent–child interaction, I did respond in a way that complemented Kathy's half of this shared interactive structure. In doing so, I confirmed for a time her original expectations. Like her mother, I allowed her to play from the safe confines of my lap, to use my hands as her hands, and to stand on my feet while she reached for something inaccessible, as if standing and reaching from her own two feet.

I do not believe that anyone operating within a psychodynamic framework would have difficulty understanding Kathy's adaptation to the therapeutic situation as a form of transference. With far less disguise and obfuscation than we are accustomed to encountering in the veiled allusions to transference implicit in the production of the more developmentally sophisticated patient, Kathy had displaced from mother to therapist (and with seeming deliberation) those very expectations that were most troubling and problematic to her. She had gone so far as to coerce from me the very kind of responsiveness that would in fact confirm and perpetuate those expectations. Like all transference phenomena, Kathy's displacement of attitudes, orientations, and expectations from mother to me contained within it an element of repetition. She had repeated with me a mode of interaction which, in the context of the mother–child dyad, had prevented her from remembering the shame, anger, and frustration she had felt when faced with the realization of her own weakness and incompetence. In this respect, the transference had served as a defense against the conscious reawakening of a painful self-representation. It contained, in other words, a kernel of conceptual-level thought. I would maintain, however, that in most other respects Kathy's active organization of the therapeutic situation around a mode of relatedness first recognized in the patterning of the mother–child interaction preserved an element of preconceptual-level transference. The initial recognition of my approach, attitude, or orientation, associated with a particular variant of responsiveness on the part of her mother, anticipated a predictable kind of interactive outcome and elicited in turn a form of response aimed at obviating or avoiding a painful or destructive consequence. The child's confused recognition and misinterpretation of my neutral, nonintrusive repose as a portentous sign of withdrawal (reminiscent of her mother's loss of empathy and withdrawal into self-absorption) led to her tyrannical insistence on my undivided attention and participation. Similarly, her distorted recognition of my solicitous overtures to participate in or expand upon her play, as a threatening prelude to the symbiotic reengulfment of a still tenuously individuated self, precipitated the explosive outbursts aimed at reestablishing an acceptable measure of distance and boundary. In both cases, Kathy's recognition of an interactive exchange and her association of the exchange with an actual and current danger outside of the treatment situation led to her inappropriately stereotyped response.

In summary, we recognize in Kathy's therapeutic transference elements of both preconceptual and conceptual-level cognitive and affective organization. At a conceptual, representational level, Kathy had repeated with me a form of complex interactive exchange which protected her, as it had protected her in her interaction with her mother, from recognizing her own inadequacy and feebleness. It was a way of acting which precluded remembering. At a preconceptual, prerepresentational level, Kathy's recognition of my relative distance or proximity as an interactive signal anticipating either withdrawal or engulfment led to a variety of counter-responses aimed at thwarting the predicted outcome with its dreaded consequences. An initial recognition, a memory, resulted in action aimed at avoiding repetition.

In both conceptual level and preconceptual level transference, the fundamental "error" is a failure to act in such a way as to make accurate discrimination possible. Not only had Kathy failed to perceive her mother and me as separate and distinct people, but she had set up her interaction with me in such a way as to mask many of the important differences between therapist and mother. Moreover, she had closed the system, structuring the various interactive motifs rigidly to preclude the introduction of new evidence or information which might disconfirm her dreaded expectations. Her fears of loss, abandonment, and symbiotic reengulfment were self-confirming and self-perpetuating.

The problem, then, from a therapeutic standpoint, was how to begin opening up Kathy's closed system of self-confirming interactions to disconfirming input and the possibility of outcomes different from those she had come to expect. In order to circumvent her defensive orientations, it was necessary to find a medium of exchange which had not yet become associated, in the context of malignant, preexisting interactional structures, with a chain of events which in Kathy's experience led inexorably toward devastating and painful outcomes. To have tried to demonstrate to her, even through well modulated and successive approximations of close physical contact, that intimacy without engulfment was in certain instances a genuine possibility, would (and in many instances indeed did) have led only to a heightening of her sensitivity to encroachment and a redoubling of her initial defensive resistance to physical proximity and contact. The converse also was true. To have helped Kathy come to terms realistically with her actual capabilities and limitations as an autonomous human being by encouraging independent play and initiative, however gradually introduced, would, with the first inadequately measured increment, have induced panicky clinging and greater insistence on the kind of confused physical and psychological intertwining that obscured effectively the relative contribution of the two interactional partners.

Clearly, Kathy's pathological response to most media of interactional exchange involving extremes of distance and proximity precluded the renegotiation of primary separation and individuation issues at a level of direct physical patterning—gradually moving closer, as we would in befriending a small child, or moving back and away, as we would in allowing a child to try out his increasing independence, were both poorly tolerated. Instead, it was necessary to frame the intervention in a mode not already associated with damaging consequences and, by carefully modulating its tone and intensity, use it to enhance rather than detract from her fragile self-regulatory capabilities. To this end, the vital bridge between therapist and child was built around words, rather than around potentially provocative sensorimotor-level interchanges which, though obviously a part of any interaction, were kept within safe, consistent, and predictable bounds. The determination of closeness and distance was left up to Kathy.

By this time, the notion of talk therapy with a child who could not talk should hardly seem strange. That Kathy did not and could not, in all probability, understand more than a few words in no way diminishes the efficacy of the intervention, provided we take into account the nonsemantic components of verbal communication which are especially salient in the primary preverbal interchange between parents and very young children and between therapists and children who, for reasons of developmental immaturity or psychopathology have yet to attain conceptual level cognitive functioning. Again, the significant therapeutic domain in this case was, at least initially, not semantics but sentience. Long before meaning becomes the specific and predominant organizing factor in the internal representation of experience, the child must begin to differentiate and discriminate periods or moments as I have described them in the continuous flux of internal and external events. A continuously changing, modulating, yet experientially seamless succession of such events must undergo a process of division and categorization in order to become humanly assimilable data. We have to mark boundaries, draw distinctions, and segregate sequences of events into coherent and identifiable physical or psychological phenomena. Nature does not often make such clear distinctions, but human beings, in order to make themselves intelligible to themselves and to others, must do so.

Talking to Kathy in a calm but expressively reflective tone, using the rhythm and cadence of my voice to follow the apparent changes in the sentient flow of her play, I marked off or "punctuated" the formerly seamless continuum of succession she experienced. Moments of special intensity were segregated, given specific designations or names, (anger, excitement, sadness, or happiness, for example) and marked off as identifiable subjective events with certain interior qualities of psychological salience and as identifiable interactional events with specific evocative qualities in the overall context of interactional exchange. Moreover, on a somewhat broader level, my presence and persistence, my attentiveness and interest in her, defined a radically different developmental experience and the foundation for interactive structures (and, ultimately, intrapsychic structures) built on a clearly articulated regulation of exchange between two separate and distinct human beings.

Starting as someone whose presence was only dimly perceived, then furiously rejected, I was gradually accepted as one benignly extraneous and, finally, pleasurably anticipated. A significant realignment of expectations had occurred through direct experiential confirmation and disconfirmation, with the result that Kathy was now willing to experiment with a range of developmentally vital interactive patterns she had formerly rejected. She had become a more flexible child, comfortable with and accepting of ever-widening variations of interactive exchange. My quiet inactivity during treatment hours was no longer perceived as a sign of impending withdrawal or abandonment but as the reliably available presence of someone ready to help, soothe, calm, console, or share, as needed. Similarly, my close, active, but clearly differentiated participation in play no longer threatened to accentuate the already unacceptable differences between the relative capabilities and limitations of the two players. In the newly developed structure of exchange, Kathy could borrow from me without demanding my complete submission. As long as constancy, reliability, and empathy were assured, domination was wholly unnecessary.

This all sounds quite hopeful, the reader may argue, but the therapist had not, after all, agreed to adopt the child. He had agreed only to treat her for two or three hours a week. The remainder of her life outside of therapy and the entirety of her life after therapy would be spent in the same developmental environment that had brought her to our attention in the first place. How long would the gratifying realignment of expectations which had evolved over the course of treatment have persisted once that which had been disconfirmed was reconfirmed and that which had been confirmed wholly disconfirmed? The answer is unequivocal: not long at all. Faced again with the old dangers, Kathy would probably respond with the old solutions she had used in the past. If her trust and hopefulness were dashed, she might well have embraced the earlier order of things with renewed ferocity and vigor.

Without significant change in the caregiving environment, comparable in scale to the change in the child herself, what Kathy had gained would quickly have been lost. What's more, there was little time in which to accomplish this. Within a very limited period, Ms. L. had herself to engage in a process of change to redefine those interactional and intrapsychic structures which preserved her past experiences as a care-receiving child in her current experience as a caregiving parent. In principle, the method of treatment was almost the same as that guiding Kathy's psychotherapy. By examining in the context of a therapeutic transference those of Ms. L.'s expectations and convictions born of the interactional outcomes of early childhood, we obtained broader insight into the origins of prevalent patterns of exchange in the present mother–child interaction. By observing interactional cues carefully and insistently, clarifying their intended rather than their anticipated significance, we devised in effect a new translation or interpretation of certain basic modes of human relatedness. The outcome of this aspect of the treatment process was understanding through broadened awareness and intellectual insight. While each of these factors stimulated a readiness for change or a preparedness for change, the actual thrust forward that broke the inertia of Ms. L.'s developmental stagnation was the result of a very different element of the therapy. Gradually, with the actual experience of positive and unexpected outcomes to complex interactional chains (some of them extending over days, weeks, or months) Ms. L. began to realign actual patterns of structured interactive behavior. The interpretation of unfounded or incongruous expectations and their derivation in the early developmental experience may have alerted Ms. L. to the essential dissimilarities between past and present and to the potential implications of these dissimilarities for her understanding of her current life. She accepted these distinctions as plausible on an intellectual level but found them unmoving until they were corroborated and in some sense verified through actual interpersonal experience. In the end, only direct experiencing fosters belief, and only belief results in the unshakable conviction which makes change in actual patterns of relatedness a reasonable risk and one worth taking. Ms. L. had been told many times by many people that she was accessible to understanding like anyone else, that her judgment was trustworthy, and that she was to be admired for her strength, authority, and control; yet, in the course of her everyday life, she was treated as incompetent, inaccessible, and out of control. Long ago, she had stopped listening to what people seemed to be telling her about herself and actually deployed a range of interactional defenses to bolster her perceived vulnerability at this level of exchange. In pulling away, however, isolating herself from human relatedness, and, in consequence, becoming increasingly "odd" and out of touch, she had unwittingly fulfilled her own expectations: no one admired her efforts, understood her predicament, or responded to her neediness. She had become, in effect, a complete unknown.

What good would my reassurances and interpretations have been if I had been unable to find in my treatment of Ms. L. a channel of interactive exchange that had not been defensively closed, avoided, or distorted beyond all interpersonal usefulness? Demonstrating to Ms. L. that some of her expectations were unfounded did not involve a deliberate manipulation of the transference, direct suggestion, or extratherapeutic education. The opportunity for this demonstration occurred spontaneously and with a force of conviction that could not possibly have been contrived or deliberately engineered. Ms. L. observed my awkward and, at the time, embarrassing struggle to coax Kathy from the waiting room into my office. Witnessing my defeat at the hands of her four-year-old forced on her, as no reassurance could have, the inescapable conclusion that now I, too, understood something of the burden she carried with her every day of her life. Suddenly she apprehended and elaborated interpretations that had fallen on deaf ears for months, incorporating them as the basis for adaptive change in her life both as a parent raising an impossibly difficult child and as an adult in her own right, pursuing goals and ambitions which, though thwarted for a time, had never been abandoned.

Where developmental psychopathology is rooted in the faulty interactional exchange of early childhood, the overriding importance of the direct experiential and reexperiential aspects of the therapeutic process is clear. In a very real sense, seeing or, more to the point, experiencing actually and spontaneously is, for such persons, tantamount to believing. Without belief, such persons cannot build solid, unshakable convictions that creative and multifarious variations are in fact possible in what were once stereotyped life situations. Nothing revitalizes hope as much as the living proof that what has occurred once can, despite countless frustrations and disappointments, occur again with a similarly favorable outcome. For many of our patients, experience must be the great teacher.

Chapter Twenty-Four

Corrective Developmental Experiences and Corrective Emotional Experiences

Medical science, like the human body, works with remarkable efficiency to protect its borders against the infiltration of alien or otherwise inimical agents which might compromise or perhaps even destroy the host organism. In both cases, the most successful infiltrations are made not by radical perpetrators of change, which are easily identified and expelled, but by agents which resemble closely in structure or function some component within the host and, by virtue of this likeness, are able to insinuate significant variations through subtle alterations. The relatively conservative or compatible agent of change is most likely to pass undetected and to perpetrate transformations constructive to the current functioning or ongoing evolution of the host.

Franz Alexander's theory of the corrective emotional experience (1924, 1946, 1958) was neither subtle nor compatible with the conservative psychoanalytic mainstream of his day. Few believed that the analyst as blank screen was feasible or even desirable, but the notion of analyst as actor, deliberately undertaking to bring a "favorable kind of emotional climate to the interview" (1961, p. 331) (one which contrasts strikingly and undeniably with the emotional climate surrounding the patient's original early life experience) was more than even the most open-minded could reconcile with the "basic model technique" (Eissler 1953) of psychoanalysis. It was expelled from the system, branded as "transference manipulation . . . gratification without interpretation."

Although Alexander is not read widely anymore, I am struck by something familiar in reading the works of such clinical investigators as Pine (1976), Modell (1980), Winnicott (1965), Kohut (1971, 1977, 1984), and Gill (1982), whose descriptions of certain noninterpretive but therapeutically active elements in the treatment situation certainly carry something of the "corrective emotional" spirit. Tolpin (1983) has proposed a reevaluation of the corrective emotional experience in connection with the treatment of analyzable disorders of the self: "The process of transmuting internalization set in motion by the analysis of self-object transference is indeed a corrective for structural deficits" (p. 364). Cast as a new edition of the "corrective developmental dialogue" between self and self-object, Tolpin's revision of Alexander's corrective emotional experience becomes an important link in the rethinking of psychoanalytic technique in cases of structural deficit psychopathology. Others, such as Gill (1982), have simply acknowledged the inevitability of certain corrective, "noninterpretive" factors in all psychodynamically oriented treatment situations: "The resolution of the transference . . . is accomplished not only by virtue of the examination of the relation between the patient's attitudes and the features of the actual analytic situation . . . but also because in the very act of interpreting the transference, the analyst behaves differently from what the patient has come to expect and even to provoke" (1982, p. 118). Still others, following Pine (1976), have measured the efficacy of "corrective emotional" or "background" elements in the treatment situation by degree, depending on the nature of the psychopathology and its origins in early development.

Clearly, there is something worth saving in Alexander's struggle to account for and correct those peculiarly recalcitrant conditions which have resisted the best efforts of psychotherapists operating under strict adherence to a drive-defense-conflict theory of psychopathology and a "basic model technique" of psychotherapeutic intervention. Taken in the context of infancy and early childhood psychopathology, pathology which predates even the cognitive-affective potential for intrapsychic conflict between differentiated intrapsychic structures, the corrective experience paradigm is not merely a factor, but a predominant factor, in the treatment process. Alexander did not address his theory specifically to children, however, and, while this alone would not have justified all of the technical deviations that are believed to be contraindicated in the psychoanalytic treatment of adults, I believe he would at least have found himself on firmer theoretical ground given the developmental status of his patients.

The corrective developmental experience is an interactional rather than intrapsychic model of treatment and is, therefore, applied most rationally at that point in the life cycle where important psychical processes are negotiated through actual exchange within a dynamic, mutually regulated interactional system. What is "corrective," however, is not limited to the emotional or affective aspects of interaction, which, after all, constitute only one developmental line. This misconception, too, probably arose from Alexander's limited consideration of developmental factors. Corrective experience as a meaningful concept applied to the treatment of early childhood psychopathology implies the facilitation of simultaneous changes across multiple developmental lines (affective, cognitive, physical-motor, social, linguistic, and so on) within a context of gradually shifting, forward moving interactional tasks (Sander 1983). Thus, I have chosen corrective developmental experience to designate a model of treatment in which the confirmation and disconfirmation of experience and expectation applies to the current and ongoing organization, disorganization, and reorganization of experience as it unfolds within a complex interactional system of which the therapist is but one formative element. While recognizing the influence of the child's past on the child's present, the corrective developmental experience is continuous and coterminous with the child's current developmental experience and its respective tasks and issues.

But what did Alexander actually say? Would it not have been better to build a new model of developmental intervention altogether, thereby avoiding association with a theory that has been largely discredited, or do we find in the corrective emotional experience a foundation for the rational treatment of certain classes of psychopathology reflecting deficits or distortions predating the onset of symbolic representational thought and the consolidation of autonomous intrapsychic personality structure?

"The essence of the therapeutic process," wrote Alexander, "consists of the difference between the physician's reactions and those of the parents, parent substitutes, and/or siblings" (1961, p. 327). Recognizing and experiencing in a deeply emotional way this discrepancy between transference feelings directed originally toward the caregiving figures of the past and the reactions of the therapist as a distinctly different kind of person ("a person in his own right") in the present constitutes, Alexander believed, living proof that cognitive insight alone cannot accomplish. The corrective emotional experience, then, is in essence a process of building contrasts and heightening the capacity for discrimination. Like the corrective developmental experience, it capitalizes on the articulation of similarity and dissimilarity as a way of confirming or disconfirming expectations based on the evidence of previous interpersonal experiences. Alexander's contrived method of demonstrating and amplifying dissimilarity, however, compromises the credibility of his treatment as a specifically psychoanalytic intervention. He recommended, for example, that the therapist alter his personality according to a plan in order to maximize the disparity between the kind of response forthcoming from the original caregivers and that which could be expected from the therapist: "If the past parental attitudes resemble those of the therapist, an interminable treatment results." That every analyst is not in fact able to "change himself" by way of becoming "a good enough actor to create convincingly an atmosphere he wants" seemed to Alexander to be a "limitation of technique" (1958, p. 331), reconcilable only by choosing with care the right analyst for the right patient.

Acting with the intention of impressing upon patients the error of their preconceptions is, to put it delicately, a transference manipulation. It promotes distortions instead of clarifying them and perpetuates convictions based on a mythical relationship with a mythical therapist whose reality as a person in his own right is pure fabrication. Furthermore, the use of this manipulation is never in and of itself subjected to interpretation; an early life disillusion is simply replaced by a later life illusion.

Alexander's method of maximizing contrast between expectation and actuality, then, was clearly dubious. His emphasis on the importance of heightening the patient's discrimination between these two aspects of experience, however, was not. The corrective developmental experience also places great emphasis on the contrast between expectation and actuality as a basis for experiential confirmation and disconfirmation. Deliberate manipulation of the transference, however, in order to amplify this contrast is not only detrimental to the treatment process but unnecessary. The therapist need not act in such a way as to accentuate his dissimilarity from the caregivers of the patient's past; dissimilarity, moreover optimal dissimilarity, is ensured already by virtue of the therapist's own developmental experience, training, physical bearing, and the kind of technically "neutral" treatment practiced. Given the person the therapist is and has become, he cannot help but be different from the child's primary caregivers, and provide a radically different interpersonal and interactional presence. The question is not whether the therapist is intrinsically like the original caregivers, but whether he can be coerced by the child into unwittingly recapitulating complementary interactive behaviors which will tend to reconfirm the child's original expectations. There will be times when the therapist must not do what might normally come most naturally—escalating, for example, his efforts to break through to an avoidant or recalcitrant child—in order to ensure understanding of the intent of the behavior and whether it might increase the likelihood of the very kind of responsiveness it is meant to avoid. Once the therapist understands the behavior, a response can be offered that is empathically informed and to this extent highly discrepant with the child's expectations.

In working with adult analytic patients, Alexander struggled with the problem of reviving early conflict situations as events essentially discontinuous with the current life experience. The problem for the therapist was one of bringing to life in a way that was cognitively as well as emotionally plausible "an emotional situation which had met with failure or trauma in the actual early life history." What followed was for all intents and purposes a deconditioning process, not altogether different from Wolpe's more recent systematic desensitization technique (1952, 1954, 1976), "re-expos[ing] the patient under more favorable circumstances to emotional situations he could not handle in the past" (Alexander 1946, p. 66). This, Alexander believed, was the "basic therapeutic principle," the underpinning of all forms of "etiological" psychotherapy.

There are two problems with Alexander's assumptions here, one endemic to the corrective emotional experience, the other endemic to working with adults and being somewhat less problematic in the treatment of children. To reactivate early attitudes based on an understanding of the patient's early development places the therapist in the role of director or choreographer, a posture that is not only active but, again, manipulative of the transference situation. Although Alexander's means of evocation are unclear, something more than the systematic interpretation of resistances to the transference in the present therapeutic relationship (Gill 1982) is implied.

I do not believe that it is necessary for the therapist, particularly the child therapist, to work actively at reviving anything in the therapeutic relationship. The child will bring to the treatment hours the only attitudes, orientations, and expectations he can possibly bring—those based on early and ongoing developmental experiences. There is little need for the therapist either to revive a particular pattern of relating by selectively responding to the child's material or to undertake deliberately to orchestrate a particular type of developmental experience, paralleling or diametrically opposed to the child's prototypic developmental situation. In a corrective developmental experience, the therapist–child interaction will build from the ground up an entirely new edition of the original and ongoing developmental environment, leading to the consolidation of new interactional structures reflecting the systematic confirmation, disconfirmation, and interpretation of phase-specific interactional issues as these arise spontaneously within the treatment process. Elucidation of the transference relationship will occur spontaneously as the therapist interprets the child's resistance to the transference. Even in the case of the very young or developmentally immature youngster, interpretive interventions (regardless of the salience to the child of their semantic component), by virtue of their unique suitability of establish contact without setting off defensive behaviors, are the most effective means of disconfirming the child's expectation of interactive clash, conflict, or frustration and of opening up the possibility of a more adaptive resolution to the problems inherent in establishing viable, growth-promoting interactive synchrony.

Alexander's second assumption—that we are working in all cases with a revival or reactivation of antiquated transference attitudes which are essentially isolated or discontinuous in time, place, and person with the current life situation—is also of questionable validity, particularly as applied to the treatment of infants or young children. In the corrective developmental experience, we make no such assumptions, but acknowledge that the therapeutic situation exists in extension of the actual caregiving situation. Ours is not a process of reactivation and undoing, but one of augmentation, of expanding an ongoing interactional process within which the preindividuated preconceptual-level child's experience of himself and his world is most important.

Because Alexander's corrective emotional experience is aimed primarily at a recovery and reorchestration of modes of interaction from the past, with certain important modifications in content, structure, and theme, it depends to a certain degree on the therapist's active reconstruction of characters, relationships, and events which the therapist can know only inferentially as they are woven into the patient's narrative. What really happened is narrative supposition which the therapist must accept as reality and utilize as he plans in the current reassemblage to avoid the kinds of predicaments that hypothetically, at least, undermined the original developmental experience and contributed to the production of symptoms and characterological deformities. Given that the original cast is no longer available to restage the patient's early experience, the therapist must study the important roles as these appear in the transference and then not only reproduce, but modify them in order to effect a more favorable outcome.

In the psychotherapy of children, particularly in the early years of life, the important experiential moments are not long gone and the original "cast" is, in most cases, still available. By working psychotherapeutically with the caregiving parents at the same time as the child, we are, in effect, correcting certain aspects of the child's developmental experience at their sources, in the original and ongoing caregiver-child interaction. This is the level at which the reorganization of recognition-expectation-response patterns is most essential if the child's reappraisal of possibilities for interactional relatedness in the therapeutic situation is to be generalized to the family system as well. Thus, if there are therapeutic manipulations in the corrective developmental experience, they are undertaken through the caregiver and caregiving family in helping family members to observe, understand, and modify patterns of interaction that are counterproductive to the child's ongoing development. Even here, however, I do not believe that the process of intervention is tantamount to manipulation. In many instances, the most effective and enduring changes in caregiving attunement and responsiveness come from insight into the sources of faulty family interaction in the caregiver's own developmental experience a generation earlier, rather than from teaching, advice or suggestion (though these may be needed in situations where the parents simply do not know how to do some things). Optimally, through the consolidation of new interactional (and, in some cases, intrapsychic) structures and the development of insight into current patterns of interaction, the caregiver's adaptive and parenting resources will expand to the point where both the therapeutic and the actual caregiving environments provide comparable and compatible growth-promoting developmental experiences for the child.

Why a Psychoanalytic Model?

As the reader will certainly have gathered, I have sought to demonstrate that the corrective developmental experience, far from being a radical departure from the basic model technique of psychoanalysis, is actually quite compatible with the mainstream of psychoanalytic theory and procedure. But why is this argument important? If the clinical model is effective as a treatment intervention and the theoretical model is plausible as an explanatory paradigm, doesn't the corrective developmental experience stand on its own, regardless of its association with a more traditional body of thought? There may be an advantage in linking a new and unconventional idea with an established discipline, but I believe that there is a far more compelling advantage with immediate clinical implications.

The discovery of precursory stages to advanced developmental processes provides an important link in our conceptualization of life span development as a continuous and coherent epigenetic sequence. Moreover, it is a first step in understanding the mechanisms through which developmental change occurs and how this is mediated by endogenous and exogenous factors. If we can see, as in the present case, that the most elemental organizations of mental life share certain structural and functional properties with phenomenally similar organizations in later life (or occupy a common developmental line), then we can also speculate that those mediating factors which alter or influence the characteristics of later organizations will, applied precociously in a form which reflects the realistic integrative and synthetic capabilities of the immature organism, have some equivalent impact on earlier organizations as well. The converse would also hold true: factors observed to influence the course of earlier developmental organizations should (again, providing appropriate adjustment for developmental status) produce parallel, if not equivalent, effects at the level of later developmental organizations. The implications of this principle for actual clinical practice are apparent in our application of a model of technical intervention that has been found useful in treating certain psychopathological disabilities of later childhood, adolescence, and adult life to the amelioration of the more precocious forms of psychopathology in infancy and early childhood. Specifically, we have found that even in the case of nonverbal, preconceptual-level child suffering from massive disruptions in the negotiation of phase-appropriate developmental tasks, a treatment methodology based on the systematic observation, articulation, interpretation, and experiential confirmation or disconfirmation of events within the psychotherapeutic process provides a rational basis for effective intervention. From a technical standpoint, then, the contribution of the corrective developmental experience to the actual mechanics of psychotherapy in infancy and early childhood is in many instances one of emphasis; to an outside observer, the treatment situation at any given moment may not look substantially different from other forms of play psychotherapy. If anything, we have demonstrated that the prevailing psychoanalytic technique is applicable to the earliest and most severe forms of psychopathology to a greater extent than has been recognized. As Gill (1982) has commented, even the most fundamental reconceptualizations of theory are not followed necessarily by equivalent changes in practice. Conceptually, however, I believe we have made some significant strides in our understanding of the therapeutic action of process-oriented psychotherapy in the context of early childhood psychopathology through our redefinition of the appropriate therapeutic field and in our rethinking of certain basic modes of experiential organization which appear to be characteristic of human beings throughout life. We have observed, for example, that even among preverbal, preconceptual-level children, interpretive interventions punctuate, identify, emphasize, and differentiate subjectively undifferentiated moments of experience within an interactional medium substantially different from any which the child has previously encountered. Unlike some psychoanalytic investigators who assert that the deep content of such interpretive statements is therapeutically active in altering psychic functioning, we place relatively greater emphasis on the structural aspects of the intervention. Content or semantic aspects, I believe, are important in working with children at this stage of development as far as they allow the therapist to track an organization of experience substantially different from the therapist's own.

Beyond the structure of the intervention and the effect it is meant to have on the sentience and organization of the child's experience is the fact of the intervention itself and its implications for the renewed negotiation of developmental and interactional issues. In many cases, we find the therapeutic process offers a different solution to interactive issues that were insufficiently or inadequately resolved in the original developmental sequence. This is the goal of a treatment in which the relevant therapeutic domain is primarily interactional rather than intrapsychic. With the understanding that all significant interactions in the child's life (not just the therapeutic ones) are formative, we treat not only the target child but also the caregivers who, by virtue of congenital or experiential compromise, have limited experiential resources to draw upon in the parenting process. We would be grateful, indeed, if as a result of our efforts the caregivers of our disturbed children could offer the interactive mix something which they themselves never had at a comparable point in their own development. Finally, we have recognized that the kind of developmental experience negotiated between child and therapist will be determined both by current factors related to the person of the therapist and the thera-

peutic milieu and by earlier factors related to the child's developmental and interactive experiences as these are manifest in patterns of recognition-expectation-response, transferred from the
original or primary caregiving system to the therapeutic interaction. The uncovering of transference and its subsequent resolution
are dependent upon a heightened capacity for discrimination between the actual and the expected and the direct experiencing of
interactional outcomes other than those anticipated.

Given these conceptual and technical modifications, it is clear
that the corrective developmental experience conforms in other
respects to Freud's basic model technique and is not as much a
radical departure as it is a developmentally compensated restate-
ment of psychoanalytic psychotherapy applied to the treatment of
the preindividuated, preconceptual-level child. The goal of our
work is conceived in terms of the facilitation of dynamic interactive
processes leading initially to the consolidation of age- and stage-
appropriate interactive structures and later to their internalization
as stable and enduring intrapsychic structures. In this respect, our
aims approximate more closely those elaborated in the structural
deficit models of psychopathology than in the more traditional
models of intrapsychic conflict resolution. (Though we do not deny
the importance of clash, ambitendency, and paradox in the early
phases of development, we recognize that these apply to interactions between the child and actual components of the child's developmental system and cannot, given the child's limited symbolic
representational capabilities, be conceived in terms of conflict involving internalized structures or agencies.) Our means of facilitating adaptive growth-promoting interactive processes, however, re-
tains an emphasis on the undoing of resistances, the heightening of
awareness and discrimination, and the confirmation and disconfirmation of expectations. Indeed, the facilitation of these processes
within the therapeutic context would appear to be the active agent
in all growth-promoting interactions as these occur throughout life,
no less in infancy and early childhood than in adulthood or later
life. To reiterate: factors which alter or influence the characteristics of later developmental organizations will, applied in a developmentally compensated mode, produce a parallel or equivalent impact upon earlier developmental organizations.

But what of the converse? In what ways do factors which
actively mediate growth early in development figure into the
scheme of ongoing development later in life? More to the point, how
do we conceive of a corrective developmental experience derived
from clinical work with infants and toddlers suffering severe psy-

chopathological disturbances being applied to the treatment of older children or adult psychiatric patients who have already achieved the capacity for mental representation, conceptual-level thought, and autonomous psychological functioning?

Spence (1982, 1983) and Schafer (1983) have discussed the psychoanalytic process in terms of narrative construction in the elaboration of a cogent and coherent account of human actions over time and throughout life. Creating a narrative account of the life experience is something all of us who are able engage in all the time, though in doing so we necessarily tolerate and even perpetuate a certain degree of incompleteness, ambiguity, and creative license. The idea of narrative is to answer such questions as "Who am I? What do I do? Why?" in terms of certain historical or biographical constants which identify the self to the self, justify choosing certain courses of action from among many alternatives as being conducive to maintaining that identity cohesively, and reaffirm the meaning and centrality of that identity in the life experience. Any narrative is only one of the many renderings that may be possible, given the actual life history. When this narrative is an adaptive one which accommodates flexibly and creatively both the foreseeable and the unforeseeable eventualities of life, the individual experiences a sense of wonder, curiosity, and emotional and intellectual expansiveness. Where the narrative construction is limited by pervasive gaps in memory and accountability or by an experiential base that is disjointed or idiosyncratic to the point of being nongeneralizable, expectancies and anticipation are characterized by terror, uncertainty, doubt, and constriction. As Spence (1983) has described it, "Part of my sense of self depends on my being able to go backward and forward in time and weave a story about who I am, how I got that way, and where I am going. . . . Take that away from me and I am significantly less . . . living [only] for the moment, I am not a person at all" (p. 458).

Not a person at all—certainly not a psychologically healthy adult person but perhaps, as we have seen, a developing person for whom moments and instants comprise the baseline of consciousness and experiential awareness. Narratives do not begin with memories, causal sequences, and descriptive internal dialogues; they begin with sensory impressions registering momentary and fluctuating internal stimuli and patterns of recognition-expectation-response which register those special stimuli that are socially interactive in nature. Gradually, through the mutual regulation of caregiver and child, these disconnected or disassociated events become correlated with certain recognitions, expectations, and, finally, cause-and-effect sequences. Where certain types of experience are excluded from the gradual interactive processes of organization, differentiation, punctuation, and articulation because of congenital defects, constitutional predispositions, or psychopathology, the individual will experience a void, an area of nonawareness, which may, depending on the centrality or salience of what is missing to the overall life experience, persist as a more or less pervasive gap in the narrative history, a break in the line of continuity which defines self and identity.

Experiential gaps can, of course, occur for a variety of reasons at any point in the life cycle. With the advent of symbolic and conceptual-level thought and the consolidation of the tripartite personality organization, we begin to think in terms of actions, internal and external events, and ideas which are rendered unconscious or are modified in such a way as to disguise or distort their original purpose, aim, or intent. The construction or reconstruction of narrative history where there is incomplete information, misapprehension, or distortion at this level of development begins with a process of uncovering or, in some cases, fabricating what had been lost, forgotten, or distorted. It then proceeds with the assembly of the various component pieces into coherent biographical totalities that are presumably more complete and fully informed than the original and to this extent are more versatile, explanatory, and adaptive as the basis for assertive action in the current life experience. When, however, the narrative gap or distortion has occurred prior to the advent of symbolic, conceptual-level thought, we begin the construction or reconstruction process much as we would with the infant or preindividuated, preconceptual-level child, by articulating and discriminating subtle variations in internal states and by punctuating the ebb and flow of experiential sentience. All of this takes place within a verbal interpretive motif aimed at tracking the patient's production at content-descriptive and process-experiential levels of organization. The relative therapeutic efficacy of this kind of intervention will depend on the developmental phase of which the experience in question is representative and the form in which it is preserved: memory, affective state, physical patterning, or interactive patterning. Where the therapeutic material evokes themes associated with relatively advanced developmental phases (oedipal themes for example) in which true intrapsychically organized mental events are registered symbolically, the efficacy of interpretation will depend to a greater extent on the therapist's ability to prove the patient's experience at the level of a specific symbolic content or representation around which various affective tones and physical-motor patterns are organized. Where, in contrast, the patient's material is evocative of themes associated with early presymbolic prerepresentational experiences that are preserved interactionally in patterns of recognition-anticipation-response or psychophysiologically as affective states or physical-motor patterns, the therapeutic action of the same intervention will depend to a greater extent on those structural aspects of the interpretation which capture the sentient characteristics of the experience under examination. This is not to say that the content aspects of early experience are unimportant in this case, because even the earliest preverbal experiential patterns serve as specific organizing factors for the later clustering of experiences sharing a similar theme or valence. Content, after all, provides the conceptual-level observer with a conceptual-level translation of mental events that are organized preconceptually within the context of a radically different sensibility of order and meaning.

Returning to the question of the narrative aspects of the psychotherapeutic situation, we can now define the process of narrative construction and reconstruction in developmental terms. In the more traditional psychoanalytic mode, which deals primarily with the dynamics and organization of intrapsychic events represented symbolically as actual or analogous experience, the generation of a cohesive narrative history derives its power and efficacy from the restoration to consciousness of specific memories, fantasies, and the affects surrounding them and the organization of these biographical artifacts into cogent, coherent, and adaptive renderings of what the life experience might have been like at some critical juncture in the early life history. We will in other words have constructed a life story, or at least a chapter of one, complete with text, explanatory notes, and perhaps pictures. If, however, we extend the concept of narrative construction to include the earliest days and weeks of life and the salient, indeed prototypic developmental experiences with which these are occupied, then we must consider the notion of filling in gaps and rectifying distortions from a very different point of view and in a very different experiential medium. Where the conceptual-level, mentally represented aspects of development provide a kind of text of the narrative life experience, the preconceptual, interactionally represented aspects provide its tone, the distinctive cadence and coloration which comprise the earliest underpinnings of a subjectively personal human identity. The corrective developmental experience, then, does not aim to fill in gaps in the awareness of time, place, and person with carefully articulated experiential scenarios, even in the treatment of adults who have attained advanced developmental status. Instead, its goal is to facilitate through the actual confirmation and disconfirmation of experience a gradual change in the kinds of background states, convictions, attitudes, and expectations which derive from the very earliest interactive patternings, yet which color all subsequent events in the life history, giving them that peculiar sentience and continuity which confirm that they are "mine," "a part of my life," and at the core of what I know to be "me."

References

Alexander, F. (1925). Contributions to the symposium held at the eighth international psychoanalytic congress, Salzburg, April 21, 1924. *International Journal of Psychoanalysis* 6: 13–34.

—— (1961). Unexplored areas in psychoanalytic theory and treatment, part II. In F. Alexander, *The Scope of Psychoanalysis, 1921–1961* (pp. 314–335). New York: Basic Books. (Originally published in *Behavioral Sciences* 1958.3)

Alexander, F., and French, T. H., eds. (1946). *Psychoanalytic Therapy: Principles and Application.* New York: Ronald Press.

Alpert, A., and Pfeiffer, E. (1964). Treatment of an autistic child. *Journal of the American Academy of Child Psychiatry* 3: 591–616.

Alter, M., and Scholenberg, R. (1966). Dermatoglyphia in rubella syndrome. *Journal of the American Medical Association* 197: 685–688.

American Psychiatric Association. (1980). *Diagnostic and Statistical Manual of Mental Disorders (DSM III).* Washington, D.C.: APA Task Force on Nomenclature and Statistics.

Ando, H., and Tsuda, K. (1975). Infrafamilial incidence of autism, cerebral palsy, and mongolism. *Journal of Autism and Childhood Schizophrenia* 5: 267–274.

Annell, A. (1955). Insulin treatment in children with psychotic disturbances. *Acta Psychotherapeutica Psychoanalytica Orthopoedica* 3: 193–205.

Arieti, S. (1974). *Interpretations of Schizophrenia.* New York: Basic Books.

Bacharach, H. M. (1976). Empathy. *Archives of General Psychiatry* 33: 35–38.

Bartak, L., Rutter, M., and Lox, A. (1975). A comparative study of infantile autism and specific developmental receptive language disorders. *British Journal of Psychiatry* 126: 127–145.

Bartolucci, G., Pierce, S. J., Streisir, D., and Eppel, P. T. (1976). Phonological investigations of verbal autistic and mentally retarded subjects. *Journal of Autism and Childhood Schizophrenia* 6: 303–316.

Basch, M. F. (1976). The concept of affect: a reexamination. *Journal of the American Psychoanalytic Association* 24 (4): 759–777.

—— (1983). Empathic understanding: a review of the concept and some theoretical considerations. *Journal of the American Psychiatric Association* 31 (1): 101–126.

Bateson, G., Jackson, P. D., Haley, J., and Weakland, J. (1956). Towards a theory of schizophrenia. *Behavioral Sciences* 1: 251–264.

Belmaker, R. H., Hattab, J., and Epstein, R. P. (1978). Plasma dopamine b-hydroxylase in childhood autism. *Journal of Autism and Childhood Schizophrenia* 8: 293–298.

Bender, L. (1947a). Childhood schizophrenia: clinical study of one hundred schizophrenic children. *American Journal of Orthopsychiatry* 17: 40–56.

—— (1947b). One hundred cases of childhood schizophrenia treated with electric shock. *Transactions of the American Neurological Association* 72: 165–169.

—— (1953). Childhood schizophrenia. *Psychiatric Quarterly* 27: 663–687.

—— (1959). Cited in B. Bettelheim, *The Empty Fortress.* New York: Free Press, 1967. (Reference omitted.)

—— (1971). Alpha and omega of childhood schizophrenia. *Journal of Autism and Childhood Schizophrenia* 1: 115–118.

Bergman, P. B., and Escalona, S. K. (1944). Unusual sensitivities in very young children. *The Psychoanalytic Study of the Child.* Vol. 3/4, pp. 333–352. New York: International Universities Press.

Bettelheim, B. (1967). *The Empty Fortress.* New York: Free Press.

—— (1974). *A Home for the Heart.* New York: Knopf.

Bleuler, E. (1950). *Dementia Praecox or the Group of Schizophrenias.* New York: International Universities Press. (Originally published 1911.)

Bradley, L., and Bowen, M. (1941). Behavioral characteristics of schizophrenic children. *Psychiatric Quarterly* 15: 296.

Brambella, F., Viani, F., and Rosotti, U. (1969). Endocrine aspects of child psychosis. *Diseases of the Nervous System* 30: 627–632.

Broen, W. E., and Nakamura, C. Y. (1972). Reduced range of sensory sensitivity in chronic, nonparanoid schizophrenia. *Journal of Abnormal Psychology* 79: 106–111.

Brown, T. A. (1980). The microgenesis of schizophrenic thought. *Archives de Psychology* 48: 215–237.

Buie, D. H. (1981). Empathy: its nature and limitations. *Journal of the American Psychoanalytic Association* 29 (2): 281–307.

Bush, M. (1977). The relationship between impaired selective attention and severity of psychopathology in acute psychotic patients. *British Journal of Medical Psychology* 50: 251–265.

Call, J. D. (1980). Some prelinguistic aspects of language development. *Journal of the American Psychoanalytic Association* 28 (2): 259–289.

Campbell, M. (1973). Biological interventions into the psychoses of childhood. *Journal of Autism and Childhood Schizophrenia* 3 (4): 347–373.

Campbell, M., Anderson, L. T., Cohen, I. L., et al. (1982). Haloperidol in autistic children: effects on learning, behavior, and abnormal involuntary movements. *Psychopharmacology Bulletin* 18 (1): 110–113.

Campbell, M., Fish, B., Shapiro, T., and Floyd, A. (1971). Imipramine in preschool autistic and schizophrenic children. *Journal of Autism and Childhood Schizophrenia* 1: 267–282.

Campbell, M., Geller, B., Small, A. M., Petti, T. A., and Ferris, S. H. (1978). Minor physical anomalies in young psychotic children. *American Journal of Psychiatry* 135: 573–575.

Campbell, M., Petti, T. A., Green, W. H., Cohen, I. L., Genieser, N. B., and David, R. (1980). Some physical parameters of young autistic children. *Journal of Child Psychiatry* 19: 193–212.

Chess, S. (1977). Follow-up report on autism in congenital rubella. *Journal of Autism and Childhood Schizophrenia* 7: 68–81.

Churchill, D. W. (1972). The relationship of infantile autism and early childhood schizophrenia to developmental language disorders of childhood. *Journal of Autism and Childhood Schizophrenia* 2: 182–197.

Ciaranello, R. D., Vandenberg, S. R., and Anders, T. F. (1978). Intrinsic and extrinsic determinants of neuronal development: relationship to infantile autism. *American Journal of Psychiatry* 135: 573–575.

Clark, P., and Rutter, M. (1977). Compliance and resistance in autistic children. *Journal of Autism and Childhood Schizophrenia* 7: 33–48.

Cohler, B. J. (1980). Developmental perspective on the psychology of the self in early childhood. In *Advances in Self Psychology*, ed. A. Goldberg, pp. 69–115. New York: International Universities Press.

Cohn, D. J. and Johnson, W. T. (1977). Cardiovascular correlates of attention in normal and psychiatrically disturbed children. *Archives of General Psychiatry* 34: 561–567.

Colbert, E. G., Koegler, R. R., and Markham, C. H. (1959). Vestibular dysfunction in childhood schizophrenia. *Archives of General Psychiatry* 1: 600–617.

Cox, A., Rutter, M., Newman, S., and Bartak, L. (1975). A comparative study of infantile autism and specific developmental receptive language disorders. II. Parental characteristics. *British Journal of Psychiatry* 126: 146–159.

Creak, E. M. (1961). Schizophrenic syndrome in children: progress of a working party. *Cerebral Palsy Bulletin* 3: 501–504.

Creak, E. M., and Pampiglione, G. (1969). Clinical and EEG studies on a group of 35 psychotic children. *Developmental Medicine and Child Neurology* 11: 218–227.

DeMyer, M. K. (1979). *Parents and Children in Autism.* Washington, D.C.: Victor H. Winston and Sons.

DeMyer, M. K., Barton, S., Alpern, G., Kimberlin, C., Allen, J., Yang, E., and Steele, R. (1974). The measured intelligence of autistic children. *Journal of Autism and Childhood Schizophrenia* 4: 42–60.

DeMyer, M. K., Barton, S., DeMyer, W. E., Norton, J. A., Allen, J., and Steele, R. (1973). Prognosis in autism: a follow-up study. *Journal of Autism and Childhood Schizophrenia* 3: 199-246.

DeMyer, M. K., Hingten, J. N., and Jackson, R. K. (1981). Infantile autism reviewed: a decade of research. *Schizophrenia Bulletin* 7: 388-451.

DeMyer, M. K., Puntius, W., Norton, J. A., Barton, S., Allen, J., and Steele, R. (1972). Parental practices and innate activity in normal, autistic, and brain-damaged infants. *Journal of Autism and Childhood Schizophrenia* 2: 49-66.

DeMyer, M. K., Schwier, H., Bryson, C. Q., Solow, E. B., and Roeske, N. (1971). Free fatty acid response to insulin and glucose stimulation in schizophrenic, autistic, and emotionally disturbed children. *Journal of Autism and Childhood Schizophrenia* 1:436-452.

Denenberg, V. H. (1977). Interactional effects in early experience research. In *Genetics, Environment, and Intelligence*, ed. A. Oliverio. Amsterdam: Elsevier.

—— (1982). Early experiences, interactive systems, and brain laterality in rodents. In *Facilitating Infant and Early Childhood Development*, eds. L. A. Bond and J. M. Jaffe, pp. 78-97. Hanover, NH: University Press of New England.

DeSanctis, S. (1973). Some variations of dementia praecox. In *Childhood Psychosis*, eds. S. Szurek and I. Berlin. New York: Brunner/Mazel.

Des Lauriers, A. (1967). The schizophrenic child. *Archives of General Psychiatry* 16: 194-201.

Eisenberg, L., and Kanner, L. (1956). Early infantile autism 1943-1955. *American Journal of Orthopsychiatry* 26: 556-566.

Eissler, K. R. (1953). The effect of the structure of the ego on psychoanalytic technique. *Journal of the American Psychoanalytic Association* 1: 104-143.

Ekstein, R., ed. (1966). *Children of Time and Space, of Action and Impulse.* New York: Appleton Century Crofts.

—— ed. (1971). *The Challenge: Despair and Hope in the Conquest of Inner Space.* New York: Brunner/Mazel.

Ekstein, R., Bryant, K., and Freedman, S. W. (1958). Childhood schizophrenia and allied conditions. In *Schizophrenia: A Review of the Syndrome*, ed. L. Bellak. New York: Logos Press.

Emde, R. N. (1980a). Towards a psychoanalytic theory of affect. I. The organizational model and its propositions. In *The Course of Life: Psychoanalytic Contributions Towards Understanding Personality Development. Vol. 1. Infancy and Early Childhood*, eds. S. I. Greenspan and G. H. Pollack. Adelphi: National Institutes of Mental Health.

—— (1980b). Towards a psychoanalytic theory of affect. II. Emerging models of emotional development in infancy. In *The Course of Life: Psychoanalytic Contributions Towards Understanding Personality Development. Vol. 1. Infancy and Early Childhood*, eds. S. I. Greenspan and G. H. Pollack. Adelphi: National Institutes of Mental Health.

Engel, G. L., and Reichsman, F. (1956). Spontaneous and experimentally induced depression in an infant with a gastric fistula: a contribution to the problem of depression. *Journal of the American Psychoanalytic Association* 4: 428-452.

Englehardt, D. M., Polizos, P., Waizer, J., and Hoffman, S. P. (1973). A double-blind comparison of fluphenazine and haloperidol in outpatient schizophrenic children. *Journal of the American Academy of Child Psychiatry* 3: 128-137.

Erikson, E. H. (1940). Studies in the interpretation of play: I. Clinical observations of play disruptions in young children. *Genetic Psychological Monographs* 22: 557-671.

—— (1950). *Childhood and Society.* New York: W. W. Norton.

—— (1959). *Identity and the Life Cycle.* Psychological Issues. Monograph 1. New York: International Universities Press.

Escalona, S. (1964). Some considerations regarding psychotherapy with psychotic children. In *Child Psychotherapy,* ed. M. R. Haworth, pp. 50-58. New York: Basic Books.

Fennichel, O. (1945). *The Psychoanalytic Theory of Neurosis.* New York: W. W. Norton.

Fenz, W. D., and Velner, J. (1970). Physiological concomitants of behavioral indexes in schizophrenia. *Journal of Abnormal Psychology* 76: 27-35.

Ferster, C. B. (1961). Positive reinforcement and behavior deficits of autistic children. *Child Development* 32: 437-456.

Ferster, C. B., and DeMyer, M. K. (1962). A method for the experimental analysis of the behavior of autistic children. *American Journal of Orthopsychiatry* 32: 89-98.

Fish, B., Campbell, M., Shapiro, T., and Floyd, A. (1969). Comparison of trifluperidol, trifluoperazine, and chlorpromazine in preschool schizophrenic children: the value of less sedative antipsychotic agents. *Current Therapeutic Research* 11 (10): 589-595.

Fish, B., Campbell, M., Shapiro, T., and Weinstein, J. (1969). Preliminary findings on thioxanthene compared to other drugs in psychotic children under five years. In *Modern Problems in Pharmacopsychiatry.* Vol. 2, ed. F. A. Freyhan, pp. 90-99. New York: Karger, Basel.

Fish, B., Shapiro, T., and Campbell, M. (1966). Longterm prognosis and the response of schizophrenic children to drug therapy: a controlled study of trifluoperazine. *American Journal of Psychiatry* 123: 32-39.

Fisher, S. M. (1975). On the development of the capacity to use transitional objects. *Journal of the American Academy of Child Psychiatry* 14: 114-124.

Folstein, S., and Rutter, M. (1977). Genetic influences and infantile autism. *Nature* 265: 726-728.

Foxx, R. M., and Azrin, N. H. (1973). The elimination of autistic self-stimulating behavior by overcorrection. *Journal of Applied Behavior Analysis* 6: 1-14.

Fraiberg, S. (1980). *Clinical Studies in Infant Mental Health.* New York: Basic Books.

—— (1982). Pathological defenses in infancy. *Psychoanalytic Quarterly* 51: 612-635.

Freud, S. (1895). Project for a scientific psychology. *Standard Edition* 1: 295-397.

—— (1900). The interpretation of dreams. *Standard Edition* 4/5: 1-627.

—— (1905). Fragment of an analysis of hysteria. *Standard Edition* 7: 3-122.

—— (1914). On narcissism: An introduction. *Standard Edition* 14: 67-107.

—— (1916-1917). Introductory lectures on psychoanalysis. *Standard Edition* 15/16: 1-477.

—— (1918). From the history of an infantile neurosis. *Standard Edition* 17: 1-204.

—— (1923). The ego and the id. *Standard Edition* 19: 1-66.

—— (1924). Neurosis and psychosis. *Standard Edition* 19: 144-153.

—— (1933). New introductory lectures on psychoanalysis. *Standard Edition* 22: 1-182.

—— (1937). Analysis, terminable and interminable. *Standard Edition* 23: 209-253.

—— (1938). An outline of psychoanalysis. *Standard Edition* 23: 141-207. London: Hogarth, 1940.

Fromm-Reichman, F. (1948). Notes on the development of the treatment of schizophrenia by psychoanalytic psychotherapy. *Psychiatry* 2: 263-273.

Furer, M. (1964). The development of a preschool symbiotic psychotic boy. *The Psychoanalytic Study of the Child.* Vol. 19, pp. 448-469. New York: International Universities Press.

Gedo, J., and Goldberg, A. (1973). *Models of the Mind.* Chicago: University of Chicago Press.

Geller, E., Ritvo, E. R., Freeman, B., and Yuwiler, A. (1982). Preliminary observations on the effect of fenfluramine on blood serotonin and symptoms in three autistic boys. *New England Journal of Medicine* 307 (3): 165-169.

Gill, M. (1982). *The Analysis of Transference. Vol. I. Theory and Technique.* New York: International Universities Press.

Goldfarb, W. (1970). The clarifying experience in the psychotherapy of psychotic children. *Current Psychiatric Therapies* 10: 52-75.

—— (1980). Pervasive developmental disorders of childhood. In *Comprehensive Textbook of Psychiatry,* eds. H. I. Kaplan, A. M. Freedman, and B. J. Sadock, pp. 2527-2537. Baltimore: Williams and Wilkins.

Goldfarb, W., Spitzer, R. L., and Endicott, J. A. (1976). A study of psychopathology of parents of psychotic children. *Journal of Autism and Childhood Schizophrenia* 6: 327-338.

Goldstein, K. (1959). Abnormal conditions in infancy. *Journal of Nervous and Mental Diseases* 128: 538–577.

Greenson, R. R. (1967). *The Technique and Practice of Psychoanalysis. Vol. I.* New York: International Universities Press.

Greenspan, S. I. (1981a). Developmental structuralist approach to the classification of adaptive and pathological personality organizations: infancy and early childhood. *American Journal of Psychiatry* 138 (6): 725–735.

—— (1981b). *Psychopathology and Adaptation in Infancy and Early Childhood.* New York: International Universities Press.

Group for the Advancement of Psychiatry. (1966). *Psychopathological Disorders in Childhood: Theoretical Considerations and a Proposed Classification.* New York: Group for the Advancement of Psychiatry.

Hammes, J. G., and Langdell, T. (1981). Precursors of symbol formation and childhood autism. *Journal of Autism and Developmental Disorders* 11 (3): 331–346.

Hanley, H. G., Stahl, S. M., and Freedman, D. X. (1978). Hyperserotonemia and amine metabolites in autistic and retarded children. *Archives of General Psychiatry* 34: 521–531.

Hanson, D. R., and Gottesman, I. I. (1976). The genetics, if any, of infantile autism and childhood schizophrenia. *Journal of Autism and Childhood Schizophrenia* 6 (3): 209–234.

Harley, M., and Sabot, L. (1980). Conceptualizing the nature of the therapeutic action of child analysis. *Journal of the American Psychoanalytic Association* 28: 161–179.

Harley, M., and Weil, A. (1979). Introduction. In M. Mahler, *The Selected Papers of Margaret Mahler: Infantile Psychosis and Early Contributions*, Vol. 1. New York: Jason Aronson.

Harris, S. L., and Wolchik, S. A. (1979). Suppression of self-stimulation: three alternative strategies. *Journal of Applied Behavior Analysis* 12: 185–198.

Hartman, H. (1939). *Ego Psychology and the Problem of Adaptation.* New York: International Universities Press, 1958.

—— (1953). Contributions to the metapsychology of schizophrenia. *The Psychoanalytic Study of the Child.* Vol. 8, pp. 177–198. New York: International Universities Press.

Heller, T. (1971). About dementia infantalis. Reprinted in *Modern Perspectives in International Child Psychiatry*, ed. J. C. Howells. New York: Brunner/Mazel.

Hermelin, B. (1978). Images and language. In *Autism: A Reappraisal of Concepts and Treatment*, eds. M. Rutter and E. Schopler. New York: Plenum Press.

Hermelin, B., and O'Connor, N. (1967). Remembering of words by psychotic and subnormal children. *British Journal of Psychiatry* 58: 213–218.

—— (1970). *Psychological Experiments with Autistic Children.* Oxford: Pergamon Press.

Hier, D. B., LeMay, M., and Rosenberger, P. B. (1979). Autism and unfavorable left-right asymmetries of the brain. *Journal of Autism and Childhood Schizophrenia* 9: 153-154.

Hill, A. L. (1977). Idiot savants: rates of incidence. *Perceptual and Motor Skills* 44 (1): 161-162.

Hingten, J. N., and Bryson, C. Q. (1972). Recent developments in the study of early childhood psychosis: infantile autism, childhood schizophrenia, and related disorders. *Schizophrenia Bulletin* 5: 8-54.

Hinton, G. G. (1963). Childhood psychosis or mental retardation: a diagnostic dilemma. II. Pediatric and neurologial aspects. *Canadian Medical Association Journal* 89: 1020-1024.

Holt, R. R. (1981). The death and transfiguration of metapsychology. *International Review of Psychoanalysis* 8: 129-143.

Hutt, C. S., Forrest, S. J., and Richer, J. (1975). Cardiac arhythmia and behavior in autistic children. *Acta Psychiatrica Scandinavia* 51: 361-372.

Hutt, S. J., and Hutt, C. S. (1968). Stereotypy, arousal, and autism. *Human Development* 11: 277-286.

Hutt, S. J., Hutt, C. S., Lee, D., and Ounsted, C. (1965). A behavioral and electroencephalographic study of autistic children. *Journal of Psychiatric Research* 3: 181-198.

Itel, T. M., Simeon, J., and Coffin, C. (1976). Qualitative and quantitative EEG in psychotic children. *Diseases of the Nervous System* 37: 247-252.

James, A. L., and Barry, R. J. (1980). A review of psychophysiology in early onset psychosis. *Schizophrenia Bulletin* 6 (3): 506-525.

Jurgensen, O. S. (1979). Psychopharmacological treatment of psychotic children. *Acta Psychiatrica Scandinavia* 59: 229-238.

Kallman, F. S. (1938). *Genetics of Schizophrenia.* New York: Augustin.

Kanner, L. (1943). Autistic disturbances of affective contact. *Nervous Child* 2: 217-250.

—— (1971). Childhood psychosis: a historical overview. *Journal of Autism and Childhood Schizophrenia* 1 (1): 14-19.

Kennard, M. A. (1959). The characteristics of thought disturbance as related to electroencephalographic findings in children and adolescents. *American Journal of Psychiatry* 115: 911-921.

Kernberg, O. (1976). *Object Relations Theory and Clinical Psychoanalysis.* New York: Jason Aronson.

—— (1980a). *Internal World and External Reality.* New York: Jason Aronson.

—— (1980b). Neurosis, psychosis, and the borderline states. In *Comprehensive Textbook of Psychiatry,* eds. H. I. Kaplan, A. M. Freedman, and B. J. Sadock. Baltimore: Williams and Wilkins.

Kernberg, P. (1980). Childhood psychosis: a psychoanalytic perspective. In *The Course of Life. Vol. 1: Infancy and Early Childhood,* eds. S. I. Greenspan and G. H. Pollack. Adelphi: National Institute of Mental Health.

King, P. D. (1975). Early infantile autism: relation to schizophrenia. *Journal of the American Academy of Child Psychiatry* 14: 666-682.

Klein, R. G. (1975-76). Pharmacotherapy and management of pathological separation anxiety. *International Journal of Mental Health* 4 (1, 2): 255-271.

Koegel, R. L., Schreibman, L., and Lovaas, O. I. (1973). A manual for training parents in behavior modifications with autistic children. Technical article, Institute for Applied Behavioral Science, University of California, Santa Barbara.

Kohut, H. (1959). Introspection, empathy, and psychoanalysis. *Journal of the American Psychoanalytic Association* 7: 459-483.

—— (1971). *The Analysis of the Self.* New York: International Universities Press.

—— (1977). *The Restoration of the Self.* New York: International Universities Press.

—— (1980). Two letters. In *Advances in Self Psychology*, ed. A. Goldberg. New York: International Universities Press.

—— (1984). *How Does Analysis Cure?* Chicago: University of Chicago Press.

Kolvin, I., Ounsted, C., and Roth, M. (1971). Cerebral dysfunction and childhood psychosis. *British Journal of Psychiatry* 118: 407-414.

Krantz, J. C., Truitt, E. B., Speers, L., and Ling, A. (1957). New pharmaco-convulsive agent. *Science* 126: 353.

Lake, C. R., Ziegler, M. G., and Murphy, D. L. (1977). Increased norepinephrine levels and decreased dopamine-b-hydroxylase activity in primary autism. *Archives of General Psychiatry* 34: 553-556.

Lichtenberg, J. D. (1981). Implications for psychoanalytic theory of research on the neonate. *International Review of Psychoanalysis* 8: 35-52.

—— (1982). Reflections on the first year of life. *Psychoanalytic Inquiry* Vol. 1, No. 4, pp. 695-729.

—— (1983). *Psychoanalysis and Infant Research.* New Jersey, Analytic Press.

Lobascher, M. E., Kingerlee, P. E., and Gobbay, S. S. (1970). Childhood autism: an investigation of etiological factors in twenty-five cases. *British Journal of Psychiatry* 117: 525-529.

Lockyer, L., and Rutter, M. (1969). A five to fifteen year follow-up study of infantile psychosis. III. Psychological aspects. *British Journal of Psychiatry* 115: 865-882.

Lotter, V. (1966). Epidemiology of autistic conditions in young children. I. Prevalence. *Social Psychiatry* 1: 124-137.

Lovaas, O. I. (1977). *The Autistic Child: Language Development through Behavior Modification.* New York: Irvington.

—— (1979). Contrasting illness and behavioral models for the treatment of autistic children: a historical perspective. *Journal of Autism and Developmental Disorders* 9 (4): 315-323.

Lovaas, O. I., Koegel, R., and Schreibman, L. (1979). Stimulus overselectivity in autism: a review of research. *Psychological Bulletin* 86 (6): 1236-1254.

Lovaas, O. I., Koegel, R., Simmons, J. Q., and Long, J. S. (1973). Some generalizations and follow-up measures on autistic children in behavior therapy. *Journal of Applied Behavior Analysis* 6: 131-166.

Lovaas, O. I., Schreibman, L., and Koegel, R. L. (1974). A behavior modification approach to the treatment of autistic children. *Journal of Autism and Childhood Schizophrenia* 4 (2): 111-129.

Lovaas, O. I., Schreibman, L., Koegel, R. L., and Rehm, R. (1971). Selective responding by autistic children to multiple sensory input. *Journal of Abnormal Psychology* 77: 211-222.

MacCulloch, M. J., and Williams, C. (1971). On the nature of infantile autism. *Acta Psychiatrica Scandinavia* 47: 295-314.

Macmillan, M. B. (1960). Extrascientific influences in the history of child psychopathology. *American Journal of Psychiatry* 116: 1091-1096.

Mahler, K. R., Harper, J. F., Macleary, A., and King, M. G. (1975). Peculiarities in the endocrine response to insulin stress in early infantile autism. *Journal of Nervous and Mental Diseases* 161: 180-204.

Mahler, M. (1979a). A psychoanalytic evaluation of tic in the psychopathology of children: Symptomatic tic and tic syndrome. In M. Mahler, *The Selected Papers of Margaret Mahler. Infancy and Early Childhood*, vol. 1. New York: Jason Aronson. (Originally published 1949.)

—— (1979b). On child psychosis and schizophrenia: autistic and symbiotic infantile psychoses. In M. Mahler, *The Selected Papers of Margaret Mahler. Infantile Psychosis and Early Contributions*, vol. 1. New York: Jason Aronson. (Originally published 1952.)

—— (1979c). On early infantile psychosis: the symbiotic and autistic syndrome. In M. Mahler, *The Selected Papers of Margaret Mahler. Infantile Psychosis and Early Contributions*, vol. 1. New York: Jason Aronson. (Originally published 1965.)

—— (1979d). Longitudinal study of the treatment of a psychotic child with the tripartite design. In M. Mahler, *The Selected Papers of Margaret Mahler. Infantile Psychosis and Early Contributions*, vol. 1. New York: Jason Aronson. (Originally published 1976.)

—— (1979e). *On Human Symbiosis and the Vicissitudes of Individuation: Infantile Psychosis*. New York: International Universities Press.

Mahler, M., and McDevitt, J. B. (1980). The separation-individuation process and identity formation. In *The Course of Life: Psychoanalytic Contributions towards Understanding Personality Development*, eds. S. I. Greenspan and G. H. Pollack, *vol. 1. Infancy and Early Childhood*. Adelphi: National Institute of Mental Health.

Masagatani, G. N. (1973). Hand gesturing behavior in psychotic children. *The American Journal of Occupational Therapy* 27: 24-29.

Massie, H. N. (1978). Blind ratings of mother-infant interaction in home movies of prepsychotic and normal infants. *American Journal of Psychiatry* 135: 1371-1374.

Menninger, K. (1958). *Theory of Psychoanalytic Technique.* New York: Harper.

Modell, A. H. (1976). The "holding environment" and the therapeutic action of psychoanalysis. *Journal of the American Psychoanalytic Association* 24: 285-307.

—— (1980). The narcissistic character and disturbances in the "holding environment." In *The Course of Life: Psychoanalytic Contributions towards Understanding Personality Development.* eds. S. I. Greenspan and G. H. Pollack, *vol. III. Adulthood and the Aging Process.* Adelphi: National Institute of Mental Health.

O'Moore, M. (1972). A study of the etiology of autism from a study of birth and family characteristics. *Journal of the Irish Medical Association* 65: 114-120.

Ornitz, E. M. (1971). Childhood autism: a disorder of sensory and motor integration. In *Infantile Autism: Concepts, Characteristics and Treatment,* ed. M. Rutter. London: Churchill.

Ornitz, E. M., and Ritvo, E. R. (1958). Perceptual inconstancy in early infantile autism. *Archives of General Psychiatry* 19: 22-27.

—— (1976). The syndrome of autism: a critical review. *American Journal of Psychiatry* 133: 609-621.

Ornstein, A. (1976). Making contact with the inner world of the child. *Comprehensive Psychiatry* 17 (1): 3-36.

Parent-Infant Development Service. (1982). *A Parent-Infant Intervention Program.* University of Chicago. Department of Child Psychiatry. (Unpublished manuscript.)

Piaget, J. (1981). *Intelligence and Affectivity: Their Relationship During Child Development.* Palo Alto: Annual Reviews Inc.

Piaget, P., and Inhelder, B. (1955). *The Psychology of the Child.* London: Routledge and Kegan Paul.

Pine, F. (1976). On therapeutic change: perspectives from a parent-child model. *Psychoanalysis and Contemporary Science* 5: 537-569.

—— (1981). In the beginning: contributions to a psychoanalytic developmental psychology. *International Review of Psychoanalysis* 8: 15.

Potter, H. W. (1933). Schizophrenia in children. *American Journal of Psychiatry* 12: 1253.

Prior, M. J. (1979). Cognitive abilities and disabilities in infantile autism: a review. *Journal of Abnormal Child Psychology* 7 (4): 357-380.

Prior, M., and Macmillan, M. D. (1973). Maintenance of sameness in children with Kanner's syndrome. *Journal of Autism and Childhood Schizophrenia* 3: 154-167.

Racker, H. (1968). *Transference and Countertransference.* New York: International Universities Press.

Rank, B. (1944). Adaptations of the psychoanalytic technique for the treatment of young children with atypical development. *American Journal of Orthopsychiatry* 19: 130-139.

Rapaport, D. (1951). The autonomy of the ego. In *The Collected Papers of David Rapaport,* ed. M. Gill. New York: Basic Books.

Resch, R. C., Grand, S., and Meyerson, K. (1981). From the object to the person: the treatment of a two-year-old girl with infantile autism. *Bulletin of the Menninger Clinic* 45 (4): 281–306.

Ricks, D. M., and Wing, L. (1975). Language, communication, and the use of symbols in normal and autistic children. *Journal of Autism and Childhood Schizophrenia* 5 (3): 191–221.

Rimland, B. (1964). *Infantile Autism: The Syndrome and Its Implications for a Neural Theory of Behavior.* New York: Appleton Century Crofts.

—— (1973). Childhood psychosis: initial studies and new insights by Leo Kanner. *Journal of Autism and Childhood Schizophrenia* 3 (1): 88–92.

Ritvo, E. R., Freeman, B. J., Geller, E., and Yuwiler, A. (1983). Effects of fenfluramine on fourteen outpatients with the syndrome of autism. *Journal of the American Academy of Child Psychiatry* 22 (6): 549–558.

Ritvo, E. R., Ornitz, E. M., Walter, R. D., and Hanley, J. (1970). Correlations of psychiatric diagnosis and EEG findings: a double blind study of 184 hospitalized children. *American Journal of Psychiatry* 126: 988–996.

Ritvo, E. R., Yuwiler, A., Geller, E., et al. (1971). Effects of l-dopa on autism. *Journal of Autism and Childhood Schizophrenia* 1: 140–205.

Roth, C. (1982a). Clinical intervention methods for disturbed parent-infant interaction. *Infant Behavior and Development* 5 (Special ICIS issue.)

—— (1982b). The conceptual framework of parent-infant interventions. Paper presented at the International Conference on Infant Studies, Austin, Texas.

Roth, C., Levin, D. S., Morrison, M., Leventhal-Belfer, L. and Leventhal, B. L. (in press). On developing interventions for infants and their families: a systems perspective.

Rutter, M. (1972). Childhood schizophrenia reconsidered. *Journal of Autism and Childhood Schizophrenia* 2: 315–337.

—— (1975). The development of infantile autism. *Annual Progress in Child Psychiatry and Development*, pp. 327–355.

—— (1978). Diagnosis and definition of childhood autism. *Journal of Autism and Childhood Schizophrenia* 8: 139–161.

Rutter, M., Greenfield, D., and Lockyer, L. A. A five to fifteen year follow-up study of infantile autism: II. Social and behavioral outcome. *British Journal of Psychiatry* 113: 1183–1189.

Rutter, M., and Lockyer, L. (1967). A five to fifteen year follow-up study of infantile autism: I. Description of the sample. *British Journal of Psychiatry* 113: 1169–1182.

Sander, L. W. (1975). Infant and caretaking environment: investigation and conceptualization of adaptive behavior in a system of increasing complexity. In *Explorations in Child Psychiatry*, ed. E. J. Anthony. New York: Plenum Press.

—— (1983). Polarity, paradox, and the organizing process in development. In *Frontiers of Infant Research*, eds. J. D. Call, E. Galenson, and R. L. Tyson. New York: Basic Books.

Sandler, J., Kennedy, H., and Tyson, R. (1980). *The Technique of Child Psychoanalysis: Discussions with Anna Freud.* Cambridge: Harvard University Press.

Schafer, R. (1959). Generative empathy in the treatment situation. *Psychoanalysis Quarterly* 28: 347–373.

—— (1976). *A New Language for Psychoanalysis.* New Haven: Yale University Press.

—— (1983). *The Analytic Attitude.* New York: Basic Books.

Schain, R. J., and Freedman, D. X. (1961). Studies on s-hydroxyindole metabolism in autistic and other mentally retarded children. *Journal of Pediatrics* 58: 315–320.

Schopler, E. (1976). The art and science of Bruno Bettelheim. *Journal of Autism and Childhood Schizophrenia* 6 (2): 193–202.

Schopler, E., Reichler, R. J., DeVillis, R. F., and Daly, K. (1980). Towards objective classification of childhood autism: childhood autism rating scale (cars). *Journal of Autism and Developmental Disorders* 10: 91–103.

Schover, B. L., and Newsome, C. D. (1976). Overselectivity, developmental level, and overtraining in autistic and normal children. *Journal of Abnormal Child Psychology* 4: 289–298.

Schreibman, L. (1975). Effects of within stimulus and extra-stimulus prompting on discrimination learning in autistic children. *Journal of Applied Behavior Analysis* 8: 91–112.

Schreibman, L., Koegel, P. L., and Craig, M. S. (1977). Reducing stimulus overselectivity in autistic children. *Journal of Abnormal Child Psychology* 5: 425–436.

Shapiro, T. (1974). The development and distortions of empathy. *Psychoanalytic Quarterly* 43: 4–25.

Shapiro, T., Roberts, A., and Fish, B. (1970). Imitation and echoing in young schizophrenic children. *Journal of the American Academy of Child Psychiatry* 9: 548–567.

Simmons, J. Q., and Baltaxe, L. (1975). Language patterns of adolescent autistics. *Journal of Autism and Childhood Schizophrenia* 5: 333–351.

Solnick, J. O., Rincover, A., and Peterson, C. R. (1977). Some determinants of the reinforcing and punishing effects of time out. *Journal of Applied Behavior Analysis* 10: 415–424.

Spence, D. P. (1976). Clinical interpretation: some comments on the nature of evidence. *Psychoanalysis and Contemporary Science* 5: 367–388.

—— (1982). Narrative truth and Historical truth. New York: W. W. Norton.

—— (1983). Narrative persuasion. *Psychoanalysis and Contemporary Thought* 6: 457–481.

Spitz, R. A. (1951). The psychogenic diseases in infancy: an attempt at their etiologic classification. In *Psychoanalytic Study of the Child,* vol. 6, pp. 255–275. New York: International Universities Press.

—— (1964). The derailment of dialogue: stimulus overload action cycles and the completion gradient. *Journal of the American Psychiatric Association* 12: 752-775.

Spitzer, R. L., and Endicott, J. (1979). Justification for separating schizo-typal and borderline personality disorders. *Schizophrenia Bulletin* 5 (1): 95-100.

Sroufe, A. L. (1979). The coherence of individual development: early care attachment and subsequent developmental issues. *American Psychologist* 34: 834-841.

Steg, J. P., and Rapaport, J. L. (1975). Minor physical anomalies in normal, neurotic, learning disabled, and severely disturbed children. *Journal of Autism and Childhood Schizophrenia* 5: 299-302.

Stern, D. (1983). The early development of schemas of self, other, and "self with other." In *Reflections on Self Psychology*, eds. J. D. Lichtenberg and S. Kaplan, pp. 49-84. New Jersey: The Analytic Press.

Szurek, S. A., and Berlin, I. N. (1973). *Clinical Studies in Childhood Psychosis.* New York: Brunner/Mazel.

Tager-Flusberg, H. (1981). On the nature of linguistic functioning in early infantile autism. *Journal of Autism and Developmental Disorders* 11 (1): 45-55.

Tolpin, M. (1971). On the beginnings of a cohesive self. *Psychoanalytic Study of the Child* 26: 316-352.

—— (1978). Self-objects and oedipal objects: a crucial developmental distinction. *Psychoanalytic Study of the Child* 33: 167-187.

—— (1980). Discussion of "psychoanalytic developmental theories of the self: an interpretation" by Martin Shane and Estelle Shane. In *Advances in Self Psychology*, ed. A. Goldberg. New York: International Universities Press.

—— (1983). Corrective emotional experience: a self-psychological reevaluation. In *The Future of Psychoanalysis*, ed. A. Goldberg. New York: International Universities Press.

Tolpin, M., and Kohut, H. (1980). The disorders of the self: the psychopathology of the first years of life. In *The Course of Life: Psychoanalytic Contributions Towards Understanding Personality Development*, eds. S. I. Greenspan and G. H. Pollack. *vol. 1. Infancy and Early Childhood.* Adelphi: National Intitute of Mental Health.

Tustin, F. (1972). *Autism and Childhood Psychosis.* New York: Science House.

Ungerer, J. A., and Sigman, M. (1981). Symbolic play and language comprehension in autistic children. *Journal of the American Academy of Child Psychiatry* 20: 318-337.

Wachtel, P. L. (1980). Transference, schema, and assimilation: the relevance of Piaget to the psychoanalytic theory of transference. In *Annual of Psychoanalysis* 13: 59-76. New York: International Universities Press.

Waters, W. F., McDonald, D. G., and Konesko, R. L. (1977). Habituation of the orienting response: a gating mechanism subserving selective attention. *Psychophysiology* 14: 228-236.

Watt, N. F. (1978). Patterns of childhood social development in adult schizophrenia. *Archives of General Psychiatry* 35: 160–165.

Watzlawick, P., Beavin, J., and Jackson, D. D. (1967). *Pragmatics of Human Communication.* New York: W. W. Norton.

Weiland, H., and Rudnick, R. (1961). Considerations of the development and treatment of autistic childhood psychosis. *Psychoanalytic Study of the Child* 16: 549–563.

Weiss, S. (1981). Reflections on the psychoanalytic process with special emphasis on child analysis and self-analysis. *Annual of Psychoanalysis* 9: 43–56.

Williams, J. M., and Freeman, W. (1953). Evaluation of lobotomy with special reference to children. *Association for Research in Nervous and Mental Disease: Proceedings* 31: 311.

Wing, L. (1970). *Early Infantile Autism.* Oxford: Pergamon.

—— (1971). Perceptual and language development in autistic children: a comparative study. In *Infantile Autism: Concepts, Characteristics and Treatment,* ed. M. Rutter. London: Churchill.

Wing, L., Gould, J., Yeates, S., and Brierly, L. (1977). Symbolic play in severely mentally retarded and autistic children. *Psychological Reports* 25: 223–227.

Wing, L., Yeates, S., Brierly, L. M., and Gould, J. (1976). The prevalence of early childhood autism: comparison of administrative and epidemiological studies. *Psychological Medicine* 6: 89–100.

Winnicott, D. W. (1960). Transitional objects and transitional phenomena. *International Journal of Psychoanalysis* 1953. Reprinted in *Collected Papers: through Pediatrics to Psychoanalysis.* New York: Basic Books.

—— (1965). *The Maturational Process and the Facilitating Environment.* New York: International Universities Press.

Wolpe, J. (1952). Experimental neurosis and learned behavior. *British Journal of Psychology* 43: 243–268.

—— (1954). Reciprocal inhibition as the main basis of psychotherapeutic effect. *Archives of Neurological Psychiatry* 72: 205–226.

—— *(1976). Theme and Variations: a Behavior Therapy Casebook.* New York: Pergamon.

Woolley, E. W., and Shaw, E. (1954). A biochemical and pharmacological suggestion about certain mental disorders. *Science* 119: 587–588.

Young, J. G., Cohen, D. J., Brown, S. L., and Caparulo, B. K. (1978). Decreased urinary free catecholamines in childhood autism. *Journal of the American Academy of Child Psychiatry* 17: 671–678.

Author Index

Subject Index

Conflict, intrapsychic
(*Continued*)
  following structural
    consolidation, 146
Congenital factors, role of, 20–21
Conservation withdrawal reaction,
    179, 191
Contingent reinforcement
    withdrawal, 78
Core developmental prototypes,
    140–142
Corrective developmental
    experience, viii–ix
  parent exclusion from, 104–105,
    111
  parent involvement in, 95–104,
    111
  perspective of, 6–8, 287–288
  prognosis with, 285–297
Corrective development
    experience, case study
  confirmation and
    disconfirmation of
    expectations, 271–279
  diagnostic assessments, 211–230
  therapist-child interactions,
    231–257
  therapist-parent interactions,
    259–284
  transference relationship, 266–
    270
  treatment termination, 279–297
Corrective development
    experience model
  confirmation and
    disconfirmation of
    experience in, 301–302
  corrective emotional experience
    versus, 299–312
  goals of, 304
  interactional perspective of, 301
  transference relationship in,
    304–305
  value of model of, 305–312
Corrective emotional experience,
    viii, 98
  critique of, 299–305
  essence of, 301–302

Corrective object-relations
    therapy, 98–100
Corrective symbiotic relationship,
    95–96, 102
Cuing, mutual, 143

Defense behaviors
  aim of, 189
  avoidant, 191, 196, 276, 278
  clinical importance of, 16, 18,
    192
  confirmation or disconfirmation
    of, 199
  definition of, 188
  freezing, 191
  precursory defensive behaviors,
    188–189
  pre-ego, 190
  provocative, 191
  repression, 86
  splitting, 85–86
  transformation of affect, 191
Delusional-autistic modes, 90
Delusional-symbiotic modes, 90
Dementia infantalis, 13
Dementia praecocissima, 12–13
Dementia praecox, 12–14, 17
Developmental experiences, core,
    140–142
Developmental stages,
    renegotiation of, 95–98
Developmental stages (Mahler),
    86–91
  normal autistic, 87
  normal symbiotic, 87
  separation-individuation, 87–89
Developmental structuralist stage
    (Greenspan) assessments,
    125–136
  attachment, 127–128
  behavioral organization,
    initiative, and
    internalization, 130–131
  epigenetic dimension of, 126,
    306
  internal representations,
    organization of, 131–133

Psychoanalysis, child (*Continued*)
  limits of, 194
  problems with, 195
  systems-interactional
    perspective of, 204-207
Psychoanalytic psychotherapy
  agent of change in, 110-111,
    195, 197
  client selection criteria for, 193-
    194
  decline of interest in, 6, 112
  goals of, 95
  operational constructs in, 194
  prognosis with, 6, 112, 193-194
  therapist function in, 110-111
  versus other modalities, 112
Psychoanalytic psychotherapy,
    types of, 95-113. *See also*
    Tripartite treatment design
  corrective and reexperiencing,
    95-106, 110
  expressive, 106-110, 111
  suppressive, 106-107
Psychoanalytic theory, 83-93
  classical conflict model, 83-84
  object relations, 85-91
  self psychology, 91-93
"Psychological birth," 86
Psychopharmacology, 47-51
  fenfluramine, 40, 50-51
  recent emphasis on, 6
  major tranquilizers, 49-50
Psychophysiological studies, 29-37
  cardiovascular and vasomotor
    activity, 32-34
  cross-validation of, 34-37
  electroencephalographic (EEG)
    studies, 31-32
  review of literature on, 29-31'
Psychotherapeutic process, 159-
    173
  aim of, 124, 146
  capacity of child for, 186-188
  context of safety and, 146
  defensive behaviors in, 188-192
  interactive fit and coherence in,
    3

  non-interpretive background
    characteristics in, 4, 135-
    136, 205
  parent-child interaction and,
    135-136
  silent features of, 146
  therapist's response in, 159-162
  transference in, 162-173, 175-
    192

Rapprochement, 88
RAS (reticular activating system)
  dysfunction, 31, 32, 36, 37,
    41-42
Reality testing, developmental
    assessment of, 129-130, 133-
    134
Reciprocal exchange patterns, 178
Reengulfment, 90, 108, 234, 243
Regulatory responsiveness, 218
  in therapist-child interactions,
    199
  as transference issue, 177-178
Response-contingent aversive
    stimuli, 78, 79, 80
Retrospective-prospective
    processes, 162

Sameness and constancy
  maintenance of, 66-67, 283
  optimal, 203-204
Schizophrenia, childhood clinical
    studies on, 14
  DSM III classification of, 24
Self-assertion, 130-131
  interactional stage of, 180-183
Self-cohesion, 91-93, 283
Self-direction, 180
Self-esteem, 68
Self-injury, 77-78, 79, 254
Self-object differentiation, 86-91,
    96, 101-103, 130-131, 133,
    235
Self and object representations
  consolidation of, 89
  fused, 90

"good-gratifying" versus "bad-frustrating", 85–86
undifferentiated, 86, 90
Self psychology, 91–93
Self-regulation, 132
Self-soothing, 92, 93
Self-stimulation, 77–78, 79
Separation
definition of, 88
empathic responding to, 155–157
premature, 180
Separation-individuation process, 87–89, 143, 252–257
differentiation, 88
object constancy, 88–89
practicing, 88
rapprochement, 88
Serotonin hypothesis, 39–40
Social reinforcers, 78–79
Somatic-psychological
differentiation, 125–126, 132
as transference issue, 179–180
Speech articulation difficulties, 43–44, 218
Splitting, 14, 84, 85–86, 225
Stimulus barrier, primitive, 35–36, 126–127
Stimulus overloading, 127
Stimulus overselectivity, 30, 56–59
behavioral theorists'
overemphasis on, 80–81
microgenesis and, 58
in "normal" preoperational
child, 57–58
receptive language deficits and, 72–73
treatment techniques, 57
Symbiotic attachment, 19, 87, 89, 90, 95, 226–227, 234, 243, 254, 260, 288
Suppressive psychotherapy, 106–107
Symbiotic-psychosis
corrective symbiotic treatment of, 97
description of, 18–19

prognosis for, 97, 100
self-object undifferentiation and, 70
Symbolic play, 65–67
Symbolic representation, 63–73, 247–250
developmental assessment of, 131–134
language and, 67–73
play as, 65–67
precursors to, 64–65
Symptomatology. *See also*
Classification systems;
Diagnostic criteria
Systematic desensitization
technique, 303
Systems-interactional perspective, 204–207, 287–288

Tantrum, distancing through, 166, 216
Termination process, 252–257, 279–297
Testing, psychological, 265, 268–269
Therapist
optimal, 145–147
as transference object, 163, 190
Therapist-child interaction, 145–147
as medium of change, 196–197
transference in, 237–238, 240, 251
Therapist as mother substitute, 97, 108, 237
Therapist and parent-child
interactions, 151–152
Therapist-parent interactions, 149–151, 259–284
confirmation and
disconfirmation of
experience in, 271–279
importance of, 204–207
Time-out procedures, 79
Transference, 162–173. *See also*
Transference of infants